Schriftenreihe des
ZENTRUMS FÜR EUROPÄISCHE RECHTSPOLITIK
der Universität Bremen (ZERP)

Band 81

Hendrik Schulze

Exploring the Uncharted Waters of European Competition Law 4.0

An approach to the regulation of abusive data-related
behaviors of dominant undertakings in the digital age

 Nomos

The Deutsche Nationalbibliothek lists this publication in the
Deutsche Nationalbibliografie; detailed bibliographic data
are available on the Internet at http://dnb.d-nb.de

a.t.: Bremen, Univ., Diss., 2020

ISBN   978-3-8487-7741-9 (Print)
          978-3-7489-2137-0 (ePDF)

British Library Cataloguing-in-Publication Data
A catalogue record for this book is available from the British Library.

ISBN   978-3-8487-7741-9 (Print)
          978-3-7489-2137-0 (ePDF)

Library of Congress Cataloging-in-Publication Data
Schulze, Hendrik
Exploring the Uncharted Waters of European Competition Law 4.0
An approach to the regulation of abusive data-related
behaviors of dominant undertakings in the digital age
Hendrik Schulze
178 pp.
Includes bibliographic references.

ISBN   978-3-8487-7741-9 (Print)
          978-3-7489-2137-0 (ePDF)

Onlineversion
Nomos eLibrary

1st Edition 2021
© Nomos Verlagsgesellschaft, Baden-Baden, Germany 2021. Overall responsibility
for manufacturing (printing and production) lies with Nomos Verlagsgesellschaft mbH
& Co. KG.

Acknowledgements

I would like to thank my doctoral supervisor Prof. Dr. Christoph Schmid, Ph.D. (EUI Florence) for his words of advice during the writing process and especially for the initial motivation to start writing my dissertation in the first place. Moreover, I would like to thank Prof. Dr. Benedikt Buchner, LL.M. (UCLA) for the quick second assessment.

Above all, however, I would like to thank my parents for their constant and unconditional support in all matters and my wife for always having my back – even though she often had to stand my moods during the rather stressful writing process. Without them, I would not have been able to pursue my goals as planned. Last but not least, I would like to thank my beloved little daughter for motivating me every day without her even knowing it yet.

Bremen, April 30, 2021   Hendrik Schulze

Table of Contents

Table of Contents

Foreword

The present work was accepted as a dissertation by the law faculty of the University of Bremen in the winter term 20/21.

For the publication of this book and for reasons of completeness, however, some updates were made to the present work in consultation with the examination committee. Firstly, Chapter E III. "The decision of the German Federal Court of Justice" was inserted summarizing the Federal Court of Justice`s decision in the *Facebook* interim proceedings (case no. KVR 69/19). The present work had already been handed in as a dissertation when the Federal Court of Justice rendered its decision in the interim proceedings. In addition, new sources, mostly those that had not been published at the time the dissertation was submitted, were included – likewise for reasons of completeness. Last but not least, misspellings and the like that had slipped into the original version were corrected.

A. Introduction

I. Background

"Competition rules weren't written with big data in mind."[1]

Nowadays, a proliferating digitalization and its effects have reached every corner of our everyday lives and we are almost witnessing a "digital gold rush". The digital economy and especially the internet are expanding on a daily basis, in the course of which they have become firmly fixed in our lives.[2] Approximately 2.5 trillion bytes of data are generated worldwide each day due to digitalization and the growing number of devices in our everyday lives – and this number is ever increasing.[3] A large part of this data classifies as so-called personal data, meaning data relating to an identified or identifiable person. Personal data has become a core asset for companies in the digital economy and its economic value is expected to increase further.[4] Some even refer to personal data as today`s currency of the internet.[5] This is based on the fact that many companies in the digital economy have data-driven business models and strategies for which they need such information in order to ultimately monetize their services/products.[6] Hence, the market positions of companies like *Facebook*, *Google* and

---

1 Commissioner Margrethe Vestager, Speech at the EDPS-BEUC Conference on Big Data, Brussels, September 29th, 2016, available on the internet under https://wayback.archive-it.org/12090/20191129222113/https://ec.europa.eu/commission/commissioners/2014-2019/vestager/announcements/big-data-and-competition_en" (last accessed: 27/03/20).
2 See Hussain, 2017, p. 1.
3 PWC, "Big Data – Bedeutung Nutzen Mehrwert", p. 7, available on the internet under https://www.pwc.de/de/prozessoptimierung/assets/pwc-big-data-bedeutung-nutzen-mehrwert.pdf (last accessed: 27/03/20).
4 See Paal, NZKart 2018, 157 (157).
5 See former Consumer Commissioner Meglena Kuneva, Keynote Speech at the Roundtable on Online Data Collection, Targeting and Profiling, Brussels, March 31st, 2009, available on the internet under http://europa.eu/rapid/press-release_SPEECH-09-156_en.htm (last accessed 01/05/19); see also Pantlin et. al., "Data use: Protecting a critical resource", March 9th, 2018, p. 3, available on the Internet under https://www.herbertsmithfreehills.com/latest-thinking/data-use-protecting-a-critical-resource (last accessed: 22/05/19).
6 See Stucke/Grunes, 2016, p. 1.

others largely depend on their ability to process vast quantities of this data – so-called "big data".[7]

The fact that personal data has developed into a valuable good in our modern digital society has made it important to create a better (legal) protection against any kind of misuse of people`s personal data. Therefore, European data protection law experienced a significant reform in 2018 by means of the General Data Protection Regulation (abbreviated: GDPR, hereinafter also referred to as "the Regulation").[8] The GDPR has replaced the Data Protection Directive from 1995,[9] and has fully harmonized data protection law in the European Union (EU) – except for a few opening clauses.[10] The GDPR aims to ensure a uniformly high level of personal data protection throughout the whole EU and is designed to enhance the free movement of personal data.[11]

The importance of personal data for today`s digital economy has reached such an extent that some consider it to be the "new oil" of our digital world:[12] just as oil is a factor for economic power, so can data make companies more powerful vis-à-vis their competitors.[13] Thus, there is a strong incentive to gain access to as much personal data as possible

---

7 For the purpose of this work, the term "big data" shall refer exclusively to vast quantities of personal data, even though big data can in principle include non-personal information as well.

8 Regulation (EU) 2016/679 of the European Parliament and of the Council of April 27th, 2016 on the protection of natural persons with regard to the processing of personal data and on the free movement of such data, and repealing Directive 95/46/EC (General Data Protection Regulation), OJ 2016 L 119, 1.

9 Directive 95/46/EC of the European Parliament and of the Council of 24 October 1995 on the protection of individuals with regard to the processing of personal data and on the free movement of such data.

10 The so-called "opening clauses" permit a member state to alter the provision of the respective Article, in which the clause is integrated. Thereby, member states may introduce a more restrictive application than provided in the GDPR itself.

11 Communication from the Commission to the European Parliament, the Council, the European Economic and Social Committee and the Committee of the Regions – A Digital Single Market Strategy for Europe, Brussels, 6.5.2015, COM(2015) 192 final, p. 3.

12 See *N. Pantlin, et al., "Data Use – Protecting a Critical Resource", PLC Magazine, January/ February 2018, 19–27*; likewise also former Consumer Commissioner Meglena Kuneva, Keynote Speech at the Roundtable on Online Data Collection, Targeting and Profiling, Brussels, March 31st, 2009, available on the internet under http://europa.eu/rapid/press-release_SPEECH-09-156_en.htm (last accessed: 01/05/19).

13 Crofts/McLeod, MLex Interview: Margrethe Vestager, MLex Special Report, January 2015, p. 5, available on the internet under https://mlexmar-

in order to achieve a competitive advantage. This incentive might even be so strong that companies resort to anti-competitive means in order to gain that access. As will be discussed in this work, these facts could make competition law an integral part of the legal framework for handling data in the digital (platform) economy.[14] This was, inter alia, also illustrated by the *Facebook* case[15] of the German Federal Competition Authority (the "Bundeskartellamt"), where the collection and use of personal data was examined from a competition law perspective. However, as stated at the very beginning, European *"competition rules weren't written with big data in mind,"* as Margrethe Vestager, the EU`s Competition Commissioner, once said.[16] In fact, the "analogue" European competition law is more than half a century old by now and had no chance of foreseeing modern business trends in the digital economy. Article 102 of the Treaty on the Functioning of the European Union (TFEU), on which this dissertation will be focused, came into force in 1958,[17] the first IBM PC was introduced more than 20 years later in 1981, public internet access started in 1989 and tech giants like *Google* and *Facebook* were founded in 1997 and 2004, respectively.[18]

II. Focus of the thesis

Against this background, this dissertation deals with the issue of whether data protection law could provide guidance for European competition law in order to secure undistorted competition in times of "big data". Therefore, the research question is as follows: "Should big data and the GDPR, with its underlying data protection considerations, constitute a

---

ketinsight.com/insights-center/reports/interview-with-margrethe-vestager (last accessed: 22/05/19).

14 See Paal, NZKart 2018, 157 (157).

15 Bundeskartellamt, case no. B6–22/16 – *Facebook*.

16 Margrethe Vestager, Speech at the EDPS-BEUC Conference on Big Data, Brussels, September 29th, 2016, available on the internet under https://wayback.archive-it.org/12090/20191129222113/https://ec.europa.eu/commission/commissioners/2014-2019/vestager/announcements/big-data-and-competition_en (last accessed: 27/03/20).

17 Art. 102 TFEU was the former Art. 86 of Treaty establishing the European Economic Community signed March 25, 1957. The Treaty was later renamed into Treaty on the Functioning of the European Union by the Treaty of Lisbon from 2007. The wording of Art. 86 (nowadays Art. 102 TFEU) remained essentially the same though.

18 See Körber, WuW 2015, 120 (120).

normative yardstick for the application of Art. 102 TFEU in the digital economy in order to provide a remedy for the challenging regulation of possibly abusive, data-related behaviour of dominant undertakings?" This question aims to clarify whether considerations in connection with big data and the GDPR should provide guidance for Art. 102 TFEU on how to assess both dominance and abusive conduct in the digital economy. In order to find an answer to that question, it must first be elaborated whether such consideration can even be internalized by, or incorporated within, Art. 102 TFEU and, secondly, whether one should also follow such an approach by which data protection and competition law considerations are bridged.

The so-called "GAFA" – as four of the world's most valuable companies, *Google, Amazon, Facebook* and *Apple*, are known – already influence to a large extent the whole digital economy and the industry is still relatively young.[19] It is therefore important to set the course now for an effective regulation of abusive data-related business practices without over-regulating the industry – the latter could exclude the drive for innovation. Based on the example of the *Facebook* case by the German Federal Competition Authority ("Bundeskartellamt"),[20] the dissertation shall explore the uncharted waters of a regulation of abusive data-related behaviour within the context of European competition law.

Additionally, the overall research question is of particular topicality since the EU has been pursuing their idea of a digital single market since 2015 in order to create *"fair competition and a level playing field"* within the digital economy.[21] The European GDPR was one of the means through which this aim – as set out in the EU`s Digital Single Market Strategy – was to be realized. However, when speaking of a "level playing field", competition law is obviously of huge importance as well, and based on its applicability in the economic sector of the "digital single market", the interplay of competition law and data protection considerations is thus of particular relevance here.

The dissertation is limited in its scope of an examination of online platforms in the digital economy and their data-related, possibly abusive,

---

19 See also Höppner, WUW 2020, 71 (71).
20 Bundeskartellamt, decision of February 6th, 2019, case no. B6–22/16 – *Facebook*.
21 Communication from the Commission to the European Parliament, the Council, the European Economic and Social Committee and the Committee of the Regions – A Digital Single Market Strategy for Europe, Brussels, 6.5.2015, COM(2015) 192 final, p. 4.

business practices in the sense of Art. 102 TFEU. The reasons for this limitation are, on the one hand, that the *Facebook* investigation by the German Bundeskartellamt has inspired this work, which is why the problems and legal questions surrounding this investigation are also at the heart of this dissertation. On the other hand, it is precisely such online platforms in the digital economy which present themselves as data-driven businesses. It is therefore the individual data-related behaviour of tech giants like *Facebook* and co. that this dissertation is focused on. The link between data protection and competition law is in this context of particular interest and infringements of data protection and competition law are more likely to overlap in the field of Art. 102 TFEU. As a result of these aspects, Article 102 TFEU will in the focus of this work and Art. 101 TFEU and the EU Merger Regulation[22] will deliberately not be considered at this point.

Additionally, discussion about difficulties in defining the relevant markets in the digital economy is omitted as well – regardless of the fact that the definition of a relevant market plays an important role for an assessment under Art. 102 TFEU. An elaboration of said difficulties is a topic for a dissertation in itself and above that, the difficulties in defining the relevant market are much more connected to the general characteristics of the digital economy such as the two-sidedness and resulting network-effects rather than to considerations concerning big data and data protection. However, the latter in particular defines the scope of this work. The importance of data for markets in the digital economy will be elaborated on below, nonetheless.

III. Structure and methodology

The following work will first discuss the background of the digital platform economy by explaining big data, the digital economy and their characteristics in order to illustrate the importance of data for undertakings in the digital (platform) economy (more under B.). Next, the core legal framework will be elaborated on in order to provide the required background information of the two fields of law (more under C.), before their relation will be assessed (more under D.). Following this, the *Facebook* case and the interim court order of the Higher Regional Court Düsseldorf will be summarized in order to provide an illustrative example of the prob-

---

22 Council Regulation (EC) No.139/2004 of 20 January 2004 on the control of concentrations between undertakings.

lem that competition law faces in the digital economy (more under E.). Following the summary, the Bundeskartellamt`s *Facebook* case will then be discussed in a European competition law context in order to examine whether such a case could also come up under the European competition law regime (more under F.) This part is divided into three main parts. Firstly, it will be discussed if and how data-related considerations could serve as a yardstick for the establishment of dominance under Art. 102 TFEU and secondly, as a yardstick for the assessment of abusive conduct. Thirdly, the arguments for and against such an approach will be discussed. Following this, is an appraisal of whether the competition authorities would even possess the competence and expertise required for such an interdisciplinary approach (more under G.). Lastly, a review of whether the data-related behaviour of online platforms such as *Facebook* might even escape the application of competition law provisions in the first place. More precisely, the so-called "Immanenztheorie"[23] might require removing such practices from Art. 102 TFEU since online platforms like *Facebook* are competition neutral and the processing of vast amounts of data is immanent in these platforms (more under H.). On the other hand, one could also take the view of the other extreme. Arguably, certain platforms constitute natural monopolies, which should make them subject to even stronger and more direct regulations (more under I.). This possibility will be discussed last in order to assess all three of the approaches – (i) prohibition of certain data-related practices on a case-by-case assessment under Art. 102 TFEU; (ii) no regulation under Art. 102 TFEU, since a vast processing of data is immanent to online platforms or (iii) strong direct regulations – that could provide an answer to the challenges that dominant online platforms cause for competition law in the digital economy. The dissertation will end with a conclusion in which the question raised in this introduction will be answered in more detail and where future prospects will be made (more under J.). The answer to the research question aims to contribute to an ongoing discussion amongst not just academics but also policy makers and legislators as to how data-related business practices should be addressed under competition law.

---

23 The "Immanenztheorie" is an unwritten ground of justification of collusive behavior under § 1 of the German Act against Restraints of Competition. According to the theory, a restriction of competition is immanent in some agreements that are, however, generally recognized by the legal system. Therefore, certain necessary restrictions of competition are accepted in such cases. The approach can be described as a teleological reduction based on the spirit and purpose of competition law.

The research methodology applied is a doctrinal legal research methodology, which comprises an analysis of the relevant literature, EU legislation, policy documents and case law from the field of (European) data protection and competition law. Additionally, the decision-making practice of the European Commission and the German Bundeskartellamt are covered in the analysis in order to highlight developments with regard to the approach for a regulation of online platforms and their data-related business practices.

B. Big data and the digital economy

Both big data and the characteristics of the digital economy have a significant importance for the following work, which is why the underlying definitions and fundamental characteristics will be discussed first in order to gain a better understanding of the topic in general (more under I. and II.). Additionally, the fact shall be highlighted and discussed that personal data is of such importance within the digital platform economy that it even shows similarities to a method of payment (more under III.) Only afterwards, with the help of this background information, can the associated legal problems of this topic be discussed.

I. Big data and its importance for the digital economy

Big data is a term that often lacks a precise definition but generally speaking, big data is used to describe a large dimension of a dataset with all kinds of data in it.[24] Big data does not necessarily have to include personal data but it is exactly this type of information that this work is focused on. Therefore, for the purpose of this work, the term "big data" shall specifically refer to a large data set with vast amounts of personal data. Personal data, on the other hand, is defined in Art. 4 (1) GDPR and is to be understood as any information relating to an identified or identifiable individual as data subject (more under C. II. 1. a)).

Notwithstanding the fact that big data lacks a precise and common definition, it is often characterized in the digital economy by four "V"s: volume, variety, velocity and value.[25] Volume refers to the characteristically complex and vast amounts of data from which the term "big data" derives

---

24 Kupik/Mikeš, E.C.L.R. 2018, 393 (393); see also Ward/Barker, "Undefined By Data: A Survey of Big Data Definitions", September 20th, 2013, pp. 1 et seq., available on the internet under https://arxiv.org/pdf/1309.5821.pdf (last accessed: 22/05/19).

25 See Stucke/Grunes, 2016, pp. 16 et seqq; see also OECD, "Big Data: Bringing Competition Policy to the Digital Era", November 29–30, 2016, p. 5, available on the internet under https://one.oecd.org/document/DAF/COMP(2016)14/en/pdf (last accessed: 22/05/19); see also Zech, "Data as a Tradeable Commodity – Implications for Contract Law", p. 3, who also speaks of volume, variety, velocity but

its prefix "big".[26] The second characteristic of big data, its variety, describes the fact that it includes various types of information like the address, age, gender or name of a person. The third "V", velocity, derives from the fact that it is characteristic for big data to be generated, processed and, above all, analysed at highest speeds and almost in real-time.[27] Those three "V"s in turn, are then connected to the fourth "V", value. The value of big data depends significantly on the volume of data, its topicality and thus on the velocity at which it is processed and analysed once collected. The latter is due to the fact that it becomes less relevant over time. Additionally, the variety is crucial for the overall value as well. Therefore, companies also have an incentive to collect a broad range of data since different kinds of data secure the best possible insight into people`s lives. This insight into the lives of people is crucial for the use of big data as a tool to anticipate consumer needs. The more accurate the data is, the better products can be developed and enhanced and the better the data can be used as a tool for targeted marketing.[28]

As mentioned above, big data plays an important role in today`s digital economy and,[29] due to the growth of the whole industry over the last number of years, the value of data has been vastly increasing, too.[30] This development is predominantly based on the fact that *"the more data you can collect, the more you know, the better product you can provide, but also the more*

---

who mentions veracity instead of value, available on the internet under https:// papers.ssrn.com/sol3/papers.cfm?abstract_id=3063153 (last accessed: 24/09/19).

26 Some, however, refer with the prefix "big" rather to the complexity of big data and less to its actual size; see Ward/Barker, "Undefined By Data: A Survey of Big Data Definitions", September 20th, 2013, p. 2, available on the internet under https://arxiv.org/pdf/1309.5821.pdf (last accessed: 22/05/19).

27 Stucke/Grunes, 2016, p. 19.

28 See Waehrer, "Online services and the analysis of competitive merger effects in privacy protections and other quality dimensions", July 8th, 2016, p. 3, available on the internet under https://papers.ssrn.com/sol3/papers.cfm?abstract_id=2701927 (last accessed: 20/06/19).

29 See Budzinski, "Diskussionspapier Nr. 103 – Aktuelle Herausforderungen der Wettbewerbspolitik durch Marktplätze im Internet", p. 10, available on the internet under https://www.tu-ilmenau.de/fileadmin/media/wth/Diskussionspapier_N r_103.pdf (last accessed: 20/06/19).

30 See OECD, "Big Data: Bringing Competition Policy to the Digital Era", p. 6, available on the internet under https://one.oecd.org/document/DAF/ COMP(2016)14/en/pdf (last accessed: 22/05/19); see also Stucke/Grunes, 2016, p. 22.

powerful will you be towards others,"[31] as Margrethe Vestager has phrased it. An analysis of the IBM Institute for Business Value has revealed that companies using big data are 36% more likely to beat their competitors in terms of revenue growth and operating efficiency.[32] Hence, the strong market positions of companies such as *Facebook*, *Google* and others largely depend on their access to such digital information. Customers or users are therefore induced to give away their data by different means, e.g. personalized accounts, rebate schemes or other extra benefits which require the supplying of personal data. The value of such data sets is illustrated by the fact that they can actually constitute an undertaking's most valuable asset, as seen in the case of the online toy store *Toysmart.com*.[33] Moreover, due to the importance of big data for companies in the digital economy and the fact that a company with access to large amounts of data has a competitive advantage over competitors with access to only a little data,[34] it does also constitute a factor that fosters market power. Consequently, companies will not only have a strong incentive to gain access to as much data as possible, but they will also have a strong incentive to limit their competitors' access to such data.[35] In this context, big data can therefore also constitute a barrier to entry to a given market since the possession of vast amounts of data is almost essential for a successful business in the digital platform economy.[36]

---

31 Crofts/McLeod, MLex Interview: Margrethe Vestager, MLex Special Report, January 2015, p. 5, available on the internet under https://mlexmarketinsight.com/insights-center/reports/interview-with-margrethe-vestager (last accessed: 22/05/19).

32 IBM Institute for Business Value, Innovative analytics – *How the world's most successful organizations use analytics to innovate*, April 2015, p. 3, available on the internet under ftp://public.dhe.ibm.com/software/pdf/de/Innovative_analytics_Exec_Report_v42.pdf (last accessed 20/09/19).

33 See Stucke/Grunes, 2016, p. 41.

34 See Crofts/McLeod, MLex Interview: Margrethe Vestager, MLex Special Report, January 2015, p. 5, available on the internet under https://mlexmarketinsight.com/insights-center/reports/interview-with-margrethe-vestager (last accessed: 22/05/19); see also see also with regard to this phenomenon in the platform economy in general: European Commission, Competition policy for the digital era – A report by Jacques Crémer, Yves-Alexandre de Montjoye and Heike Schweitzer, p. 24, available on the internet under https://ec.europa.eu/competition/publications/reports/kd0419345enn.pdf (last accessed: 01/04/20).

35 Stucke/Grunes, 2016, p. 40.

36 See Kupik/Mikeš, E.C.L.R. 2018, 393 (395).

II. The digital (platform) economy and its characteristics

Before delving deeper into the topic of the present dissertation – namely the influence of big data and data protection considerations on competition law – the digital economy and its characteristics shall be discussed first. It is this sector of the economy in particular where big data plays such an important and prominent role.

Generally speaking, the digital economy refers to an economy that finds its base in digital technologies – as the name suggests. However, the term "digital economy" is nowadays often used to refer specifically to the "internet economy" and especially to online platforms and (business) activities in this context.[37] As pointed out in the introduction, this work is limited in its scope to such online platforms. Hence, the following part will in particular highlight the characteristics of the digital platform economy.

1. The term "online platform"

Before the characteristics of the digital (platform) economy are highlighted, the term "online platform" shall be explained. Online platforms have shaped the internet to a large extent over the last decade and they play an essential role in the digital economy. However, the term "online platform" itself lacks a precise and generally accepted definition.[38] This is to a large extent due to the fact that these platforms come in different shapes and various sizes. They cover all kinds of activities such as online marketplaces, search engines, online advertising and social media networks – just to name a few.[39] Nevertheless, they all share some specific characteristics, which shall be briefly summarized in the following in order to provide a better understanding of the term "online platform".

---

37 International Monetary Fund, "Measuring the Digital Economy", Policy Paper, April 5th, 2018, p. 7, available on the internet under https://www.imf.org/en/Publications/Policy-Papers/Issues/2018/04/03/022818-measuring-the-digital-economy (last accessed: 27/03/20).

38 See House of Lords – Select Committee on European Union, Online Platforms and the Digital Single Market, HL Paper 129 2015–16, marginal no. 38, available on the internet under https://publications.parliament.uk/pa/ld201516/ldselect/ldeucom/129/129.pdf (last accessed: 22/06/19).

39 See European Commission, Communication from the Commission – Online Platforms and the Digital Single Market Opportunities and Challenges for Europe, Brussels, May 25th, 2016, COM(2016) 288 final, p. 2.

Generally speaking, in a competition law context, a platform can be described as a multi-sided market that acts as an intermediary between two or more groups of customers or users, thus creating indirect network effects.[40] This definition can be applied not only to "offline" platforms in the brick-and-mortar economy such as shopping malls or dating bars but also to online platforms in the digital economy. Therefore, the latter are likewise characterized by so-called two- or even multi-sided markets, where providers of goods or services and their customers can meet. The European Commission is even more precise and defines an online platform as "*an undertaking operating in two (or multi)-sided markets, which uses the internet to enable interactions between two or more distinct but interdependent groups of users so as to generate value for at least one of the groups.*"[41] In practice, however, online platforms are often not just mere platforms as such, but also show elements of so-called "networks".[42] The most famous example of such an online platform is the social network *Facebook*. In contrast to a platform, a network allows interaction between users of the same user-group, thereby creating direct network effects.[43]

Due to the use of the internet by online platforms, it is also characteristic for them that they are software based. This software-based nature and the resulting quick adaptability to new trends ultimately also affects the competitive process in the digital economy, the characteristics of which shall be highlighted in the following.

---

40 See Bundeskartellamt, Working Paper, "Market Power of Platforms and Networks", June 2016, p. 8, available on the internet under https://www.bundeskartellamt.de/SharedDocs/Publikation/EN/Berichte/Think-Tank-Bericht-Langfassung.pdf?__blob=publicationFile&v=2 (last accessed: 22/06/19).
41 European Commission, "Public Consultation on the regulatory environment for platforms, online intermediaries, data and cloud computing and the collaborative economy", September 2015, p. 5, available on the internet under http://ec.europa.eu/newsroom/dae/document.cfm?doc_id=10932 (last accessed: 27/03/20).
42 See Bundeskartellamt, Working Paper, "Market Power of Platforms and Networks", June 2016, p. 87, available on the internet under https://www.bundeskartellamt.de/SharedDocs/Publikation/EN/Berichte/Think-Tank-Bericht-Langfassung.pdf?__blob=publicationFile&v=2 (last accessed: 29/03/20).
43 See Bundeskartellamt, Working Paper, "Market Power of Platforms and Networks", June 2016, p. 88 et seqq., available on the internet under https://www.bundeskartellamt.de/SharedDocs/Publikation/EN/Berichte/Think-Tank-Bericht-Langfassung.pdf?__blob=publicationFile&v=2 (last accessed: 29/03/20).

2. Characteristics of the digital platform economy

Predominantly, the economics of competition in the digital sector cannot be considered as completely detached from the principles that we know from competition in the brick-and-mortar economy. Nonetheless, some economic aspects have a significantly higher role for online platform markets in the digital economy than for markets outside the internet.[44] This is especially the case with multi-sided platform markets and their two-sidedness. As mentioned in the last paragraph, multi-sided platform markets are no exclusive peculiarity of the internet and they can be found in the "analogue economy" as well – e.g. in the form of classic commercial directories, credit cards or shopping malls. However, in contrast to the "analogue economy", in the digital economy multi-sided platform markets are the rule rather than the exception. Hence, they play a bigger role here.

A typical characteristic of multi-sided platform markets are the interactions between the respective sides leading to direct and indirect network effects.[45] In the case of social media platforms, for instance, this means that the more users a social media platform like *Facebook* has, the more attractive it will be to new users (direct network effect). On the other hand, the more users a platform has and the more users such a platform can win, the more attractive it will be for companies on the other side to pay for a placement of their advertisement on the platform`s website (indirect network effect).[46] Combined with the first mover advantage, meaning the competitive advantage a company has by being the first in a market,[47] the network effects foster concentration tendencies and are one of the

---

44 See Budzinski, "Diskussionspapier Nr. 103 – Aktuelle Herausforderungen der Wettbewerbspolitik durch Marktplätze im Internet", p. 2, available on the internet under https://www.tu-ilmenau.de/fileadmin/media/wth/Diskussionspapier_N r_103.pdf (last accessed: 20/06/19).

45 Körber, ZUM 2017, 93 (94); Federal Ministry for Economic Affairs and Energy, "Ein neuer Wettbewerbsrahmen für die Digitalwirtschaft – Bericht der Kommission Wettbewerbsrecht 4.0" (= A New Competition Framework for the Digital Economy – Report by the Commission Competition Law 4.0), p. 16, available on the internet under https://www.bmwi.de/Redaktion/DE/Publikationen/Wirtschaft/bericht-der-kommission-wettbewerbsrecht-4-0.html (last accessed 01/04/21).

46 See Budzinski, "Diskussionspapier Nr. 103 – Aktuelle Herausforderungen der Wettbewerbspolitik durch Marktplätze im Internet", p. 5, available on the internet under https://www.tu-ilmenau.de/fileadmin/media/wth/Diskussionspapier_N r_103.pdf (last accessed: 20/06/19).

47 Jones/Sufrin, 2016, p. 83.

reasons why companies in this economy often have high market shares. However, high market shares do not necessarily imply market power in these highly innovative online platform markets.[48] This is based on the fact that innovation is crucial in this industry and the boundaries of markets are constantly redefined through a process of "disruptive innovation".[49] This phenomenon describes a process whereby a small company, usually one that is new to the market, successfully challenges the incumbent by introducing an innovative alternative at lower costs to segments that the incumbent may have neglected with their own product/service.[50] After gaining a first foothold in the market, the entrant will ultimately move up-market and will expand its position due to its innovative product/service, thereby diminishing the incumbent`s market share. The disruptive nature of markets in the digital economy can be illustrated by Sten Franke`s "Social Media Prismas".[51] Franke, who is, according to the German business magazine *Wirtschaftswoche*, one of the most influential internet people in Germany,[52] points out that more than 50 % of the platforms that were included in his last publication from 2014 have disappeared over the course of only three years.[53] However, not only Franke but many

---

48 Körber, ZUM 2017, 93 (95); See Jones/Sufrin, 2016, pp. 344 et seq.

49 See European Parliament, Challenges for Competition Policy in a Digitalised Economy", July 2015, p. 9, available on the internet under http://www.europarl.europa.eu/RegData/etudes/STUD/2015/542235/IPOL_STU%282015%29542235_EN.pdf (last accessed: 15/07/19); see also Christensen/Raynor/McDonald, "What is Disruptive Innovation", Harvard Business Review, December 2015, available on the internet under https://hbr.org/2015/12/what-is-disruptive-innovation (last accessed: 15/07/19); Graef, "Stretching EU Competition Law Tools for Search Engines and Social Networks", Internet Policy Review 2015, pp. 2 et seq., available on the internet under https://papers.ssrn.com/sol3/papers.cfm?abstract_id=2655555 (last accessed: 23/07/19).

50 See Christensen/Raynor/McDonald, "What is Disruptive Innovation", Harvard Business Review, December 2015, available on the internet under https://hbr.org/2015/12/what-is-disruptive-innovation (last accessed: 15/07/19).

51 See for the latest version, the Social Media Prisma 2017/2018: Franke, "Das neue Social Media Prisma 2017/2018 – Wandel durch Disruptive Innovation", 16/10/2017, available on the internet under https://ethority.de/2017/10/16/das-neue-social-media-prisma-20172018-wandel-durch-disruptive-innovation/ (last accessed: 15/08/19).

52 Wirtschaftswoche, "Welche Menschen die deutsche Internetwirtschaft bewegen", 07/05/2012, available on the internet under https://www.wiwo.de/technologie/digitale-welt/plaetze-21-bis-100-plaetze-61-bis-100/6598926-2.html (last accessed: 15/08/19).

53 Franke, "Das neue Social Media Prisma 2017/2018 – Wandel durch Disruptive Innovation", 16/10/2017, available on the internet

more point out that there is a permanent threat in these digital industries that an innovative competitor could outperform the dominant undertaking.[54] Consequently, this leads to the fact that market power has a rather ephemeral nature in these industries. This is especially the case because dynamic competition is much more intense for online platforms that are software based. The software-based nature makes it easier to add new services/features in competition with others.[55] Admittedly, the sunk costs of developing software from scratch can constitute a barrier for potential competitors, preventing them from entering into competition with the dominant undertaking in the first place. However, the fact that there are various platforms such as *Facebook, Amazon, Google* and others that started in college bedrooms, garages and the like illustrates that developing software does not necessarily cost millions of euros. In addition, it is especially true for existing competitors already active in the market that they will find it easier to develop their software-based products further by editing an already existing source code, thus introducing new services/features in competition with others.[56]

Moreover, due to their multi-sidedness, platforms have to attract not just one type of customer but different groups of them.[57] In this context, it is a typical phenomenon that at least one side of the market does not pay a monetary sum for the product/service offered. That way, online platforms are able to attract the attention of users more easily. Additionally, gaining access to the user`s data, which they provide in return instead of paying

---

under https://ethority.de/2017/10/16/das-neue-social-media-prisma-20172018-wandel-durch-disruptive-innovation/ (last accessed: 15/08/19).

54 See for instance GC in case T-79/12, *Cisco Systems and Messagenet v Commission*, ECLI:EU:T:2013:635, para. 69; Bundeskartellamt, B6–113/15, Arbeitspapier Marktmacht von Plattformen und Netzwerken, June 2016, pp. 80 et seqq., available on the internet under https://www.bundeskartellamt.de/SharedDocs/Publikation/DE/Berichte/Think-Tank-Bericht.pdf?__blob=publicationFile&v=2 (last accessed: 23/08/19); Körber, ZUM 2017, 93 (94); Grave/Nyberg, WUW 2017, 363 (363); Jones/Sufrin, 2016, pp. 344 et seq.

55 Evans, "Multisided Platforms, Dynamic Competition, and the Assessment of Market Power for Internet-Based Firms", University of Chicago Coase-Sandor Institute for Law & Economics Research Paper No. 753, p. 16, available on the internet under https://ssrn.com/abstract=2746095 (last accessed: 03/12/19).

56 See also Körber, ZUM 2017, 93 (94).

57 Graef, "Stretching EU Competition Law Tools for Search Engines and Social Networks", Internet Policy Review 2015, p. 2, available on the internet under https://papers.ssrn.com/sol3/papers.cfm?abstract_id=2655555 (last accessed: 23/07/19).

a monetary price, is easier as well.[58] This means – in reference to the four "V"s of big data – that big platforms like *Facebook* or *Google* can gather particularly large and complex data sets (volume and variety),[59] which they can process almost instantly (high velocity) due to its software-based nature. Thereby, the overall value of the data collected (value) will be increased, too.[60] With the help of this data, advertisements can be personalized and the spaces where they can be placed are then sold to companies. That way, the business model can be monetized, even though it is free of a monetary charge on one side.

Despite the fact that the monetary price normally constitutes an important parameter of competition, undertakings are nonetheless in competition with each other on non-price-related parameters and, in the context of this dissertation, the level of data protection must be highlighted as one of those non-price-related parameters of competition.[61] The circumstance that companies like *Facebook* offer their services free of a monetary charge finds its base in the data-driven nature, which is characteristic of companies in the digital platform economy.

According to Hartman et al., a company can be considered as data-driven if its business model relies on data as a key resource.[62] However, such

---

58 Evans, "Multisided Platforms, Dynamic Competition, and the Assessment of Market Power for Internet-Based Firms", University of Chicago Coase-Sandor Institute for Law & Economics Research Paper No. 753, p. 10, available on the internet under https://ssrn.com/abstract=2746095 (last accessed: 03/12/19).

59 See European Commission, Commission Staff Working Document, A Digital Single Market Strategy for Europe – Analysis and Evidence, SWD(2015) 100 final, p. 53, available on the internet under https://eur-lex.europa.eu/legal-content/EN/TXT/PDF/?uri=CELEX:52015SC0100&from=EN (last accessed: 23/08/19).

60 See with regard to the interplay between the four "V"s of big data p. 5, B. I. "Big data and its importance for the Digital Economy".

61 See European Commission in case no. COMP/M.7217, *Facebook/Whatsapp*, marginal no. 87 where it is stated that "consumer communications apps compete for customers by attempting to offer the best communication experience", which includes, inter alia, "privacy and security, the importance of which varies from user to user but which are becoming increasingly valued, as shown by the introduction of consumer communications apps (such as Threema) specifically addressing privacy and security issues"; see also Waehrer, "Online services and the analysis of competitive merger effects in privacy protections and other quality dimensions", July 8th, 2016, p. 1, available on the internet under https://papers.ssrn.com/sol3/papers.cfm?abstract_id=2701927 (last accessed: 20/06/19).

62 Hartman et al., "Big Data for Big Business? A Taxonomy of Data-driven Business Models used by Start-up Firms", March 2014, available on the internet under https://cambridgeservicealliance.eng.cam.ac.uk/resources/Down-

a broad definition needs some clarification. A data-driven business model can be defined more precisely as a model that collects and analyses large amounts of data in order to make business decisions based on this data and, in particular, create value out of it.[63] It is particularly this latter aspect, the transformation of mere information into a monetizable asset by which revenue streams are created, that is immanent in a data-driven business model. Consequently, these business models are aimed at acquiring user data instead of charging the user a monetary price for their service. Besides the data-driven nature of such companies in the digital (platform) economy and the resulting importance of personal data, this is also what connects the data protection considerations to competition law concerns. Competition law concerns, such as the incentive of companies to get access to as much data as possible – sometimes using anti-competitive means to the disadvantage of the data subjects – or the incentive to prevent competitors from acquiring access to valuable data, is strongly connected to the data-driven nature.

III. Personal data as consideration in the digital platform economy

As outlined above, the collection and processing of vast amounts of data is one of the peculiarities of the digital platform economy and of significant importance for the competitive process in this industry. Likewise, it was highlighted above that this is why companies often do not charge the user a monetary price but instead aim at gathering user data. In the digital economy and its data-driven business models, big data is often considered to be the *"new currency of the internet"*[64] for services that might be free

---

loads/Monthly%20Papers/2014_March_DataDrivenBusinessModels.pdf (last accessed: 12/09/19).

63 See for similar characteristics Hein/Hendricks, "Data-Driven-Company", Business Intelligence Magazine, available on the internet under https://www.bi-magazine.net/data-driven-company.html (last accessed: 12/09/19).

64 Margrethe Vestager during her confirmation hearing before the European Parliament, October 2014, available on the internet under http://www.europarl.europa.eu/hearings-2014/resources/library/media/20141022RES75845/20141022RES75845.pdf (last accessed: 30/11/18); see also Monopolkommission, Wettbewerb 2018 – XXII. Hauptgutachten der Monopolkommission gemäß § 44 Abs. 1 Satz 1 GWB, July 3rd, 2018, p. 253, stating that personal data would function as a method of payment, available on the internet under https://www.monopolkommission.de/images/HG22/HGXXII_Gesamt.pdf (last accessed: 24/08/19).

of charge at first glance. For instance, companies like *Google* or *Facebook* might not charge private users a certain monetary price but they still require something in return for their service: the user`s data. The supposedly free services companies often offer in the digital economy are therefore not really free of any charge but are rather aimed at acquiring valuable personal data from their customers and/or users.[65] Due to the importance of data as a resource for these data-driven business models and its similarity to a method of payment, the question comes up whether the data provided by the users has to be regarded as some sort of payment in kind sui generis. This question is of particular relevance in order to illustrate that the competition law approach to abusive price mechanisms might also be applicable to data due to its alleged function as a method of payment.

In order to deal with the notion of data being the *"new currency of the internet"*[66] in a legal manner, the contractual relationship between platforms such as *Facebook* and their users has to be taken into account. Only on the basis of this can it be assessed whether or not data can be regarded as a payment in kind within the contractual relationships in this context. For the purpose of this work, this avenue of investigation will be based on a German legal perspective – more precisely on the provisions of the German Civil Code (hereinafter referred to as "BGB", abbreviation for "Bürgerliches Gesetzbuch"). This is not least based on the fact that the EU´s new *Directive (EU) 2019/770 of 20 May 2019 on certain aspects concerning contracts for the supply of digital content and digital services,*[67] explicitly states that the legal nature of such contracts where personal data is supplied in return for a service shall be determined by national law.[68]

---

65 Stucke/Grunes, 2016, p. 37; see also Franceschi, in: Schmidt-Kessel/Kramme, 2017, p. 115.
66 Margrethe Vestager during her confirmation hearing before the European Parliament, October 2014, available on the internet under http://www.europarl.europa.eu/hearings-2014/resources/library/media/20141022RES75845/20141022RES75845.pdf (last accessed: 30/11/18).
67 Directive (EU) 2019/770 of the European Parliament and of the Council of 20 May 2019 on certain aspects concerning contracts for the supply of digital content and digital services, OJ L 136/1.
68 See recital 12 of directive EU 2019/770, stating, inter alia, that "the question of whether such contracts constitute, for instance, a sales, service, rental or sui generis contract, should be left to national law."

1. Classification of contract typology

Before dealing with the question whether or not data can be regarded as a payment in kind, the user agreements of platforms such as *Facebook* shall first be placed within the German BGB system to accordingly assess whether a payment other than money would be allowed under that contract according to the provisions of the BGB.[69]

It is acknowledged that the German BGB system is not conclusive with regard to the different types of contracts provided for in the §§ 433 et seqq.[70] This finds its base in contractual freedom which entails the so-called "type freedom" ("Typenfreiheit"). The latter explicitly acknowledges that certain types of contracts may be combined with each other (mixed contracts) or may even be alien to the typological classification of the BGB (atypical contracts). Hence, the user agreements of platforms like *Facebook* do not necessarily have to fall under one of the BGB`s contractual categories. Nonetheless, most of them do indeed classify as one of those contract types – even though there is much discussion as to which type exactly.[71]

More precisely, the literature discusses the so-called "Software-as-a-Service" agreements of *Facebook, Google* and co. predominantly as a contract for work ("Werkvertrag" according to § 631 BGB), a service contract ("Dienstvertrag" according to § 611 BGB) or – due to the missing monetary remuneration – as a mandate ("Auftrag" according to § 662 BGB).[72] The latter, however, is not a valid option, as can be shown based on the example of *Facebook*.[73] Generally speaking, the classification of the con-

---

69 Contracts such as the purchase agreement in the sense of § 433 BGB specifically require a monetary purchase price. Here, a payment in kind would not be possible.

70 Stürner, in: Prütting/Wegen/Weinreich, § 311 BGB, marginal no. 16; Grüneberg, in: Palandt, § 311 BGB, marginal no. 11; Gehrlein, in: BeckOK BGB, § 311, marginal no. 18 (effective 01/08/19); see also German Federal Constitutional Court, decision of February 2nd, 1990, 1 BvR 26/84, NJW 1990, 1469 (1469 et seq.).

71 German Federal Court of Justice, judgement of March 4th, 2010, III ZR 79/09, MMR 2010, 398 (399); see Bräutigam, MMR 2012, 635 (636); Seidler, 2016, pp. 129 et seqq.; Kutscher, 2015, pp. 45 et seqq.; Redeker, in: Hoeren/Sieber/Holznagel, Handbuch MMR, part 12 B. II., marginal nos. 17 et seq.

72 Seidler, 2016, pp. 129 et seqq.; Kutscher, 2015, pp. 45 et seqq.; Bräutigam, MMR 2012, 635 (636); Redeker, in: Hoeren/Sieber/Holznagel, Handbuch MMR, part 12 B. II., marginal nos. 17 et seq.

73 Bräutigam, MMR 2012, 635 (636).

tract typology depends on the obligations of the parties.[74] A user`s main intention when concluding the user agreement with *Facebook* is to get access to the social network and its IT infrastructure. The use of the IT infrastructure entails the uploading of information, the storage of this information and the ability to send messages to another user.[75] Due to the fact that *Facebook* uses its own servers for their social network, one could argue that the company is therefore also responsible for the successful delivery of messages to other users or the correct storage of uploads.[76] Accordingly, *Facebook* could owe a certain result as the main contractual duty rather than the execution of an order, as would be characteristic for a mandate.[77] This would rather match the characteristics of a contract for work in the sense of § 631 BGB and would contradict a classification as a mandate. Jandt and Roßnagel, on the other hand, classify the user agreements of *Facebook* and co. as service agreements in the sense of § 611 BGB.[78] They are of the opinion that *Facebook* does not owe a certain result but merely provides access to the company`s social network.[79] However, even if the user agreement is not to be classified as a result-related contract for work but rather as an activity-related service agreement, classifying it as a mandate seems to be unsuitable either way.

Additionally, what further contradicts the classification as a mandate is the fact that this would result in the application of § 667 and § 670 BGB.[80] Consequently, the user could have a claim according to which the advertising revenues generated by the social network in the course of the mandate would need to be handed over to the user in accordance with § 667 BGB. Additionally, *Facebook* could offset claims for reimbursement of expenses for the use of the IT infrastructure based on § 670 BGB. It is obvious that such a result is not intended by the parties when entering into the platform agreement.

---

74 See for instance German Federal Court of Justice, judgement of August 30th, 2018, VII ZR 243/17, NJW 2018, 3380, marginal nos. 21 et seqq.; German Federal Court of Justice, judgement of July 19th, 2018, VII ZR 19/18, ZfBR 2018, 775, marginal nos. 19 et seqq.; see also Voit, in: BeckOK BGB, § 631, marginal no. 6 (effective 01/02/19); Busche, in: MüKo BGB V, § 631, marginal no. 9; Seidler, 2016, p. 130.
75 Seidler, 2016, p. 130.
76 Seidler, 2016, p. 130.
77 See also Seidler, 2016, p. 130.
78 See Jandt/Roßnagel, MMR 2011, 673 (679).
79 See Jandt/Roßnagel, MMR 2011, 673 (679).
80 Redeker, in: Hoeren/Sieber/Holznagel, Handbuch MMR, part. 12 C. VIII., marginal no. 424; Bräutigam, MMR 2012, 635 (636).

Speaking of the parties' intention, Seidler denies a classification as a contract for work or a service contract, arguing that users are not conscious of disclosing their data in return for access to the network.[81] Therefore, the necessary meeting of the minds would be missing in this context.[82] However, in the case of *Facebook*, for instance, the terms of service make the user`s consent to the collection of data an explicit requirement for accessing the platform. *Facebook*`s terms of service explicitly state:

> We don't charge you to use Facebook *or the other products and services covered by these Terms. Instead, businesses and organizations pay us to show you ads for their products and services. By using our Products, you agree that we can show you ads that we think will be relevant to you and your interests. We use your personal data to help determine which ads to show you.*[83]

By using the word "instead", it must become perfectly clear to the user that *Facebook* does not charge a monetary price but monetizes its business through personalized advertisements for which they need the user`s personal data. In that context, it is also evident that *Facebook* collects user data in return for access to the platform. Moreover, *Facebook's* stock market launch has brought the highly successful business strategy of "platform-access against data" more into the public spotlight.[84] This "deal" was also highlighted by the Irish Data Protection Commissioner stating that *"this basic "deal" is acknowledged by the user when s/he signs up to FB"*.[85] Additionally, topics such as privacy, targeted marketing and big data have experienced an increasing awareness over the last decade. Tech giants and their data-related business practices have been regularly featured in the media, too.[86] Consequently, people are indeed aware of the fact that *Face-*

---

81 Seidler, 2016, p. 130.
82 Seidler, 2016, p. 130.
83 Facebook, Terms of Service, Date of Last Revision: July 31st, 2019, available on the internet under https://www.facebook.com/legal/terms/update (last accessed: 22/09/19).
84 See also Bräutigam, MMR 2012, 635 (638).
85 Irish Data Protection Commissioner, Facebook Ireland Ltd. – Report of Audit, December 21st, 2011, p. 4, available on the internet under https://www.pdpjournals.com/docs/87980.pdf (last accessed: 06/08/19).
86 See for instance Dworschak/Rosenbach/Schmundt, "Planet der Freundschaft", May 7th, 2012, available on the internet under https://www.spiegel.de/spiegel/print/d-85586231.html (last accessed: 06/08/19), stating that user would not pay Facebook with money but with the data track of their lives; Nocun, "Habe meine Daten runtergeladen: Was Facebook alles

book and co. are only able to monetize their businesses by the use of the data collected from their users as a de facto "payment".[87] People are also aware that companies like *Facebook* have a strong interest in collecting user data, which is why they only grant the users access to the platforms in order to obtain access to their data in return. Thus, one cannot deny that both parties know about the other parties` intention when concluding the user agreements. As a result, the user agreements of online platforms can either be classified as a contract for work ("Werkvertrag" in the sense of § 631 BGB) or a service contract ("Dienstvertrag" in the sense of § 611 BGB). For the purpose of this dissertation, however, the exact classification can be left undecided between these alternatives. Both the contract for work and the service contract allow for a consideration other than money. The whole purpose of the contract typology classification was to illustrate that competition law principles regarding abusive price mechanisms might also be applicable to the excessive collection of personal user data. The rationale behind this thought is based on the parallel that both data and money might function as consideration for a dominant undertaking`s performance.[88]

The service contract, § 611 BGB, only speaks of "remuneration" ("Vergütung") as consideration for the other party`s performance. The

---

über mich weiß, hat mich schockiert", June 26th, 2018, available on the internet under https://www.focus.de/digital/experten/facebook-ich-wusste-dass-facebook-daten-speichert-doch-das-ausmass-hat-mich-erschreckt_id_9145326.html (last accessed: 06/08/19); Mansholt, "Zugriff auf Facebook-Daten: Hier sehen Sie, welche Apps bei Ihnen schnüffeln", March 21st, 2018, available on the internet under https://www.stern.de/digital/online/zugriff-auf-facebook-dat-en--hier-sehen-sie--welche-apps-bei-ihnen-schnueffeln-7908578.html (last accessed: 06/08/19); Müller, "Der große Google-Test", July 2nd, 2019, available on the internet under https://www.focus.de/digital/computer/chip-exklusiv/tid-18904/suche-datenschutz-nutzbarkeit-der-grosse-google-test_aid_525753.html (last accessed: 06/08/19); Hasse, "So entziehen Sie sich Googles Datensammlung", March 3rd, 2012, available on the internet under https://www.abendblatt.de/ratge-ber/wissen/article107752170/So-entziehen-Sie-sich-Googles-Datensammlung.html (last accessed: 06/08/19).

87 See also Hoffer/Lehr, NZKart 2019, 10 (19); Schmidt-Kessel/Grimm, ZfPW 2017, 84 (85); Schmidt-Kessel et al., GPR 2016, 54 (58).

88 If a dominant undertaking requires the payment of excessive prices in return for its contractual performance, this behavior might be classified as abusive under Art. 102 (2) (a) TFEU. Behind this background, it must then be seen as equally abusive, if the dominant undertaking requires a different consideration (e.g. the provision of personal data) of an equally undue amount in return for its own performance under the contract.

remuneration, however, does not necessarily have to consist of money.[89] The contract for work, § 631 BGB, only speaks of a "remuneration" as well and neither does it say anything about the exact kind of payment that is required under a contract for work.[90] It follows from the wording of § 631 BGB alike that the remuneration may consist not only of money but may take another form.[91] Therefore, both types of contracts match the characteristics of the platform agreements since neither of them requires the payment of a monetary sum. Accordingly, both types of contracts make it, in theory, possible to consider the provision of personal user data as consideration – i.e. as payment in kind sui generis.

Payments (contributions) in kind are often known from corporate law, for instance, as a contribution by the shareholder to the company`s share capital (see § 5 (4) of the German Limited Liability Companies Act (hereinafter referred to as "GmbHG")). These contributions in kind are often associated with physical objects. Thus, one might question the terminology when considering data as "payment in kind". The parallel to the German GmbHG makes it clear though that such payments/contributions in kind do not necessarily refer to physical objects. Contributions in kind may be any object – tangible or intangible – with a certain economic value.[92] The German legislator has a rather broad understanding of the term "payment in kind" which is why rights of use and other intangible assets can also classify as such.[93] Hence, the terminology itself does not preclude classifying data as payment in kind. However, what could preclude classifying the provision of personal data as consideration (i.e. payment in kind sui generis) is the question of whether it can constitute a suitable subject of performance/counter-performance (=consideration) ("Leistungsgegenstand"). This question will be discussed next.

---

89 Baumgärtner, in: BeckOK BGB, § 611, marginal no. 42 (effective 01/08/19); Müller-Glöge, in: MüKo BGB IV, § 611, marginal no. 696; Mansel, in: Jauernig, § 611 BGB, marginal nos. 30 et seq.

90 In contrast to § 433 (2) BGB, which specifically speaks of the "purchase price" as a monetary payment.

91 Busche, in: MüKo BGB V, § 631, marginal no. 89; Voit, in: BeckOK BGB, § 631, marginal no. 88 (effective 01/02/2019).

92 Ziemons, in: BeckOK GmbHG, § 5, marginal no. 177 (effective 01/05/19); Fastrich, in Baumbach/Hueck, GmbHG, § 5, marginal no. 23.

93 See Ziemons, in: BeckOK GmbHG, § 5, marginal no. 194 (effective 01/05/19); see also Schwandtner, MüKo GmbHG, § 5, marginal nos. 94 et seqq.

2. Data as subject of performance

As mentioned above, data is often considered "the new currency of the internet".[94] This phrase highlights the economic value of data and its function as a de facto method of payment. What is more, though, it likewise suggests that data can constitute the actual subject of a performance/counter-performance.

Generally speaking, the term "counter-performance" (=consideration) shall mean any performance which one party owes within the context of a mutual agreement as "payment" for the other party's performance. Hence, every consideration is a performance in itself. According to § 241 (1) BGB, the term "performance" has a rather broad definition and can consist of (i) a positive action, (ii) mere tolerance of an action or (iii) an omission.[95] Therefore, classifying personal data and the provision of it as a subject of performance does not cause any problems under the definition of "performance" at first glance.[96] Hacker, on the other hand, has defined the term "consideration" in more specific terms for the conditions of the digital economy.[97] According to him, the term consideration can be understood as transaction specific, typically (i) wealth-enhancing equivalent to performance which (ii) characterizes the exchange relationship and (iii) was not explicitly excluded from the concept of consideration.[98]

The first requirement, the wealth-enhancing requirement of the consideration, does not raise any problems when users provide their personal data based on their consent.[99] Personal data presents itself in the context of the digital (platform) economy as an essential "raw material", which is without doubt of a certain economic value.[100] The users` consent regarding the collection of data secures the legality of the processing and the value created by it. However, even in cases where the processing of data lacks such a valid legal base, the provision of user data has a certain economic

---

94 Margrethe Vestager during her confirmation hearing before the European Parliament, October 2014, available on the internet under http://www.europarl.europa.eu/hearings-2014/resources/library/media/20141022RES75845/20141022RES75845.pdf (last accessed: 30/11/18).
95 Bachmann, in: MüKo BGB II, § 241, marginal no. 19.
96 Schmidt-Kessel/Grimm, ZfPW 2017, 84 (88 et seq.).
97 Hacker, ZfPW 2019, 148 (158 et seq.).
98 Hacker, ZfPW 2019, 148 (158 et seq.).
99 Hacker, ZfPW 2019, 148 (159).
100 See Zech, GRUR 2015, 1151 (1152); Hacker, ZfPW 2019, 148 (159); Schmidt-Kessel/Grimm, ZfPW 2017, 84 (85).

value nonetheless.[101] *Facebook,* for instance, is a prime example showing that personal data has an immense economic value for undertakings in the digital (platform) economy, even if the collection of this data relies on an insufficient legal base – e.g. an insufficient consent.

Additionally, according to Hacker, the provision of data can only be regarded as consideration if it characterizes the exchange relationship as the main counter-performance.[102] With regard to user agreements for services that are free of any monetary consideration, the provision of user data is the only relevant performance by the user in return for the service.[103] Hence, it obviously characterizes the exchange relationship as the main counter-performance.

Lastly, the provision of user data must not be explicitly excluded from the concept of consideration. As seen above,[104] user agreements can be classified as types of contracts all of which allow for a consideration other than money so that there is no exclusion in that regard. However, in order to regard the provision of personal data as suitable for the concept of consideration, it would have to be possible that one can actually dispose one`s personal data in a property-like way. A report commissioned by the Federal Ministry of the Interior on the "modernisation of data protection law" states that there would be no such right similar to a property-like right of disposal of one`s personal data.[105] Likewise, Roßnagel et al. argue that personal data could not be the subject of performance for a legal transaction.[106]

Whether or not one can transfer personality rights has indeed been the subject of discussion amongst legal scholars for decades now.[107] This

---

101 Sometimes it is suggested that the provision of personal data cannot have an economic value without a sufficient legal base (see for instance Schmidt-Kessel/ Grimm, ZfPW 2017, 84 (89 et seq.)).

102 Hacker, ZfPW 2019, 148 (162); see also Bachmann, in: MüKo BGB II, § 241, marginal no. 29.

103 See also Hacker, ZfPW 2019, 148 (163); see also Buchner, WRP 2019, 1243 (1246).

104 See pp. 31 et seqq.; B. III. 1. "Classification of contract typology".

105 See Roßnagel/Pfitzmann/Garstka, "Modernisierung des Datenschutzrechts", report commissioned by the Federal Ministry of the Interior, Berlin 2002, p. 37, available on the internet under https://pdfs.semantic-scholar.org/fa68/4e56317983fb6c379f29de8f61b4e22d3087.pdf (last accessed: 12/08/19).

106 See footnote 105.

107 See for instance Forkel, GRUR 1988, 491 et seqq., who addressed the issue already back in 1988; Weichert, NJW 2001, 1463 et seqq.; Kilian, CR 2002, 921

whole dissertation illustrates, however, that it would contradict today`s reality and business trends if one would deny such a possibility. Of course, this cannot be the only argument in order to prove that there is actually the possibility to transfer rights to one`s own personal data but, contrary to various voices in literature, the possibility to transfer such rights is indeed backed by case law. In fact, even the earliest case law of the highest German courts on this matter certainly leaves room for such a possibility.[108] Therefore, both Kilian and Bräutigam rightly argue that personal data, as an objectified manifestation of the general right of personality, must be contractually transferable.[109] It becomes even clearer when drawing the parallel to the German Act on Copyright and Related Rights (UrhG) and its § 11 UrhG. The latter, § 11 UrhG, ensures the protection of "the author in his intellectual and personal relationships to the work and in respect of the use of the work". The principle behind § 11 UrhG takes into account the work as an intangible asset but also the personal relationship between the author and the work. Both are closely intertwined, which is why the author can indeed transfer certain rights of use without transferring his author`s rights completely. A similar limited transferable right of use should also be recognized in the present case with regard to personal data. The fact that today`s business trends call for such a transferability of personal data is evident. However, the regulatory framework for the commercialization of data, especially the regulatory notion in private law regarding its transferability, is by no means sufficiently developed yet.

Even the EU`s new directive 2019/770 also provides very little clarification.[110] As mentioned above,[111] the directive does deal with digital services that are provided in return for personal user data – in so far it does not differentiate between the payment of a monetary price or the "payment

---

et seqq.; Unseld, GRUR 2011, 982 et seqq.; Langhanke/Schmidt-Kessel, EuCML 2015, 218 et seqq.; Hacker, ZfPW 2019, 148 et seqq.

108 See German Federal Constitutional Court, judgement of December 15th, 1983, 1 BvR 209/83, NJW 1984, 419 (421), stating that it follows from the idea of self-determination that the individual has the power to decide for himself when and within what limits personal data shall be revealed; see also German Federal Court of Justice, judgement of October 14th, 1986, VI ZR 10/86, NJW-RR 1987, 231 – *Nena*; German Federal Court of Justice, judgement of December 1st, 1999, I ZR 49/97, NJW 2000, 2195 – *Marlene Dietrich*.

109 See Kilian, CR 2002, 921 (925 et seqq.); see also Bräutigam, MMR 2012, 635 (639).

110 See footnote 67.

111 See p. 30; B. III. "Personal data as consideration in the digital platform economy".

in kind" of providing personal data. On the other hand, it leaves aspects such as the legal nature of the contracts or the exact organization of the transferability of personal data to the national law of the member states. The lack of certainty regarding the transferability of personal data could indeed exclude the provision of personal data from the concept of consideration, as stipulated by Hacker as a third (negative) requirement for consideration. The problem of the lacking framework for such a transferability in German private law is not the primary concern of this work, though. Therefore, a detailed examination of this matter would go beyond the scope of this dissertation, which is why the discussion will be left to future studies. Apart from that, directive 2019/770 nonetheless suggests that a parallel can be drawn between the payment of a monetary price and the provision of user data – de facto a payment in kind sui generis.[112] The former proposal of the directive even classified the provision of personal data explicitly as "counter-performance".[113] Recital 13 of the former proposal specifically stated:

> *In the digital economy, information about individuals is often and increasingly seen by market participants as having a value comparable to money. Digital content is often supplied not in exchange for a price but against counter-performance other than money, i.e. by giving access to personal data or other data. [...] Introducing a differentiation depending on the nature of the counter-performance would discriminate between different business models; it would provide an unjustified incentive for businesses to move towards offering digital content against data. A level playing field should be ensured. In addition, defects of the performance features of the digital content supplied against counter-performance other than money may have an impact on the economic interests of consumers. Therefore the applicability of the rules of this Directive should not depend on whether a price is paid for the specific digital content in question.*

Even though the wording of recital 13 of the former proposal did not make its way into the final directive 2019/770, the rationale behind it remains true, nevertheless. A differentiation depending on the nature of

---

112 See. Art. 3 directive 2019/770, stating that the directive shall apply not only in cases where the digital content/service is provided for a monetary price but also in cases where personal data is provided in return.

113 See Proposal for a Directive of the European Parliament and of the Council on certain aspects concerning contracts for the supply of digital content, COM(2015) 634 final – 2015/0287 (COD), recital 13.

the counter-performance would not adequately address the peculiarities of the digital platform economy. Consequently, even though the regulatory framework of German private law regarding the transferability of personal data is not sufficiently developed yet, one can still draw a parallel between the payment of a price and the quasi payment in kind sui generis – e.g. the provision of personal data.

3. Interim conclusion

It has been shown that the user agreements of online platforms can either be classified as a contract for work ("Werkvertrag" in the sense of § 631 BGB) or a service contract ("Dienstvertrag" in the sense of § 611 BGB). For the purpose of this dissertation, though, the exact classification can be left undecided between these alternatives. This is based on the fact that both types of contract allow for a consideration other than money. In that context, the parallels between money and personal data as consideration under the aforementioned contracts were highlighted. The purpose was to illustrate that competition law principles regarding (abusive) price mechanisms can also be applied to the excessive collection of personal user data. The rationale behind this thought is based on the parallel that not only money but also personal data functions, de facto, as consideration in the digital platform economy.[114] This is also recognized by the directive 2019/770. However, German private law lacks the exact regulatory framework regarding the transferability of personal data, which needs to be developed in the near future. As shown throughout the previous pages, the business trends and practices in today`s digital (platform) economy call for legal certainty in that regard, but that is not the research matter of this dissertation.

---

114 If a dominant undertaking requires the payment of excessive prices in return for its contractual performance, this behavior might be classified as abusive under Art. 102 (2) (a) TFEU. On this basis it must then be seen as equally abusive, if the dominant undertaking requires a different consideration (e.g. the provision of personal data) of an equally undue amount in return for its own performance under the contract.

C. Overview of the core legal framework

The previous pages have outlined the characteristics of the digital economy and the special features of personal data in this context. The foregoing info should help to understand how the actual legal framework, namely European data protection and competition law, can be applied to cope with the new legal challenges that the digital platform economy raises.

The following section will present the core legal framework of this dissertation in order to provide the required background knowledge for the chapters to follow. Based on the fact that the following dissertation is limited in its scope to the example of strong online platforms with a certain "platform power" and their data-related business practices within the EU, the legal framework of this work particularly consists of data protection and competition law. More precisely, the European GDPR and Art. 102 of the TFEU constitute the core legal framework for this work. The following part will first elaborate Art. 102 TFEU (more under I.), followed by an explanation of the GDPR (more under II.).

I. Article 102 of the Treaty on the Functioning of the European Union

Generally speaking, Art. 102 TFEU deals with the unilateral conduct of undertakings and is aimed at preventing them from abusing their dominant position within the internal market or a substantial part of it. In order to apply Art. 102 TFEU, five general elements have to be fulfilled: There has to be (i) one or more undertakings, meaning an entity or entities engaging in an economic activity,[115] with (ii) a dominant position (iii) within the internal market or a substantial part of it, and in addition there has to be (iv) an abuse of said dominant position with (v) a possible effect on

---

115 ECJ in case C-41/90, *Höfner and Elser v Macrotron GmbH*, ECLI:EU:C:1991:161, para. 21.

inter-state trade.[116][117] In the context of the digital economy, the crucial elements of Art. 102 TFEU are the establishment of a dominant position and the abuse of said position. These elements will be mostly under the influence of big data with regard to their application and interpretation. Therefore, these two requirements of Art. 102 TFEU will be elaborated on in more detail below (more under I. 1. respectively I. 2.). Lastly, the possibility of an objective justification will be briefly explained (I. 3.).

1. The establishment of dominance and the resulting "special responsibility"

Art. 102 TFEU does not provide a definition of the term "dominant position" but the European Court of Justice (ECJ) has stated inter alia in *United Brands* that an undertaking holds a dominant position where it enjoys a position of such economic strength that it is able *"to prevent effective competition being maintained on the relevant market by giving it* (the undertaking) *the power to behave to an appreciable extent independently of its competitors, customers and ultimately of its consumers"*.[118] Additionally, the ECJ has stated that dominance exists only in relation to a particular market.[119] Thus, the definition of the relevant market is an essential first step to be made in order to later establish the dominance of an undertaking.[120] In order to define the relevant market, it is necessary to look at the market in the light of its product aspect (the product market), its geographical aspect (the geographic market) and even in the light of its temporal aspect (the temporal market). That way, potential substitutes for the goods and/or

---

116 The requirement of a possible effect on trade between member states (inter-state trade) limits, together with the requirement that the dominant position has to be held in the internal market or within a substantial part of it, the EU's jurisdiction and shall exclude an application of the provision in cases without any Union interest. The focus of this part will, however, lie on an elaboration of the two main requirements: the establishment of a dominant position and the abuse of this position.

117 Jones/Sufrin, 2016, p. 259.

118 ECJ in case C-27/76, *United Brands v Commission*, ECLI:EU:C:1978:22, para. 65.

119 ECJ in case C-6/72, *Europemballage Corporation and Continental Can Company v Commission*, ECLI:EU:C:1973:22, para. 32.

120 See Jones/Sufrin, 2016, p. 290.

services in question can be identified, which then determines the exact market.[121]

Once the relevant market is defined, a set of factors has to be taken into account in order to establish the dominance of the respective undertaking. Generally speaking, two steps can be distinguished here: firstly, the undertaking's market share will be analysed and afterwards, the market structure in general has to be considered.[122] With regard to the undertaking's market share, it has to be noted that the significance of market shares can vary from one market to another.[123] Nevertheless, an undertaking that has a particularly high market share, perhaps even for a long period of time, can be presumed to be dominant. The ECJ has affirmed such a legal presumption of dominance for market shares of at least 50 %.[124] Anything below that threshold requires certain "plus factors" as extra indicators of an "unhealthy" market structure.[125] However, even the presumption of dominance based on a high market share does not automatically make the second step, the look at the general market structure, obsolete. The Court of Justice of the European Union (CJEU) has been rather reluctant to decide on dominance solely based on high market shares.[126] Therefore, other factors of the market structure have to be taken into account such

---

121 Schröter/Bartl, in: von der Groeben/Schwarze/Hatje, AEUV, Art. 102, marginal no. 127; Weiß, in: Calliess/Ruffert, AEUV, Art. 102, marginal no. 6; see also Paal, in: BeckOK InfoMedienR, AEUV, Art. 102, marginal no. 6 (effective 01/05/19); Jones/Sufrin, 2016, pp. 291 et seqq.

122 See Weiß, in: Calliess/Ruffert, AEUV, Art. 102, marginal nos. 10 et seqq.; see also Herz/Vedder, "A Commentary on Article 102 TFEU", marginal no. 11, available on the internet under https://papers.ssrn.com/sol3/papers.cfm?abstract_id=2977195 (last accessed: 27/03/20).

123 See Weiß, in: Calliess/Ruffert, AEUV, Art. 102, marginal no. 11; see also ECJ in case C-85/76, *Hoffmann-La Roche v Commission*, ECLI:EU:C:1979:36, para. 41.

124 ECJ in case C-62/86, *AKZO Chemie BV v Commission of the European Communities*, ECLI:EU:C:1991:286, para. 60.

125 See GC in case T-219/99, *British Airways plc. v Commission of the European Communities*, ECLI:EU:T:2003:343, paras. 210 et seqq.; GC in case T-321/05, *AstraZeneca v Commission*, ECLI:EU:T:2010:266, paras. 242–243.

126 See e.g. ECJ in case C-85/76, *Hoffmann-La Roche v Commission*, ECLI:EU:C:1979:36, paras. 40–42; ECJ in case C-62/86, *AKZO Chemie BV v Commission of the European Communities*, ECLI:EU:C:1991:286, para. 61; GC in case T-30/89, *Hilti AG v Commission of the European Communities*, ECLI:EU:T:1991:70, paras. 92–94.

as, for instance, the market shares of the closest competitors,[127] network-effects[128], barriers to entry and/or expansion such as the access to key inputs[129] or the bargaining power of customers and their resulting so-called countervailing buying power[130]. The existence of a dominant position usually derives from a combination of several of these factors which do not necessarily have to be determinative if taken separately, each by itself.[131]

A crucial consequence resulting from the establishment of a dominant position is the so-called "special responsibility" a dominant undertaking has under Art. 102 TFEU.[132] This idea of the special responsibility was first developed by the ECJ in *Michelin I* where it was stated that, irrespective of the exact reasons leading to the dominant position, *"the undertaking concerned has a special responsibility not to allow its conduct to impair genuine undistorted competition on the common market."*[133] Consequently, something like a positive duty is imposed on a dominant undertaking according to which such an undertaking has to act in a way by which it observes the general EU goal of the internal market.[134] However, *"the actual scope of the special responsibility imposed on a dominant undertaking must be considered in the light of the specific circumstances of each case"*, as the Court has stated

---

127 See for instance ECJ in case C-85/76, *Hoffmann-La Roche v Commission*, ECLI:EU:C:1979:36, paras. 60, 63 and 66; see also ECJ in case C-27/76, *United Brands v Commission*, ECLI:EU:C:1978:22, para. 58.

128 Network-effects describe an increase in the utility that a user of a product/service experiences when more people start using the respective product/service, too. With regard to network-effects as a factor for the assessment of dominance under Art. 102 TFEU, see GC in case T-79/12, *Cisco Systems and Messagenet v Commission*, ECLI:EU:T:2013:635, paras. 78 et seqq.

129 See e.g. ECJ in case C-27/76, *United Brands v Commission*, ECLI:EU:C:1978:22, paras. 121–124.

130 Countervailing buying power refers to the ability of customers to create competition between suppliers or to pave the way for new entrants due to the size or commercial significance of the customers.

131 See for instance ECJ in case C-85/76, *Hoffmann-La Roche v Commission*, ibid, para. 39.

132 ECJ in case C-209/10, *Post Danmark A/S v Konkurrencerådet*, ECLI:EU:C:2012:172, para 23.

133 ECJ in case C-322/81, *NV Nederlandsche Banden Industrie Michelin v Commission of the European Communities*, ECLI:EU:C:1983:313, para. 57; see also ECJ in joined cases C-395 and 396/96 P, *Compagnie Maritime Belge Transport SA v Commission*, ECLI:EU:C:2000:132, para. 37.

134 See Jones/Sufrin, 2016, p. 358; see Herz/Vedder, "A Commentary on Article 102 TFEU", marginal no. 34, available on the internet under https://papers.ssrn.com/sol3/papers.cfm?abstract_id=2977195 (last accessed: 27/03/20).

it in *CMB* and *Tetra Pak II*.[135] Thus, exactly what conduct the dominant undertaking might be required to refrain from in order for it to not be classified as abusive, depends on the specificities of each case and the market background. Consequently, this means for the case at hand that the special responsibility of a dominant undertaking can also be affected by the peculiarities of the digital economy.

2. The abuse of a dominant position

As seen from the elaborations above, an undertaking has to abuse its dominant position in order to fall under Art. 102 TFEU. This is based on the fact that Art. 102 TFEU does not prohibit dominance itself, but purely the abuse of such a dominant position.[136] However, neither Art. 102 TFEU nor the TFEU in general provide any legal definition of the term "abuse" – as is the case with dominance. The ECJ, on the other hand, has defined the term "abuse" in *Hoffmann-La Roche* as *"an objective concept relating to the behaviour of an undertaking in a dominant position"* that further weakens the structure of competition in a market *"through the recourse to methods different from [...] normal competition"*, *"where, as a result of the very presence of the undertaking in question, the degree of competition is weakened"* anyway.[137] The notion of abuse is understood as such an "objective concept", so that the intention of the respective undertaking to infringe Art. 102 TFEU does not constitute a requirement in order to classify the conduct as abusive.[138] Moreover, regardless of the fact that Art. 102 TFEU does not provide any legal definition of the term abuse, it does name several examples that

---

135 ECJ in joined cases C-395 and 396/96 P, *Compagnie Maritime Belge Transport SA v Commission*, ECLI:EU:C:2000:132, para. 114; ECJ in case C-333/94 P, *Tetra Pak International SA v Commission of the European Communities*, ECLI:EU:C:1996:436, para 24.

136 ECJ in case C-209/10, *Post Danmark A/S v Konkurrencerådet*, ECLI:EU:C:2012:172, para 21; ECJ in case C-322/81, *NV Nederlandsche Banden Industrie Michelin v Commission of the European Communities*, ECLI:EU:C:1983:313, para. 57; GC in case T-65/98, *Van den Bergh Foods Ltd v Commission of the European Communities*, ECLI:EU:T:2003:281, para. 158; see also Jung, in: Grabitz/Hilf/Nettesheim, Art. 102 TFEU, marginal. no. 119.

137 See ECJ in case C-85/76, *Hoffmann-La Roche & Co AG v Commission*, ECLI:EU:C:1979:36, paras. 91, 123.

138 ECJ in case C-549/10 P, *Tomra Systems ASA and Others v European Commission*, ECLI:EU:C:2012:221, paras. 18–21; Weiß, in: Calliess/Ruffert, AEUV, Art. 102, marginal no. 29.

constitute such an abuse in particular. However, the ECJ has emphasized several times that this list is not exhaustive and that there may be other forms of abusive conduct prohibited by Art. 102 TFEU.[139]

Predominantly though, two categories of abuses can be distinguished: exploitative and exclusionary abuses.[140] The first category describes conduct of an undertaking in the course of which it takes advantage of its market power resulting in an exploitation of trading partners – e.g. customers and/or suppliers.[141] The second category, exclusionary abuse, refers to conduct of an undertaking that has a negative impact on the competition structure in a market. Thereby, it becomes clear that the conduct of an undertaking does not necessarily have to result in an exploitation of consumers in order to be classified as abusive. Conduct that negatively affects the effective competition structure within a given market can also constitute an abuse.[142] However, due to the rather indefinite spectrum of conduct that may fall under these two categories of abuse, it might be difficult to distinguish illegitimate from legitimate conduct. This problem was noted by the ECJ as well. Therefore, the Court stated in *Hoffmann-La Roche* that the key factor for a distinction between legitimate and illegitimate conduct is the question whether the dominant undertaking`s conduct can be classified as a *"recourse to methods different from those which condition normal competition in products or services on the basis of the transactions of commercial operators."*[143] This rather complicated phraseology

---

139 ECJ in case C-6/72, *Europemballage Corporation and Continental Can Company Inc. v Commission of the European Communities*, ECLI:EU:C:1973:22, para. 26; ECJ in case C-333/94 P, *Tetra Pak International SA v Commission*, ECLI:EU:C:1996:436, para. 37; cases C-395 and 396/96 P, *Compagnie Maritime Belge Transport SA v Commission*, ECLI:EU:C:2000:132, para. 112; case C-95/04 P, *British Airways v Commission*, ECLI:EU:C:2007:166, paras. 57–58; case C-280/08, *Deutsche Telekom v Commission*, ECLI:EU:C:2010:603, para. 173.

140 See ECJ in case C-6/72, *Europemballage Corporation and Continental Can Company Inc. v Commission of the European Communities*, ECLI:EU:C:1973:22, para. 26; Schröter/Bartl, in: von der Groeben/Schwarze/Hatje, AEUV, Art. 102, marginal no. 172; see Herz/Vedder, "A Commentary on Article 102 TFEU", marginal nos. 49–46, available on the internet under https://papers.ssrn.com/sol3/papers.cfm?abstract_id=2977195 (last accessed: 27/03/20); Jones/Sufrin, 2016, p. 351.

141 Jones/Sufrin, 2016, p. 351.

142 See ECJ in case C-6/72, *Europemballage Corporation and Continental Can Company Inc. v Commission of the European Communities*, ECLI:EU:C:1973:22, para. 26; Jones/Sufrin, 2016, p. 351.

143 ECJ in case C-85/76, *Hoffmann-La Roche v Commission*, ECLI:EU:C:1979:36, para. 91; see also ECJ in case C-322/81, *NV Nederlandsche Banden Industrie*

essentially means that, in order to fall outside the scope of Art. 102 TFEU, the conduct in question has to present itself as mere competition on performance factors such as price or quality – so-called "competition on the merits"[144].[145] Additionally, it should also be mentioned that Art. 102 TFEU does not protect less efficient competitors from being forced out of the market.[146] However, drawing an exact line between anti-competitive conduct on the one hand and legitimate competition on the merits on the other hand can be difficult, nonetheless.[147]

3. The possibility of an objective justification for abusive conduct

Even though a given behaviour of a dominant undertaking might classify as abusive, there is the possibility that such behaviour may be objectively justified. Should an undertaking`s abusive conduct be objectively justified, it escapes an infringement of Art. 102 TFEU.[148] In *Post Danmark I*, the

---

Michelin v Commission of the European Communities, ECLI:EU:C:1983:313, para. 70, where it says: "recourse to methods different from those governing normal competition in products or services based on traders' performance".

144 Exemplified, "competition on the merits" means that an undertaking provides a superior product/service at a low price which can force competitors out of the market. However, the undertaking is solely competing on performance based factors so that there is no problem with Art. 102 TFEU. It is required, however, that the low price reflects the actual production/running costs and does not just constitute a temporary loss-making business in order to force other competitors out of the market.

145 See e.g. ECJ in case C-457/10 P, *AstraZeneca AB and AstraZeneca plc v European Commission*, ECLI:EU:C:2012:770, paras. 93 and 134; ECJ in case C-549/10 P, *Tomra Systems ASA and Others v European Commission*, ECLI:EU:C:2012:221, para 42; see also in principle ECJ in case C-202/07 P, *France Télécom SA v Commission of the European Communities*, ECLI:EU:C:2009:214, para. 106.

146 ECJ in case C-209/10, *Post Danmark A/S v Konkurrencerådet*, ECLI:EU:C:2012:172, para. 21.

147 See Temple Lang/O'Donoghue, "Defining Legitimate Competition: How to Clarify Pricing Abuses Under Article 82 EC", Fordham International Law Journal 2002, 83 (83 et seqq.), available on the internet under https://ir.lawnet.fordham.edu/cgi/viewcontent.cgi?article=1866&context=ilj (last accessed: 01/10/19); Jones/Sufrin, 2016, pp. 361 et seq.

148 ECJ in case C-209/10, *Post Danmark A/S v Konkurrenceradet*, ECLI:EU:C:2012:172, para. 41–42; ECJ in case C-418/01, *IMS Health GmbH & Co. OHG v NDC Health GmbH & Co. KG*, ECLI:EU:C:2004:257, para. 51; GC in case T-201/04, *Microsoft Corp. v Commission of the European Communities*, ECLI:EU:T:2007:289, para. 688.

ECJ stated that conduct with anti-competitive effects can be objectively justified if it is either objectively necessary by means of health and safety concerns or if it is outweighed by efficiency gains that directly result from the respective conduct necessary for the achievement of those efficiency gains. Additionally, said gains would have to counteract any likely negative effects on competition and consumer welfare without eliminating effective competition overall.[149] As can be seen, the requirements of the concept of objective justification are stringent and subject to a high standard of proof.[150] Hence, the objective justification of an abusive conduct presents itself as hard to realize in practice since the burden of proof lies on the undertaking.[151] However, the need to comply with other legal provisions must also allow the possibility to objectively justify allegedly abusive conduct. In the context of the present dissertation, such legal provisions can be found in particular within the GDPR, which will be explained next.

II. The General Data Protection Regulation (GDPR)

In May 2018, the GDPR replaced the Data Protection Directive from 1995.[152] It now regulates the collection, processing and storing of personal data in all member states of the EU. The GDPR is part of the EU`s Digital Single Market Strategy[153] and constitutes a comprehensive reformation as well as harmonization of the former data protection law throughout the Union. The coherent data protection framework was implemented in order to prevent obstacles that might impede the free movement of data within the EU`s internal market. Additionally, it is to create both legal certainty and transparency in order to facilitate the development of the digital economy.[154] The digital economy offers great opportunities but as

---

149 ECJ in case C-209/10, *Post Danmark A/S v Konkurrenceradet*, ECLI:EU:C:2012:172, paras. 41–42.
150 Jones/Sufrin, 2016, p. 375.
151 GC in case T-201/04, *Microsoft Corp. v Commission of the European Communities*, ECLI:EU:T:2007:289, para. 688.
152 Directive 95/46/EC of the European Parliament and of the Council of 24 October 1995 on the protection of individuals with regard to the processing of personal data and on the free movement of such data.
153 See European Commission, Communication from the Commission to the European Parliament, the Council, the European Economic and Social Committee and the Committee of the Regions – A Digital Single Market Strategy for Europe, Brussels, 6.5.2015, COM(2015) 192 final.
154 See recitals 7, 10 and 13 of the GDPR.

Vestager said recently: The great task *"is to put the right policies in place, to help get European industry ready to grasp those opportunities."*[155]

Due to the fact that this second part of the legal framework refers to the GDPR as a legal act in itself, the approach in its explanation will differ from the approach applied above with regard to Art. 102 TFEU. This is based on the fact that the GDPR is relatively new and thus in various aspects still alien to many people so that the scopes of application shall be explained in more detail. Based on the novelty of the Regulation, this also enhances legal certainty. Additionally, this dissertation is addressed to readers, who are familiar with European competition law but those readers might be less familiar with data protection law. Thus, the explanation of the scopes of application of the GDPR shall provide the reader with the necessary background information with regard to the circumstances under which the Regulation may apply to a certain undertaking.

The following part will first provide an overview of the scope of application of the GDPR in the context of the digital economy (more under 1.). Afterwards, the decisive cornerstones of the Regulation – especially those of particular relevance for the digital economy – will be briefly discussed (more under 2.).

1. The scope of application of the GDPR

The scope of application of the GDPR has to be defined in material, territorial and personal terms and at least with respect to the first two aspects, the GDPR provides specific articles.

a) The material scope

Regarding the material scope of application, Art. 2 (1) GDPR is crucial and states that the EU`s new data protection law in form of the GDPR applies to every processing of so-called "personal data" – with only few exceptions. Thus, it is already apparent that the material scope is rather broad. Both

---

155 Vestager, Speech "Keeping the EU competitive in a green and digitial world", College of Europe, Bruges, March 2nd, 2020, available on the internet under https://ec.europa.eu/commission/commissioners/2019-2024/vestager/announcements/keeping-eu-competitive-green-and-digital-world_en (last accessed: 28/03/20).

the vague terms "processing" and "personal data" are defined in Art. 4 (1) respectively (2) GDPR. Generally speaking, according to Art. 4 (1) GDPR, personal data means any information that can be used to identify, directly or indirectly, any natural person – the so-called "data subject". Due to the fact that the mere possibility of an indirect identification is sufficient to classify data as personal data under the GDPR, even IP addresses[156] or pseudonymized data[157] are both to be regarded as personal data within the meaning of Art. 2 (1) GDPR.[158] This broad application affects especially the digital economy where vast amounts of data are based on these two data-categories of IP addresses and pseudonymized data.

Moreover, the word "processing" has a rather broad definition too. It is defined as any operation in connection with personal data. In particular, this refers to operations such as the collection, transmission or storage of personal data. This wide scope of application is only limited by the very few exemptions listed under Art. 2 (2) GDPR. According to those exemptions, the GDPR does not apply in cases of national security or security policy and neither in cases where there is a processing by either a natural person in the course of a purely personal or household activity or by competent authorities for matters of criminal law.[159] However, these exemptions do not apply by their very nature to the normal business conduct of companies in the digital (platform) economy. Therefore, they will not be explained in more detail.

b) The territorial scope

In order to determine the various obligations for undertakings under the GDPR, it is also important to elaborate the territorial and personal scope of application of the GDPR. The former is defined in Art. 3 of the Regulation.

---

156 ECJ in case C-582/14, *Patrick Breyer v. Bundesrepublik Deutschland*, ECLI:EU:C:2016:779, paras. 47, 48.
157 See recital 26 GDPR.
158 This is based on the fact that, in order to assess whether a person is identifiable or not, account should be taken of all the means reasonably likely to be used for such an identification as it is stated in recital 26 of the GDPR. Therefore, a data subject can be still classified as "identifiable" even if the data controller would require the help of a third person for such an identification.
159 See Ernst, in: Paal/Pauly, DSGVO/BDSG Kommentar, Art. 2 DSGVO, marginal nos. 11 et seqq.

Nowadays, national borders hardly play a role when it comes to the processing of personal data.[160] Therefore, according to Art. 3 (1) GDPR, the Regulation is not only applicable to undertakings that are purely active within the EU – this goes without saying. In fact, the Regulation applies also to European companies processing their data in an establishment outside the EU or, vice versa, to non-European companies processing data for their European establishments.[161] Facebook for instance is a prime example of the latter scenario, where the mother company Facebook Inc., USA, processes data from its European subsidiaries – e.g. Facebook Ireland Ltd.[162]

Above that, Art. 3 (2) GDPR sets out another extension regarding the territorial scope. Art. 3 (2) GDPR declares the Regulation applicable where personal data from European persons is processed by a controller outside the EU, regardless whether or not said controller has a European subsidiary. However, in such cases it is at least required that the processing activity is related to (i) either the offering of goods or services or (ii) the monitoring of people`s behaviour in the EU. It is important to mention that offering goods or services includes, inter alia, also goods and services free of charge like the services of internet search engines or social networks in the digital economy.[163] Hence, for an application of the GDPR, it is not important where the data processing takes place or where the head office of the processing body is located. This fact is even more important in the digital economy, where national boundaries have become largely obsolete.

c) The personal scope

With regard to the personal scope of the GDPR, no specific article can be found similar to articles 2 and 3 of the GDPR, which define the material,

---

160 See Buttarelli, International Data Privacy Law 2016, 77 (77).

161 Ernst in: Paal/Pauly, DSGVO/BDSG Kommentar, Art. 3 DSGVO, marginal nos. 5 et seqq.

162 Facebook Inc., the US-American mother company, processes vast amounts of personal data from European users transferred to them by their Irish daughter company Facebook Ireland Ltd. with which the European users concluded their contracts. This can be seen in the case of Mr. Schrems for instance in ECJ in case C-362/14, *Maximillian Schrems v Data Protection Commissioner*, ECLI:EU:C:2015:650.

163 Ernst in: Paal/Pauly, DSGVO/BDSG Kommentar, Art. 3 DSGVO, marginal no. 17.

respectively territorial scope. However, it is at least clearly illustrated by Art. 5 GDPR whom the obligations of the Regulation are aimed at. Art. 5 (1) GDPR sets out certain general principles relating to the processing of personal data. More precisely, Art. 5 (1) (a) GDPR sets out the general obligation to process personal data lawfully, fairly and transparently. Art. 5 (2) GDPR on the other hand defines the accountability of the data controller, stating that it is the controller who is responsible for compliance with the general principles laid down in Art. 5 GDPR. However, processing data "lawfully" constitutes an obligation of such generality that it includes the more specific obligations of the whole GDPR, too. Hence, it is clearly the data controller who is the main body being bound by the GDPR and the rules in it.[164] According to Art. 4 (7) GDPR, controller is to be defined as "the natural or legal person, public authority, agency or any other body which, alone or jointly with others, determines the purposes and means of the processing of personal data".

2. The decisive cornerstones of the GDPR

There is not only a need for clarification regarding the applicability of the Regulation but also with regard to the decisive provisions of the GDPR. The Regulation consists of a whole set of rules – 99 Articles in fact. The following passage shall give an insight into the decisive provisions and principles of the GDPR, where it would be most plausible that an infringement of those provisions by a dominant undertaking might also trigger Article 102 TFEU. Other provisions than the following, especially Art. 17 GDPR, which stipulates the right to be forgotten known from the *Google-Spain* case[165] and which is amongst the provisions that are often mentioned in the context of "big data", are deliberately not discussed at this point. Article 5 and 6 GDPR, which will be discussed in the following, constitute the pivotal elements of the GDPR and are most likely to be breached when other provisions of the GDPR are infringed as well.[166] Thus, the focus lies particularly on them. These Articles especially are

---

164 See also Rücker/Kugler, 2018, para. 120; Kamann/Miller, NZKart 2016, 405 (408).

165 See ECJ in case C-131/12, *Google Spain SL and Google Inc. v Agencia Española de Protección de Datos (AEPD) and Mario Costeja González*, ECLI:EU:C:2014:317.

166 See for instance with regard to Art. 17 GDPR Worms, in: BeckOK DatenschutzR, Art. 17 DSGVO, marginal no. 26 (effective 01/08/18).

relevant for the research question as it shall be clarified whether a violation of the pivotal elements of the GDPR could lead to an infringement of Art. 102 TFEU.

a) The admissible grounds for processing personal data

The starting point for an examination under data protection law is usually the question whether the data was processed lawfully or not.[167] This is based on the fact that one normally reviews whether the controller was allowed to collect the data in the first place before one examines any further actions the controller took or should have taken. Hence, it is especially the question whether the respective processing of data is lawful or not that takes on an important role within the system of the GDPR. The GDPR follows the principle of prohibition with reservation of authorization.[168] This means that any processing of personal data is prohibited unless it is based on one of the admissible grounds. Therefore, especially Art. 6 GDPR – respectively Art. 9 with regard to special categories of personal data such as medical data or data concerning ethnic origin, political belief or sexual orientation – are of particular importance.[169] Those articles name the admissible grounds that may serve as a legal basis for the processing. However, in most cases the applicability of those grounds in the free economy and especially in digital markets is by their very nature limited. Big tech-companies will, for instance, hardly ever process data according to Art. 6 (1) (d) GDPR in order to protect the vital interests of a data subject. Rather, the intention for processing the data of customers and/or platform-users will be the economic value resulting from the processing – namely for example the ability to enhance one's products according customer's preferences or the placing of advertisements tailored to the customer's needs. Thus, in the context at hand, processing of personal data can in most cases only be based on either the explicit and genuinely freely given consent of the relevant person (Art. 6 (1) (a) GDPR), a contract for which the processing is provably necessary (Art. 6 (1) (b) GDPR), a

---

167 Steinrötter, EWS 2018, 61 (65).
168 Frenzel in: Paal/Pauly, DSGVO/BDSG Kommentar, Art. 6 DSGVO, marginal no. 1.
169 Processing of data that falls under the "special categories of data" within the meaning of Art. 9 GDPR will be an exception in the digital economy, which is why Art. 9 GDPR will not be explained in more detail within this dissertation. The focus will lie on non-special data and thus on Art. 6 GDPR.

legal obligation to which the controller is subject such as certain legal obligations to preserve records (Art. 6 (1) (c) GDPR) or the legitimate interests of the controller (Art. 6 (1) (f) GDPR).[170]

b) The principles of purpose limitation and data minimization

The provisions about the legal bases are accompanied by the general obligation of Art. 5 (1) (b) GDPR stating that data has to be collected for a specific and legitimate purpose. Accordingly, processing is bound to those purposes for which the personal data was originally collected and may not go further in a way that is incompatible with those purposes. Any processing incompatible with the original purposes cannot be simply compensated with a separate legal basis either since this would undermine the actual intention behind this principle.[171] The provision about the purpose limitation is not only a cornerstone of the GDPR but of data protection law in general.[172]

Moreover, the principle of data minimization stipulated in Art. 5 (1) (c) GDPR is of particular importance and also affects the admissible grounds mentioned in Art. 6 GDPR. More precisely, it specifically affects Art. 6 (1) (b), (c) and (f) GDPR. Generally speaking, it entails that any processing based on these grounds must pass a three-stage test similar to a proportionality test consisting of an examination whether the collection of personal data is appropriate for the purpose for which the data is meant to be used, whether it is limited to what is necessary and whether it is actually suitable for achieving the specific purpose.[173] That way, Art. 5 (1) (c) GDPR explicitly defines the principles of data avoidance and data

---

170 See also Steinrötter, EWS 2018, 61 (66 et seq.); see also Bundeskartellamt, case summary of case no. B6–22/16 – *Facebook*, published February 15th, 2019, pp. 10 et seq. where those legal grounds were likewise in the focus, available on the internet under https://www.bundeskartellamt.de/SharedDocs/Entscheidung/EN/Fallberichte/Missbrauchsaufsicht/2019/B6-22-16.pdf?__blob=publicationFile&v=3 (last accessed: 27/03/20).

171 Schantz, in: BeckOK DatenschutzR, Art. 5 DSGVO, marginal no. 23 (effective 01/02/19).

172 Schantz, in: BeckOK DatenschutzR, Art. 5 DSGVO, marginal no. 12 (effective 01/02/19).

173 Frenzel, in: Paal/Pauly, DSGVO/BDSG Kommentar, Art. 5 DSGVO, marginal nos. 34 et seqq.; Schantz, in: BeckOK DatenschutzR, Art. 5 DSGVO, marginal nos. 24 et seqq. (effective 01/02/19).

economy, which require that the amount of personal data processed by the controller be reduced as much as possible.[174] Thus, extensive collection of data, as practiced by Facebook for instance, is only justifiable based on the explicit and freely given consent of the user.

c) The requirement of transparency

Independent of the question of the legal base but similarly linked to Art. 5 GDPR and occupying a similarly important role within the whole system of the Regulation are the transparency obligations. As mentioned above, Art. 5 (1) (a) GDPR states that "personal data shall be processed lawfully, fairly and in a transparent manner". The principle of transparency is an important cornerstone of the GDPR and has been significantly strengthened compared to previous data protection laws in the member states of the EU.[175] The intention behind this requirement is to ensure that data subjects are actually aware of the fact that their personal data are being processed, as well as being aware of their rights in this context.[176] Moreover, the whole GDPR might come to nothing without a sufficient degree of transparency since a breach of data protection could remain unnoticed.[177] Hence, the required transparency is particularly important for an effective enforcement of the GDPR and for the protection of the data subjects.

---

174 Pötters, in: Gola, DSGVO Kommentar, Art. 5, marginal no. 22.
175 See Heberlein, in: Ehmann/Selmayr, DSGVO Kommentar, Art. 5 DSGVO, marginal no. 11; Pötters, in: Gola, DSGVO Kommentar, Art. 5, marginal no. 10.
176 Paal/Hennemann, in: Paal/Pauly, DSGVO/BDSG Kommentar, Art. 13 DSGVO, marginal no. 4.
177 Pötters, in: Gola, DSGVO Kommentar, Art. 5, marginal no. 11.

D. The relation between data protection and competition law

From the elaboration of the legal acts above, data protection and competition law are indeed rather different at first glance. In addition, when thinking of "traditional scenarios", the relation between data protection and competition law might not be too obvious, either. For instance, an employer who secretly records an employee at his workplace without his consent obviously does not violate competition law in any way. However, the employer clearly violates data protection law. On the other hand, the recent Intel case[178] did not raise any privacy related concerns but Intel was fined 1.6 billion euros by the Commission for an infringement of Art. 102 TFEU. Nevertheless, in some areas privacy concerns do play a role when it comes to competition law concerns. This is particularly obvious in the digital economy as recent developments such as the Facebook case of the German Bundeskartellamt have shown. In this digitalized industry, these two fields of law are becoming more and more intertwined[179] – even though such a connection might contradict the traditional understanding of these two legal acts. Therefore, the following part shall assess in which aspects data protection and competition law overlap in order to find an answer to one of the aspects covered by the research question: Can European data protection and competition law be considered "compatible" with each other based on their respective objectives and other parallels?

This question is important since such parallels constitute an essential foundation, by which the rationale behind the research question of the present dissertation can be underpinned: The fact that linking data protection considerations to competition law concerns may not present itself as an artificial approach.

In this context, the traditional understanding regarding the relationship between these two fields of law will be briefly summarized first and it will be shown that a turning point in the understanding has indeed been

---

178 European Commission in case no. COMP/C-3 /37.990, D(2009) 3726final – *Intel*.
179 See also Cornelius, NZWiST 2016, 421 (421); Zanfir-Fortuna, Ianc, "Data Protection and Competition Law: The Dawn of "Uberprotection", p. 2, available on the internet under https://papers.ssrn.com/sol3/papers.cfm?abstract_id=3290824 (last accessed: 16/03/20).

reached (more under I.). Afterwards, the respective objectives of European data protection and competition law will be discussed (more under II. 1.), before further parallels in particular between the GDPR and Art. 102 TFEU will be elaborated (more under II. 2.). Lastly, an interim conclusion will be given (more under III.).

I. The evolving opinion on the relation between data protection and competition law

Traditionally, competition and data protection law were regarded as two separate fields of law with no relation whatsoever. This was illustrated by the ECJ in 2006 in the case of *Asnef-Equifax*.[180] The case was based on a register the purpose of which it was to exchange information between competing financial institutions about their debtors. The information exchanged gave an insight into the solvency of their debtors in order to evaluate the risks undertaken when engaging in credit or lending activities with them. Here, the ECJ explicitly stated that *"any possible issues relating to the sensitivity of personal data are not, as such, a matter for competition law, they may be resolved on the basis of the relevant provisions governing data protection."*[181] However, one has to point out that this case differed from today's data-related business practices in so far as the usage of data in *Asnef-Equifax* served a common interest rather than the sake of a specific undertaking as is the case today. Nowadays, undertakings have an interest in keeping as much data as possible for themselves.

The Commission of the European Union, on the other hand, was likewise reluctant to link data protection considerations to competition law cases. In its Google/DoubleClick-decision of 2008, the Commission stated in its conclusion that the proposed concentration between Google Inc. and DoubleClick Inc. was cleared solely from a competition law point of view and without prejudice to any other obligation arising under data protection law.[182] This approach was affirmed by the Commission's decision in the Facebook/WhatsApp-merger in 2014.[183] In its decision, the

---

180 ECJ in case C-238/05, *Asnef-Equifax v Ausbanc*, ECLI:EU:C:2006:734.
181 ECJ in case C-238/05, *Asnef-Equifax v Ausbanc*, ECLI:EU:C:2006:734, para. 63.
182 European Commission in case no. COMP/M.4731, C(2008) 927 final, *Google/DoubleClick*, para. 368.
183 European Commission in case no. COMP/M.7217, C(2014) 7239 final, *Facebook/Whatsapp*.

Commission stated explicitly that it "*has analysed potential data concentration only to the extent that it is likely to strengthen Facebook's position in the online advertising market*" and "*any privacy-related concerns flowing from the increased concentration of data [...] as a result of the Transaction do not fall within the scope of the EU competition law rules but within the scope of the EU data protection rules.*"[184]

However, Joaquín Almunia, Vice President of the European Commission responsible for Competition Policy, had already indicated a point of rethinking in 2012. In a speech at an event called "Competition and Privacy in Markets of Data", Almunia highlighted the strong incentive for companies to gain access to personal data in order to gain a commercial advantage. Almunia had stated that due to the value of data in the digital economy, it may become a competition law issue in the future.[185] Likewise, Margrethe Vestager, the current European Commissioner for Competition, explicitly stated that "*competition rules weren't written with big data in mind*" but that big data can constitute a competition law concern so that she will have a close eye on companies and how they use data.[186]

II. The similarities between data protection and competition law

In the following, it will be assessed in which aspects data protection and competition law overlap and whether they are indeed to be regarded as two fundamentally different fields of law, which could exclude an interdisciplinary approach.

---

184 European Commission in case no. COMP/M.7217, C(2014) 7239 final, *Facebook/Whatsapp*, para. 163.

185 Almunia, "Competition and personal data protection", Speech at the Privacy Platform event: Competition and Privacy in Markets of Data, Brussels 26 November 2012, available on the internet under http://europa.eu/rapid/press-release_SPEECH-12-860_en.htm (last accessed: 09/02/20).

186 Vestager, Speech at the EDPS-BEUC Conference on Big Data, Brussels 29 September 2016, available on the internet under https://wayback.archive-it.org/12090/20191129222113/https://ec.europa.eu/commission/commissioners/2014-2019/vestager/announcements/big-data-and-competition_en (last accessed: 27/03/20).

1. The objectives of data protection and competition law

An approach to competition law assessments in the digital (platform) economy, by which data protection and competition law considerations are combined, would present itself as even more plausible, if data protection and competition law pursued to some extent the same or at least similar objective(s). *Kamann and Miller* argue, that the EU`s new data protection law in form of the GDPR and European competition law would indeed serve the same goals.[187] Taking a closer look, it can be argued that they are, inter alia, both aimed at enhancing market integration[188] and at a certain consumer protection.[189] However, such a statement is rather generalized and does not sufficiently address the intention behind data protection and competition law.[190] Therefore, this statement shall be assessed in more detail in the following.

---

187 Kamann/Miller, NZKart 2016, 405 (406).

188 Costa-Cabral/Lynskey, CML Rev. 2017, 11 (21 et seqq.); with regard to competition law see also Cseres, Competition Law Review 2007, 121 (151); Immenga/Mestmäcker, in: Immenga/Mestmäcker, KartellR Kommentar, Einl. EU. B, marginal no. 17; Bunte, in: Langen/Bunte, EU KartellR Kommentar, Einl., marginal no 1; see with regard to data protection law von Lewinski, in: Eßer/Kramer/von Lewinski, DSGVO/BDSG Kommentar, Art. 1 DSGVO, marginal nos. 3 et seq.; Selmayr/Ehmann, in: Ehmann/Selmayr, DSGVO Kommentar, Einführung, marginal no. 18.

189 See Vestager and her speech "Competition is a consumer issue" in front of the BEUC General Assembly, May 13th, 2016,stating that *"It`s* (compeition policy) *is there to defend consumers"*, available on the internet under https://wayback.archive-it.org/12090/20191129205633/https://ec.europa.eu/commission/commissioners/2014-2019/vestager/announcements/competition consumer-issue_en (last accessed: 27/03/20); see also Vestager and her speech "Competition in changing times" on the occasion of the FIW Symposium in Innsbruck (Germany), February 16th, 2018, stating *"Our rules are clear that consumers come first.",* available on the internet under https://wayback.archive-it.org/12090/20191129215248/https://ec.europa.eu/commission/commissioners/2014-2019/vestager/announcements/competition-changing-times-0_en (last accessed: 27/03/20); see also Säcker, in: MüKoEuWettbR, Einl., marginal no. 4; Costa-Cabrel/Lynskey, CML Rev. 2017, 11 (21); Kadar, ZWeR 2015, 342 (362); see with regard to data protection law also von Lewinski, in: Eßer/Kramer/von Lewinski, DSGVO/BDSG Kommentar, Einführung, marginal no. 69; Selmayr/Ehmann, in: Ehmann/Selmayr, DSGVO Kommentar, Einführung, marginal no. 18; Weitbrecht, NZKart 2020, 45 (46).

190 See also Kamann/Miller, NZKart 2016, 405 (406).

a) The objectives of European competition law

Arguably, one of the main objectives of European competition law is market integration. The market-oriented aspect of the objective of European competition law is explicitly mentioned in Protocol No. 27 on the Internal Market and Competition[191]. There it is stated that the internal market, as set out in Article 3 of the Treaty on European Union (TEU), "shall include a system ensuring that competition is not distorted". This phrase refers to the competition law system of the EU and illustrates that it constitutes an essential cornerstone of the creation and maintenance of the internal market in general.[192] In addition, in *Telia Sonera* Sverige, the ECJ even explicitly stated that Art. 102 TFEU is one of the competition rules necessary for the functioning of the internal market.[193] Thus, European competition law is primarily concerned with the prevention of market failure and the functioning of the internal market.

However, European competition law does not only have the purpose of protecting competition as such and thereby the internal market, it also has the purpose of protecting the interests of certain individual market participants – especially consumer interests.[194] For instance, in *Continental Can*, the very first judgement on Art. 102 TFEU, the Court explicitly stated: *"the provision* (meaning todays Art. 102 TFEU) *is not only aimed at practices which may cause damage to consumers directly, but also at those which are detrimental to them through their impact on an effective competition structure such as is mentioned in Article 3 (f) of the Treaty."*[195] The part of the Court`s judgement where it is explicitly stated that Art. 102 TFEU is aimed at preventing "practices which may cause damage to consumers directly", already indicates a certain consumer protective orientation within

---

191 Protocol No 27 on the internal market and competition, annexed to the Treaty of the Functioning of the European Union, OJ 2010 C 83/309.

192 Schröter, in: von der Groeben/Schwarze/Hatje, Art. 101 AEUV, marginal no. 18.

193 ECJ, judgement of 17/02/11 in case C-52/09, Konkurrensverket v *Telia Sonera Sverige AB*, ECLI:EU:C:2011:83, paras. 20 et seq.

194 See Eilmansberger/Bien, in: MüKo EuWettbR, Art. 102 AEUV, marginal nos. 10 et seqq.; see also Jones/Sufrin, 2016, p. 362; Kamann/Miller, NZKart 2016, 405 (407); see also 1st Cartel Senate of the Higher Regional Court Düsseldorf in its decision of August 26th, 2019, VI-Kart 1/19 (V) – "Facebook", p. 8, speaking of the concept of consumer protection implemented in Art. 102 TFEU.

195 ECJ in case C-6/72, *Europemballage Corporation and Continental Can Company v Commission*, ECLI:EU:C:1973:22, para. 26; ECJ, judgement of 17/02/11 in case C-52/09, Konkurrensverket v *Telia Sonera Sverige AB*, ECLI:EU:C:2011:83, para. 24.

European competition law. But what is more, the Court also emphasizes the element of an "effective competition structure", which European competition law is also aimed at.[196] This concept of effective competition was directly derived from Art. 3 (f) of the Treaty establishing the European Economic Community[197], which corresponds to Art. 3 (1) (g) of the Treaty establishing the European Community[198]. The respective Article 3 of those treaties names a catalogue of Community activities and states that the activities of the Community shall include, inter alia, a system ensuring undistorted competition in the internal market. As a result of the Lisbon Treaty, the provision about the system of undistorted competition as a building block of the internal market was shifted to "Protocol No. 27 on the Internal Market and Competition"[199]. However, since this is a full-fledged component of primary Union law, the normative rank of the provision has not changed.[200] The concept behind this provision focusses on the long-term consequences of anti-competitive behaviour and aims to prevent any market failure in the long run alike. That way, consumer welfare can be maximized in the long run, too.[201] Moreover, it is to be guaranteed that, by protecting the structure of competition, competition as a process is protected. Ultimately, this creates value for consumer in turn.[202] In the context of Art. 102 TFEU, this aim is illustrated by Advocate

---

196 In addition to the Court's statement in Continental Can regarding the aim of Art. 102 TFEU, see with regard to Art. 101 TFEU the ECJ in case C-26/76, *Metro SB-Großmärkte GmbH & Co KG v Commission*, ECLI:EU:C:1977:167, para. 20; GC in case T-168/01, *GlaxoSmithKline Services Unlimited v Commission*, ECLI:EU:T:2006:265, para. 109.

197 An English version of the Treaty was never published in the Official Journal but one can be found in the United Nations Treaty Series, available on the internet under https://treaties.un.org/doc/Publication/UNTS/Volume%20298/v298.pdf (last accessed: 27/03/20).

198 Treaty establishing the European Community, *OJ C 325*, 24/12/2002, pp. 33–184.

199 Consolidated version of the Treaty on European Union – PROTOCOLS – Protocol (No 27) on the internal market and competition, OJ C 115, 9.5.2008, p. 309.

200 See Fuchs, in: Immenga/Mestmäcker, KartellR Kommentar, Art. 102 TFEU, marginal no. 1.

201 Nazzini, 2011, p. 172.

202 See Michael Albers (Consultant to European and Asian Competition Authorities, who was entrusted with the task of developing a "more economic approach" to the application of the prohibition of abuse (Art. 102 TFEU)), "Der „more economic approach" bei Verdrängungsmissbräuchen: Zum Stand der Überlegungen der Europäischen Kommission", Lecture on the occasion

General (AG) Jacobs in the case of *Bronner,* where he explicitly stated that *"the primary purpose of Article [102] is to prevent distortion of competition – and in particular to safeguard the interests of consumer"*.[203] Additionally, Art. 3 (3) TEU postulates the model of the "social market economy" for the EU, which is another indicator of a consumer oriented approach.[204] Furthermore, the Commission already indicated years ago that they pursue an approach by which they aim to bring competition law into line with the other objectives of the Treaty.[205] In its "Report on competition policy" from 1993, the Commission explicitly stated that competition policy plays an important role in the implementation of other policies such as consumer protection.[206] In addition, the Commission explicitly stated in its 1998 *Football World Cup*-decision[207] that Art. 102 TFEU does not only protect consumer interests by prohibiting conduct of dominant undertakings which impairs free and undistorted competition, but also by prohibiting conduct which is direct prejudicial to consumers.[208] Consequently, Art. 102 TFEU can be even applied *"to situations in which a dominant undertaking's behaviour direct prejudices the interests of consumers – notwithstanding the absence of any effect on the structure of competition."*[209]

Moreover, the consumer-oriented direction of competition law was reinforced in the course of the Commission`s so-called "more economic approach" and its focus on the consumer welfare standard as "the guiding principle of EU competition policy"[210]. It has to be mentioned though, that the case law of the CJEU is not wholly uniform in this respect and

---

of the Hamburg Antitrust Law Symposium 2006, available on the internet under http://ec.europa.eu/competition/antitrust/art82/albers.pdf (last accessed: 27/03/20).

203 Case C-7/97, *Oscar Bronner GmbH & Co KG v Mediaprint,* ECLI:EU:C:1998:264, opinion of AG Jacobs, para. 58.

204 See also Kamann/Miller, NZKart 2016, 405 (407).

205 See European Commission, XXIIIrd Report on Competition Policy 1993, para. 2.149, available on the internet under https://publications.europa.eu/en/publication-detail/-/publication/7db4a243-39f3-4ba4-a5b7-1cb48f8ca6d3 (last accessed: 05/09/19); Weiß, in: Callies/Ruffert, Art. 101 AEUV, statement in footnote 362.

206 See European Commission, XXIIIrd Report on Competition Policy 1993, para. 2.149, available on the internet under https://publications.europa.eu/en/publication-detail/-/publication/7db4a243-39f3-4ba4-a5b7-1cb48f8ca6d3 (last accessed: 05/09/19).

207 European Commission, case no. IV/36.888 – *1998 Football World Cup.*

208 European Commission, case no. IV/36.888 – *1998 Football World Cup,* para. 100.

209 See footnote 208.

210 See Commissioner Almunia and his speech "Competition – what's in it for consumers?" on the occasion of the European Competition and Consumer

has not adopted the approach unreservedly in line with the Commission`s (at least theoretical) alignment and various pronouncements regarding the consumer welfare standard.[211] Instead, the CJEU emphasizes consumer welfare in some cases more than in others.[212] Nonetheless, one can discern an approach under which European competition law is ultimately also aimed at benefitting consumers.[213] This is realized either directly, by pro-

---

Day in Poznan, 24 November 2011, available on the internet under http://europa.eu/rapid/press-release_SPEECH-11-803_en.htm (last accessed: 11/03/20).

211 See for instance Commissioner Monti and his speech "The Future for Competition Policy in the European Union", Merchant Taylor`s Hall, London, July 9th, 2001, extracts available on the internet under http://europa.eu/rapid/press-release_SPEECH-01-340_en.htm?locale=de (last accessed: 12/03/20), where it was stated that *"the goal of competition policy [...] is to protect consumer welfare"*; see also Commissioner Kroes, "European Competition Policy – Delivering Better Markets and Better Choices", European Consumer and Competition Day, London, September 15th, 2005, available on the internet under http://europa.eu/rapid/press-release_SPEECH-05-512_en.htm?locale=en (last accessed: 12/03/20) where it was stated that *"Consumer welfare is now well established as the standard the Commission applies when assessing mergers and infringements of the Treaty rules on cartels and monopolies."*; see also See Commissioner Almunia and his speech "Competition – what's in it for consumers?" on the occasion of the European Competition and Consumer Day in Poznan, November 24th, 2011, available on the internet under http://europa.eu/rapid/press-release_SPEECH-11-803_en.htm (last accessed: 11/03/20); Commission, Guidance on the Commission's enforcement priorities in applying Article 82 of the EC Treaty to abusive exclusionary conduct by dominant undertakings, OJ 2009 C 45/02, marginal no. 5; see also Daskalova, Competition Law Review 2015, 133 (151 et seqq.).

212 See for instance ECJ in case C-457/10 P, *AstraZeneca v Commission*, ECLI:EU:C:2012:770, para. 186 or GC in case T-201/04, *Microsoft v Commission*, ECLI:EU:T:2007:289, para. 229, where the respective Courts were more concerned about the protection of effective competition than the direct protection of consumer welfare; on the other hand, see GC in the joined cases T-213/01 and T-214/01, *Österreichische Postsparkasse and Bank für Arbeit und Wirtschaft v Commission*, ECLI:EU:T:2006:151, para. 115; GC in case T-168/01 *GlaxoSmithKline Services Unlimited v Commission of the European Communities*, ECLI:EU:T:2006:265, para. 118, where the General Court was in both cases predominantly concerned about the well-being of consumers.

213 See for instance ECJ in case C-52/09, Konkurrensverket v *Telia Sonera Sverige AB*, ECLI:EU:C:2011:83, para. 24; ECJ in joined Cases C-468/06 to C-478/06, *Sot. Lélos kai Sia EE and others v GlaxoSmithKline AEVE Farmakeftikon Proïonton*, ECLI:EU:C:2008:504, para. 66, where a special focus was on the "final consumer"; ECJ in case C-28/77, *Tepea v Commission*, ECLI:EU:C:1978:133, para. 56, where it was regarded as incompatible with the internal market that an agreement had the effect to "deprive consumers of the benefits flowing from

hibiting any kind of exploitative abuse or indirectly, by securing (effective) competition within a market. The latter also protects competitors but, ultimately, securing effective competition primarily creates values for consumers in the long run.[214] Thus, European competition law does indeed serve, inter alia, the aim of consumer interests. In a competition law context, it is simply called consumer welfare, which is nonetheless similarly aimed at the protection of consumer rights and especially the protection of consumer interests.[215]

b) The objectives of the GDPR and data protection law in general

According to Art. 1 para. 2 GDPR, European data protection law in the form of the GDPR serves the protection of the rights of individuals – as is to a certain extend the case with competition law. Regardless of the fact that the GDPR cannot be classified as a consumer (protection) law as such, it does nonetheless have a consumer protective function and objective.[216] This is based on the fact that it is largely concerned with equalizing the imbalance of power between the data controller, on the one hand, and individuals as data subjects on the other.[217] To a large extent, it aims to protect the right to informational self-determination as one of the main objectives of European data protection law. The right to data protection is even secured by Art. 8 (1) of the Charter of Fundamental Rights of the

---

effective competition"; see also GC in the joined cases T-213/01 and T-214/01, *Österreichische Postsparkasse and Bank für Arbeit und Wirtschaft v Commission,* ECLI:EU:T:2006:151, para. 115; *see* also Andriychuk, 2017, p. 111.

214 See e.g. ECJ in case C-28/77, *Tepea v Commission,* ECLI:EU:C:1978:133, para. 56.

215 See for instance Cseres, Competition Law Review 2007, 121 (173); Jones/Sufrin, 2016, pp. 34 et seq. and p. 362; Kamann/Miller, NZKart 2016, 405 (407). It has to be noted, however, that the concept of consumers in a European competition law context encompasses in principle not only private end users but also other companies along the supply chain. In principle, the term "consumer welfare" can thus not be reduced to end-user-welfare. Nonetheless, a special emphasis is usually placed on the individual end user as it can be seen, inter alia, in the judgement of the GC in case T-168/01 *GlaxoSmithKline Services Unlimited v Commission of the European Communities,* ECLI:EU:T:2006:265, para. 118, where the GC was concerned with *"the welfare of the final consumer".*

216 Von Lewinski, in: Eßer/Kramer/von Lewinski, DSGVO/BDSG Kommentar, Einführung, marginal nos. 67 et seqq.

217 See von Lewinski, in: Eßer/Kramer/von Lewinski, DSGVO/BDSG Kommentar, Einführung, marginal no. 69.

European Union, which constitutes another cornerstone of the internal market. The fact that the protection of personal data has the character of a fundamental right emphasizes the status of data protection in general and the objective pursued by it: the protection of the rights of individuals.

However, protecting the idealistic interest of informational self-determination is not the only objective of (European) data protection law. In fact, it can be argued that data protection law also serves the aim of protecting commercial interests by securing people`s free choice regarding whether and how they want to grant access to their data for the commercial interests of others.[218] Buchner rightly sees users of online platforms like *Facebook* not just as mere consumers but also as "data suppliers" in a global market for (personal) data.[219] In that context, data protection law also serves a market-oriented purpose by securing the data supplier`s position as an equal party to the data transaction.[220]

Additionally, European data protection law is also essential for the internal market. According to Art. 1 paras. 1 and 3 GDPR, it aims to guarantee the free movement of data and is meant to abolish barriers to digital data trade. Such barriers can consist of different legal requirements amongst the European member states, such as national restrictions on data localization.[221] The full harmonization that goes with the GDPR intends to prevent this. The Commission explicitly stated with regard to the overall approach of data protection in the EU that data protection law serves ...

> ... *two of the oldest and equally important objectives of the European integration process: the protection of fundamental rights and freedoms of the individual, in particular the fundamental right to data protection, and the completion of the internal market.*[222]

It is especially the latter part that highlights one of the points of intersection between European data protection and competition law.

---

218 Buchner, WRP 2019, 1243 (1245); see also Mohr, EuZW 2019, 265 (272).
219 Buchner, WRP 2019, 1243 (1245).
220 See Buchner, Buchner, WRP 2019, 1243 (1245).
221 Brühann, in: von der Groeben/Schwarze/Hatje, Art. 16 AEUV, marginal nos. 72 et seq.; Schantz, in: BeckOK DatenschutzR, Art. 1 DSGVO, marginal nos. 2 et seq. (effective 01/02/19); Ernst, in: Paal/Pauly, DSGVO/BDSG Kommentar, Art. 1 DSGVO, marginal no. 14.
222 Communication from the Commission, "A comprehensive approach on personal data protection in the European Union", Brussels, 04/11/2010, COM(2010) 609 final.

2. Other links between data protection and competition law

In addition to the similarities in their respective objectives, European data protection law and competition law also show similarities and links in other aspects. To start with, they are two of the few areas of Union law which are of a Union constitutional law nature and which result directly from the TFEU – namely Art. 16[223] respectively Art. 101 et seqq. TFEU. This illustrates their similar status within the legal system of the Union. In addition to that, data protection law is also established in the Charter of Fundamental Rights of the European Union (CFREU), where it is explicitly mentioned in Art. 7 CFREU (right to privacy) respectively Art. 8 CFREU (right to protection of personal data). This, on the other hand, leads to another link between data protection and competition law. Article 51 (1) CFREU explicitly stipulates that the provisions of the Charter are addressed to, inter alia, the institutions of the Union,[224] which shall not only respect the respective rights and observe the principles but which shall also promote the application thereof. Consequently, institutions such as the Commission have to observe the fundamental rights of the CFREU in all their actions – i.e. also when it comes to the application of competition law.[225] Thus, the constitutional values of the Charter,[226] such as those of Art. 7 and Art. 8 CFREU, also have an indirect influence on competition law. However, this will be discussed in more detail as part of the elaborations regarding the normative influence of data protection law on competition law.[227]

Additionally, Europe`s data protection law in the form of the GDPR and likewise European competition law are both characterized by a dual system of administrative control and sanction measures on the one hand, and instruments of private enforcement such as claims for damages on the

---

223 Art. 16 (2) TFEU also formed the legal base for the General Data Protection Regulation.

224 The institutions of the Union are named in Art. 13 (1) subsec. 2 TEU. The European competition authority, the European Commission, is one of those institutions named in Art. 13 (1) subsec. 2 TEU.

225 See Jarass, GRCh Kommentar, Art. 51, marginal no. 14; see also Ladenburger/Vondung, in: Stern/Sachs, GRCh Kommentar, Art. 51, marginal nos. 6 et seq.; Kamann/Miller, NZKart 2016, 405 (407).

226 According to Art. 6 (1) TEU, the CFREU has the same legal status as the Treaties and forms thus likewise the EU`s constitutional base.

227 See pp. 106 et seqq.; F. I. 2. b) aa) "The influence of data protection considerations on the notion of abuse under Art. 102 (1) TFEU".

other.[228] With regard to the administrative sanction measures, the GDPR is heavily influenced by European competition law with regard to the imposition of fines for undertakings and applies the same methodology.[229] Firstly, the structure is similar, allowing the data protection authority according to Art. 83 (5) and (6) GDPR to impose fines on undertakings of up to 4 % of the total worldwide annual turnover of the preceding financial year. Secondly, the GDPR refers specifically to Art. 101 and 102 TFEU regarding the definition of an undertaking.[230] In this respect, it should also be mentioned that such a close link regarding the imposition of fines on undertakings is indeed logical since infringements of the relevant legal acts are in both areas often equally motivated by a pursuit of profit – either deriving from the economic value of big data or, in a competition law context, from the profit that comes from the exploitation of a market-dominating position.

III. Interim conclusion

Overall, one can see that contrary to the traditional view of the relation between data protection and competition law, the two fields of law show several parallels. Both competition and data protection law can be considered to be consumer-oriented to some extent. In addition, both legal acts also serve the internal market by securing its correct functioning. Nonetheless, based on the fact that the "traditional" core objectives of both laws differ – informational self-determination on the one hand and the functioning of the market/correction of market failure on the other hand – one could argue that such an analogy might present itself as

---

228 Such claims for damages are in a competition law context directly based on Art. 101/102 TFEU (see with regard to Art. 101 TFEU ECJ in case C-453/99, *Courage Ltd. v Crehan*, ECLI:EU:C:2001:465, paras. 26, 36, the principles of which must be also applicable in case of Art. 102 (see Eilmansberger/Bien, in: MüKoEuWettbR, Art. 102 AEUV, marginal no. 678) and in case of the GDPR, it is Art. 82 (1) GDPR that explicitly stipulates the right to damages (see Nemitz, in: Ehmann/Selmayr, DSGVO Kommentar, Art. 82 DSGVO, marginal no. 3).

229 See Golla, in: Eßer/Kramer/von Lewinski, DSGVO/BDSG Kommentar, Art. 83 DSGVO, marginal no. 13; see also Nemitz, in: Ehmann/Selmayr, DSGVO Kommentar, Art. 83 DSGVO, marginal no. 6; Schwartmann/Jacquemain, in: Schwartmann/Jaspers/Thüsing/Kugelmann, DSGVO/BDSG Kommentar, Art. 83 DSGVO, marginal no. 62; see also recital 120 of the GDPR explicitly referring to Art. 101/102 TFEU.

230 See recital 120 of the GDPR.

far-fetched at first glance. However, in reference to the case law of the ECJ, it was substantiated above that the two fields of law are indeed, inter alia, concerned with the interests of individuals. Likewise, the analogy in the internal market objective of the two fields of law cannot be fully denied, either. As mentioned, the Commission has explicitly stated that data protection law also serves *"the completion of the internal market"* as an *"equally important objective"* alongside the protection of the informational self-determination.[231] Thus, one can find a parallel with competition law in so far as the completion of the internal market is another regulatory objective of competition law alike.[232] In fact, a certain conduct can fall under Art. 102 TFEU precisely because it isolates the markets of individual member states within the EU.[233] Hence, it is by no means false when Becker, Director at the German Bundeskartellamt, states that both fields of law are *"pointing in the same direction"*.[234] In fact, the protection of competition is an important component of a complete approach to consumer protection and vice versa.[235] Above that, both fields of law even show parallels in their structure. Ultimately, the character of data protection law as a fundamental right must also have an influence on other fields of law, such as competition law.

Consequently, one can indeed note that data protection and competition law are "compatible" with each other based on their respective objectives and the further parallels shown above. Hence, linking these two fields of law is by no means an artificial and far-fetched approach. This is also a crucial difference to other fields of law such as construction law, environmental law, employee protection law and others. Körber, on the other hand, argues that a violation of these aforementioned fields of law could (theoretically) result in an infringement of Art. 102 TFEU too if one

---

231 Communication from the Commission, "A comprehensive approach on personal data protection in the European Union", Brussels, 04/11/2010, COM(2010) 609 final.

232 See for instance ECJ in joined Cases C-468/06 to C-478/06, *Sot. Lélos kai Sia EE and others v GlaxoSmithKline AEVE Farmakeftikon Proïonton*, ECLI:EU:C:2008:504, where Art. 102 TFEU was applied to refusals to supply, designed to prevent parallel trade in medicinal products; Fuchs, in: Immenga/Mestmäcker, KartellR Kommentar, Art. 102 TFEU, marginal no. 7.

233 See for instance ECJ in joined Cases C-468/06 to C-478/06, *Sot. Lélos kai Sia EE and others v GlaxoSmithKline AEVE Farmakeftikon Proïonton*, ECLI:EU:C:2008:504.

234 See also Becker, ZWeR 2018, 229 (237).

235 Becker, ZWeR 2018, 229 (237 et seq.).

extends the scope of competition law beyond its actual core objectives.[236] However, it is precisely the unique similarity in their nature and the wide congruence of objectives that connects European competition law and data protection law within the field of the digital economy.[237] Due to the lack of fundamental similarities between competition law and the other fields of law mentioned by Körber, his argumentation cannot be followed.

Additionally, recent developments have shown that the awareness of this relation between data protection and competition law is increasing – not just in Germany but in all major countries. Not least, this might be connected to the proliferating digitalization and the fact that the digital economy is expanding on a daily basis.[238] The resulting need for such an approach was also highlighted by the investigation of the German Bundeskartellamt into *Facebook*, which will be discussed next. The case is a prime example showing that the development of the digital economy causes several challenges for competition law. These challenges have to be addressed by an effective enforcement of competition rules,[239] and an effective enforcement of competition rules might require emphasizing the relation between data protection and competition law in the digital platform economy.

---

236 See Körber, NZKart 2019, 187 (195).
237 See with regard to the congruence of objectives: Becker, ZWeR 2018, 299 (238).
238 See p. 13; A. I. "Background".
239 See von Danwitz, DuD 2015, 581 (584).

E. The *Facebook* case of the Bundeskartellamt

The interplay between data protection and competition law is illustrated by the German Bundeskartellamt and its case against *Facebook*.[240] Due to the contemporary relevance of this case and the fact that it serves as an illustrative base for the present dissertation, it shall be summarized in the following (more under I.). Following this, the court order of the Higher Regional Court of Düsseldorf shall be summarized, too. The Court expressed some essential points of criticism in its order for provisional suspension of the Bundeskartellamt's decision which shall be discussed as well (more under II.).

I. The investigation and decision by the German Bundeskartellamt

In 2016, the German Federal Competition Authority, the Bundeskartellamt, initiated an investigation against *Facebook* Inc., USA, and its Irish and German subsidiaries. The investigation was based on a potential abuse of *Facebook*'s presumably dominant position in the social network market.[241] More specifically, the Bundeskartellamt was suspicious about whether *Facebook* had been abusing its possibly dominant position with its specific terms of service. Those terms of service allowed *Facebook*, inter alia, to excessively collect and process user data from other websites. This had been done, for instance, by the implementation of tools on third-party websites such as the "*Facebook* Like Button", the "*Facebook* Login" and the tracking tool "*Facebook*-Pixel".

In this context, *Facebook*'s data policy states:

> *Advertisers, app developers, and publishers [...] provide* (by means of such tools) *information about your activities off Facebook – including informa-*

---

240 Bundeskartellamt, case no. B6–22/16, *Facebook*.
241 Bundeskartellamt, press release "Bundeskartellamt initiates proceeding against Facebook on suspicion of having abused its market power by infringing data protection rules", March 2nd, 2016, available on the internet under https://www.bundeskartellamt.de/SharedDocs/Meldung/EN/Pressemitteilungen/2016/02_03_2016_Facebook.html?nn=3591568 (last accessed: 27/03/20).

tion about your device, websites you visit, purchases you make, the ads you see, and how you use their services – whether or not you have a Facebook *account or are logged into* Facebook.[242]

Additionally, it states: "*We also receive information about your online and offline actions and purchases from third-party data providers.*"[243]

These sentences were present in a similar wording in *Facebook*'s data policy when the Bundeskartellamt initiated its proceedings back in 2016. The problem with those passages is that they enable *Facebook* to collect data from third-party websites without the explicit consent of users. However, the explicit consent would normally be required under the GDPR for such an extensive collection of data. Consequently, data from different sources is being merged and the affected persons have no way of avoiding the merging unless they refrain from joining the social network in the first place. It is particularly this "all-or-nothing approach" that the Bundeskartellamt criticized. Firstly, customers are not left with a real choice to either accept or reject the terms of service as *Facebook* makes the use of the social network entirely conditional on the acceptance of these terms. Secondly, users will often be unable to foresee the actual extent of the data collection, which makes them oblivious as to which data from which sources is being merged.[244] According to the Bundeskartellamt, the resulting loss of control suffered by users as a result of losing the ability to control the use of their data must be regarded as a harm to them even though no actual financial loss is suffered. Due to the fact that *Facebook* is predominantly only able to hold on to this practice because it has a large market power, it also becomes a competition law concern, according to the Bundeskartellamt.[245] In addition, the Bundeskartellamt points out that there is a harm to competition since competitors may not be able to amass such data pools.[246] *Facebook* is able to offer more and better personalized

---

242 See Facebook Data Policy (date of last revision: April 19, 2018), available on the internet under https://www.facebook.com/privacy/explanation (last accessed: 27/03/20).

243 Loc. cit.

244 Bundeskartellamt, "Background information on the Facebook proceeding", December 19th, 2017, p. 4, available on the internet under https://www.bundeskartellamt.de/SharedDocs/Publikation/EN/Diskussions_Hintergrundpapiere/2017/Hintergrundpapier_Facebook.pdf?__blob=publicationFile&v=6 (last accessed: 27/03/20).

245 Bundeskartellamt. loc. cit.

246 See Bundeskartellamt, press release "Bundeskartellamt prohibits Facebook from combining user data from different sources", February 7th, 2019,

advertisements through the collected data, which strengthens *Facebook*'s position in the advertising market.[247]

In order to pursue its case, the Bundeskartellamt relied on § 19 (1) of the German Competition Act called "Act against Restraints of Competition" (ARC), according to which the abuse of a dominant position is prohibited.[248] More specifically, the Bundeskartellamt focused on the relation between § 19 (1) ARC and data protection principles. Thereby, they pursued the question of whether the data processing terms of *Facebook* could be regarded as exploitative and thus as an abuse of *Facebook*'s dominant position. As seen from the outcome of the case, this question was answered in the affirmative by the Bundeskartellamt.[249] According to the Bundeskartellamt, *Facebook* is dominant in the social network market and has abused this position with its extensive collection and merging of personal user data.[250] Therefore, the Bundeskartellamt's decision now obliges *Facebook* to obtain the users informed and freely given consent before data from third-party websites may be assigned to user accounts. Andreas Mundt, President of the Bundeskartellamt, said they were *"carrying out what can be seen as an internal divestiture of* Facebook's *data"*.[251]

The approach behind this decision is based on the VBL-Gegenwert II judgement of the German Federal Court of Justice (FCJ).[252] According to that judgement, an abuse under the general clause of § 19 (1) ARC can consist in the imposition of exploitative business terms, if the imposition

---

available on the internet under https://www.bundeskartellamt.de/Shared-Docs/Meldung/EN/Pressemitteilungen/2019/07_02_2019_Facebook.html;jsessionid=832649993354525E65A66B820BEC5711.1_cid378?nn=3591568 (last accessed: 27/03/20).

247 Loc. cit.

248 Bundeskartellamt, case summary of case no. B6–22/16 – *Facebook*, published February 15th, 2019, p. 1, available on the internet under https://www.bundeskartellamt.de/SharedDocs/Entscheidung/EN/Fallberichte/Missbrauchsaufsicht/2019/B6-22-16.pdf?__blob=publicationFile&v=3 (last accessed: 27/03/20).

249 See Bundeskartellamt, press release "Bundeskartellamt prohibits Facebook from combining user data from different sources", February 7th, 2019, available on the internet under https://www.bundeskartellamt.de/Shared-Docs/Meldung/EN/Pressemitteilungen/2019/07_02_2019_Facebook.html;jsessionid=832649993354525E65A66B820BEC5711.1_cid378?nn=3591568 (last accessed: 27/03/20).

250 Loc. cit.

251 Loc. cit.

252 German Federal Court of Justice, judgement of January 24th, 2017, KZR 47/14, *VBL-Gegenwert II*, NZKart 2017, 242.

of such terms is a manifestation of the market dominance of the undertaking in question and if those terms are additionally incompatible with other legal provisions or principles.[253] Consequently, in the context of the latter requirement, the legal valuation behind the GDPR played a particularly important role in the assessment of the exploitative nature of the terms in the Facebook case. Additionally, in Pechstein,[254] another judgement about exploitative business terms, the FJC specifically took account of constitutionally protected rights in order to assess the exploitative nature of the business terms in question under § 19 ARC. The FCJ stated that in cases where one party is powerful enough to almost dictate the terms of a contract, § 19 ARC must take account of the fundamental rights possibly infringed in such cases in order to secure the protection of those fundamental rights. In the light of the case law of the FCJ and especially due to the judgement in VBL-Gegenwert II,[255] the Bundeskartellamt stated that the violation of European data protection rules to the detriment of users resulted in an infringement of § 19 (1) ARC. Additionally, the infringement could not be outweighed by any *"efficiencies in a business model based on personalized advertising"*.[256] *Facebook* could not rely on a sufficient legal base regarding the extent to which data was collected and merged.[257] Moreover, this violation of the GDPR lead to a manifestation of *Facebook*`s market power since the company *"gained a competitive edge over its competitors in an unlawful way and increased market entry barriers, which in turn secures* Facebook's *market power towards end customers"*.[258]

As seen above, the case is strongly connected to *Facebook*`s data policy and data protection considerations in general. However, notwithstanding this fact, it is still a case involving a competition authority and this illustrates that data protection concerns can become a highly relevant question for competition authorities, too. As the Bundeskartellamt has pointed out,

---

253 German Federal Court of Justice, judgement of January 24th, 2017, KZR 47/14, *VBL-Gegenwert II*, NZKart 2017, 242 (243).

254 German Federal Court of Justice, judgement of June 6th, 2016, KZR 6/15, *Pechstein*, NJW 2016, 2266 (2271 et seq.).

255 See footnote 252.

256 Bundeskartellamt, case summary of case no. B6–22/16 – *Facebook*, published February 15th, 2019, p. 1, available on the internet under https://www.bundeskartellamt.de/SharedDocs/Entscheidung/EN/Fallberichte/Missbrauchsaufsicht/2019/B6-22-16.pdf?__blob=publicationFile&v=3 (last accessed: 27/03/20).

257 Loc. cit, p. 10.

258 Loc. cit., p. 11.

social networks like *Facebook* are data-driven products and where access to data plays such a vital role for the market position in general, the way this data is handled becomes a competition law concern, too.[259] However, as will be seen next, this highly revolutionary approach suffered a substantial setback by the interim court order of the Higher Regional Court Düsseldorf and the criticism regarding the Bundeskartellamt`s decision expressed therein.

II. The court order of the Higher Regional Court Düsseldorf

After the Bundeskartellamt announced its decision in the *Facebook* case, *Facebook* applied for a temporary suspension of the decision by way of interim relief. That way, *Facebook* wanted to have the measures imposed by the Bundeskartellamt suspended until a decision had been made in the actual appeal proceedings. The Higher Regional Court Düsseldorf, before which the proceedings for interim relief were pending, announced its decision on August 26th, 2019.

The court expressed its serious doubts as to the lawfulness of the decision. Accordingly, it has indicated that an annulment of the Bundeskartellamt`s decision in the main appeal proceedings was likely. Predominantly, the court order is based on the view that *Facebook*`s data-related business practices would not result in a relevant damage to competition.[260] However, the Court explicitly stated that this does not mean that it would be a priori ruled out that a certain damage to consumer protection may be regarded as a relevant damage to competition.[261] It was not the general approach of considering data protection concerns in competition law assessments that was heavily criticized by the Court but the reasoning on which the Bundeskartellamt based its finding of an abuse – i.e. the theory of harm – that the Court doubted.[262]

---

259 Bundeskartellamt, "Background information on the Facebook proceeding", December 19th, 2017, pp. 1 et. seq., available on the internet under https://www.bundeskartellamt.de/SharedDocs/Publikation/EN/Diskussions_Hintergrundpapiere/2017/Hintergrundpapier_Facebook.pdf?__blob=publicationFile&v=6 (last accessed: 27/03/20).

260 1st Cartel Senate of the Higher Regional Court Düsseldorf, decision of August 26th, 2019, VI-Kart 1/19 (V) – "Facebook", marginal no. 25.

261 Loc. cit., marginal no. 29.

262 See for similar conclusion also Dowse/Dück, NZKart 2020, 80 (82); see also the statement of Thomas Kühnen, presiding judge at the Higher Regional

More precisely, the Court took the view that a dominant undertaking does not have a special responsibility to comply with the whole legal system in general but only a responsibility not to impair competition.[263] However, as will be explained later, this statement does not sufficiently consider the competitive advantage that results from an extensive collection of data when the provisions of the GDPR are bypassed. Additionally, the Court was of the opinion that users would give their consent to the extensive processing of data by accepting both *Facebook*'s terms of service and data policy.[264] Thus, one could not speak of a loss of control with regard to the personal data of the users.[265] On the contrary – according to the Court's opinion, the processing of data would take place with the knowledge and will of the users.[266] The fact that the acceptance of *Facebook*'s terms of service is a condition for joining the social network would not result in a loss of control or a predicament either.[267]

However, the view taken by the Court neglects essential principles of data protection law with regard to the requirements for valid consent. Predominantly, the imbalance of power between *Facebook* and the users is used to *Facebook*'s advantage. *Facebook* demands the user's consent regarding the extensive processing of data if he/she wants to join the network. According to the European Art. 29 Data Protection Working Party, *"the situation of "bundling" consent with acceptance of terms or conditions [...] is considered highly undesirable. If consent is given in this situation, it is presumed to be not freely given"*.[268] This presumption is neglected by the Court. In

---

Court Düsseldorf, in the later main proceedings, cited by Podszun, who attended the oral hearing: "Grundsätzlich kann ein Missbrauch von Marktmacht durch einen Verstoß gegen verbraucherschutzrechtliche Normen bewirkt werden" (= "In principle, an abuse of market power can be brought about by a violation of norms of consumer protection law"), Podszun, D'KART Antitrust Blog, "Facebook: Next Stop Europe", 25. March 2021, available on the internet under https://www.d kart.de/en/blog/2021/03/25/facebook-next-stop-europe/ (last accessed: 17/04/21).

263 1st Cartel Senate of the Higher Regional Court Düsseldorf, decision of August 26th, 2019, VI-Kart 1/19 (V) – "Facebook", marginal no. 44.

264 Loc. cit., marginal no. 35.

265 See footnote 264.

266 See footnote 264.

267 See footnote 264.

268 Art. 29 Data Protection Working Party, WP 259 – Guidelines on consent under Regulation 2016/679, p. 8, available on the internet under https://iapp.org/resources/article/wp29-guidelines-on-consent/ (last accessed: 07/09/19); see also recital 43 of the GDPR stating that "Consent is presumed not to be freely given if it does not allow separate consent to be given to different personal data

addition, surveys show that an average of 80 % of *Facebook* users have not or only sporadically read the data policy.[269] Consequently, one cannot argue that the processing of data would take place with the knowledge and will of the users – for the majority of people, that is simply not true.[270]

Furthermore, the Court rejects the argument that *Facebook's* breach of data protection law could not have been committed in such a way by competitors without a dominant market position. Therefore, the Court denies the relevant causality between *Facebook*`s market power and the infringement of data protection law.[271] According to the Court, *Facebook*`s dominant position does not affect users' consent to the excessive processing of data.[272] More precisely, the Court takes the view that each user could freely choose whether or not he/she wants to join the social network without fearing any negative consequences if he/she chooses not to.[273] A clear indication in favour of that statement would be the fact that 50 million people, of the roughly 83 million people living in Germany, do not use the platform at all.[274]

Caspar, the Data Protection Officer of Hamburg, criticizes the Court`s reasoning as "unrealistic".[275] According to him, the Court`s decision raises

---

processing operations despite it being appropriate in the individual case, or if the performance of a contract, including the provision of a service, is dependent on the consent despite such consent not being necessary for such performance".

269 See for instance Rothmann/Buchner, DuD 2018, 342 (344 et seqq.).

270 In fact, the survey by Rothmann and Buchner (footnote 269) shows that only 37 % of the people who took part in the survey, were aware of the fact that they had granted Facebook access to their personal data. 43 % were not aware of this fact and 20 % were even of the opinion that they did not consent to Facebook`s data policy. Additionally, 75 % stated that they would not have agreed to the extensive processing of data by Facebook, if they had had an alternative (Buchner, WRP 2019, 1243 (1246 et seq.).

271 1st Cartel Senate of the Higher Regional Court Düsseldorf, decision of August 26th, 2019, VI-Kart 1/19 (V) – "Facebook", marginal no. 52; other opinion Bundeskartellamt, decision of February 6th, 2019, case no. B6–22/16 – *Facebook*, pp. 276 et seq., marginal no. 880, available on the internet under https://www.bundeskartellamt.de/SharedDocs/Entscheidung/DE/Entscheidungen/Missbrauchsaufsicht/2019/B6-22-16.pdf?__blob=publicationFile&v=8 (last accessed: 03/09/19).

272 See 1st Cartel Senate of the Higher Regional Court Düsseldorf, decision of August 26th, 2019, VI-Kart 1/19 (V) – "Facebook", marginal no. 71.

273 See footnote 272.

274 See footnote 272.

275 Holzki/Neuerer, "OLG Düsseldorf kassiert Vorwürfe des Kartellamts gegen Facebook", August 26th, 2019, available on the internet under https://www.handelsblatt.com/technik/it-in-

the question whether the judges have properly acknowledged the complex relationships between the market power of companies in the digital (platform) economy and the users' consent to the extensive processing of their data.[276] The question is indeed justified as the Court did not consider that not using *Facebook* does result in disadvantages for people. For instance, certain raffles are only offered via *Facebook*, some web services can only be used if you log in via *Facebook* and some events only allow participation via prior *Facebook* sign-up, as an article published by the well-known newspaper *ZEIT* shows.[277] In addition, in order to stay connected with friends, *Facebook* and its services such as *Instagram* or *WhatsApp* are often the only actual option for communication. For instance, international telephone calls, which would provide a similarly fast way of communication, can be expensive and internet-based services like *WhatsApp* do not charge you any additional monetary costs. Moreover, the Court`s argument that 50 million people out of Germany`s total population do not use *Facebook*`s services is too general and does not sufficiently take into account the different age groups. For instance, more than 4.5 million of Germany`s population are aged 0–5,[278] of the 18 million people that are 65 or older, only roughly 40 % actually use the internet at all.[279] These numbers put the 50 million people that the Court referred to in perspective. In fact, these numbers alone illustrate that rather every second German who uses the internet also uses *Facebook*. However, only 3 % of the German population

---

ternet/datenschutz-olg-duesseldorf-kassiert-vorwuerfe-des-kartellamts-gegen-face-book/24943100.html?ticket=ST-10780336-fQe2mQy0vL0ak5RT1F5e-ap4 (last accessed: 10/09/19).

276 See loc. cit.

277 Mielczarek, "Digitale Diskriminierung – Ohne Facebook geht nichts mehr", November 19th, 2012, available on the internet under https://www.zeit.de/digital/internet/2012-11/leserartikel-ohne-facebook (last accessed: 09/09/19).

278 Statista, "Bevölkerung – Zahl der Einwohner in Deutschland nach Altersgruppen am 31. Dezember 2017 (in Millionen)", available on the internet under https://statista.extdb.e-fellows.net/statistik/daten/studie/1365/umfrage/bevoelkerung-deutschlands-nach-altersgruppen/ (last accessed: 09/09/19).

279 Statista, "Anteil der Internetnutzer nach Altersgruppen in der Generation 50-plus in Deutschland in ausgewählten Jahren von 2011 bis 2017", available on the internet under https://statista.extdb.e-fellows.net/statistik/daten/studie/5 68561/umfrage/anteil-der-internetnutzer-in-deutschland-in-der-generation-5 0plus/ (last accessed: 09/09/19); Statista, "Bevölkerung – Zahl der Einwohner in Deutschland nach Altersgruppen am 31. Dezember 2017 (in Millionen)", available on the internet under https://statista.extdb.e-fellows.net/statistik/daten/studie/1365/umfrage/bevoelkerung-deutschlands-nach-altersgruppen/ (last accessed: 09/09/19).

do not care about how their personal data is processed.[280] This suggests the conclusion that people give their consent to *Facebook*'s extensive data processing solely because of the platform's dominant position and due to the fact that they have no real alternative.[281] This conclusion is also backed by the above-mentioned survey conducted by Rothmann and Buchner and the results thereof.[282]

Another argument brought forward by the Court was that the data which people provide to *Facebook* could easily be duplicated.[283] In theory, that might be true. However, such an argument does not adequately address the network and lock-in effects. Firstly, social media especially are of much more interest to people the more users the platform has. Hence, it would be possible, in theory, to join another social network, thereby "duplicating" the data. Yet people will refrain from doing so due to the unique market position of *Facebook*. Other social networks simply do not offer the chance to connect with as many users. Secondly, even though joining another network does not necessarily result in any monetary switching costs, lock-in effects in the broader sense are present, nonetheless. This is based on the fact that providing social networks with all the information about oneself requires a considerable amount of time – not to mention the time required to familiarize yourself with a new platform.[284] What is more, though, people might be "locked-in" because social networks like *Facebook* also constitute what can be seen as a digital storage facility for old memories. For instance, old messages sent via the instant messenger or old "posts" written after a special event would be lost if one

---

280 Engels/Grunewald, Institut der deutschen Wirtschaft, IW-Kurzbericht Nr. 57: "DAS PRIVACY PARADOX – Digitalisierung versus Privatsphäre", August 14th, 2017, available on the internet under https://www.iwkoeln.de/studien/iw-kurzb erichte/beitrag/barbara-engels-mara-grunewald-das-privacy-paradox-digitalisieru ng-versus-privatsphaere-356747.html (last accessed: 09/09/19).

281 See Bundeskartellamt, decision of February 6th, 2019, case no. B6–22/16 – *Facebook*, p. 121, marginal no. 385, available on the internet under https://www.bundeskartellamt.de/SharedDocs/Entscheidung/DE/Entschei-dungen/Missbrauchsaufsicht/2019/B6-22-16.pdf?__blob=publicationFile&v=8 (last accessed: 03/09/19).

282 See footnotes 269, 270.

283 See in that context for instance 1st Cartel Senate of the Higher Regional Court Düsseldorf, decision of August 26th, 2019, VI-Kart 1/19 (V) – "Facebook", marginal no. 31.

284 See Varian, "Economic of Information Technology", p. 20, available on the internet under http://people.ischool.berkeley.edu/~hal/Papers/mattioli/mat-tioli.pdf (last accessed: 01/10/19); see also Tamke, ZWeR 2017, 358 (366).

were to quit the network. However, people might want to preserve these things.[285] All in all, "duplicating" the data is not as easy as suggested by the Court. The fact that Art. 20 GDPR describes the right to data portability does not alter this fact, either.[286] However, the Higher Regional Court Düsseldorf did not have the last word in the interim proceedings anyway – even though the decision did provide an important outlook regarding the Court's opinion in the main proceedings. The Bundeskartellamt appealed the decision of the Higher Regional Court Düsseldorf so that the FCJ had to made a final decision in the interim proceedings on *Facebook*'s application for suspension. The decision of the FCJ shall be briefly discussed next as not only does it offer an outlook on the chances of success regarding the interdisciplinary approach in general, but it also provides an outlook on the possible outcome of the main proceedings before the Higher Regional Court Düsseldorf.

---

285 See also Tamke, ZWeR 2017, 358 (366), who is also of the opinion that the loss of data can lead to lock-in effects.

286 Inter alia, Art. 20 GDPR intends to prevent lock-in effects. However, in practice, the right to data portability lacks its significance in the digital economy, which is to a large extent based on the fact that Art. 20 GDPR does not create an obligation for the data controllers to develop processing systems, which would be technically compatible with systems of other data controllers (see recital 68 of the GDPR). Additionally, due to the fact that there is no "commonly used format" in the digital economy yet (see von Lewinski, in: BeckOK DatenschutzR, Art. 20 DSGVO, marginal no. 78 (effective 01/05/19)), as stated in Art. 20 GDPR, the actual use for data subjects of the right to data portability is strongly limited (see von Lewinski, in: BeckOK DatenschutzR, Art. 20 DSGVO, marginal no. 78 (effective 01/05/2019); see also Spiecker genannt Döhmann, GRUR 2019, 341 (348), stating for the same reasons that Art. 20 GDPR will currently provide very little assistance in overcoming lock-in effects; see for a discussion of the practical problems of Art. 20 GDPR also Federal Ministry for Economic Affairs and Energy, "Ein neuer Wettbewerbsrahmen für die Digitalwirtschaft – Bericht der Kommission Wettbewerbsrecht 4.0" (= A New Competition Framework for the Digital Economy – Report by the Commission Competition Law 4.0), p. 39 et seq., available on the internet under https://www.bmwi.de/Redaktion/DE/Publikationen/Wirtschaft/bericht-der-kommission-wettbewerbsrecht-4-0.html (last accessed 01/04/21)). Most importantly, however, Art. 20 GDPR does only apply at the initiative of the data-subject. Most people do not even want to switch platforms due to the network-effects. Therefore, Art. 20 GDPR is of only limited value for competitors in order to get access to the big data pools of Facebook and co.

III. The decision of the German Federal Court of Justice

After the Higher Regional Court Düsseldorf had expressed its serious doubts as to the lawfulness of the Bundeskartellamt`s order, the approach of linking data protection law considerations to competition law cases seemed to have been off the table – once again. However, the Bundeskartellamt successfully appealed the Higher Regional Court`s decision on points of law. The FCJ overruled the Higher Regional Court Düsseldorf with its decision of 23 June 2020.[287] Bearing in mind that the standard of review in interim proceedings based on Sec. 65 para. 2 ARC is rather limited – as the Federal Court of Justice only examines whether or not the lower court`s decision was plausible, i.e. whether the serious doubts of the lower court were justifiable – this outcome came by surprise.[288] The FCJ`s decision indicates that the lower court`s opinion was not reasonable at all. The decision therefore reignited the debate about an interdisciplinary approach for competition law cases in the digital economy. Podszun[289] even sees in the judgement to some extent *"a significant re-adjustment of* [German] *competition policy with a stronger focus on consumer choice and the sovereignty of users to decide for themselves"*.[290]

   In its reasoning, the FCJ made it clear that it had no serious doubts regarding *Facebook*`s dominant position within the German social network market.[291] Interestingly, the Court also had no serious doubts regarding the abuse of *Facebook*`s dominant position.[292] According to the FCJ, *Facebook* abuses its dominant position by making the private use of the network – without the users` further consent – dependent on the users` acceptance of *Facebook's* authority to link user data generated outside of

---

287 German Federal Court of Justice, decision of June 23rd, 2020, KVR 69/19, *Facebook*, GRUR-RS 2020, 20737.

288 German Federal Court of Justice, decision of June 23rd, 2020, KVR 69/19, *Facebook*, GRUR-RS 2020, 20737, marginal no. 12.

289 Prof. Dr. Rupprecht Podszun is the holder of the Chair for Civil Law, German and European Competition Law at the Heinrich Heine Universität Düsseldorf and also Director of the Institute for Competition Law at the Heinrich Heine Universität Düsseldorf.

290 Podszun, D'Kart Antitrust Blog, "Facebook Case: The Reasoning", August 28th, 2020, available on the internet under https://www.d-kart.de/blog/2020/08/28/facebook-case-the-reasoning/#comments (last accessed: 26/10/20).

291 See German Federal Court of Justice, decision of June 23rd, 2020, KVR 69/19, *Facebook*, GRUR-RS 2020, 20737, marginal no. 14.

292 German Federal Court of Justice, decision of June 23rd, 2020, KVR 69/19, *Facebook*, GRUR-RS 2020, 20737, marginal no. 53.

facebook.com ("off-*Facebook*" data) with the users´ personal data resulting from the immediate *Facebook* activity itself.[293] However, according to the FCJ, the decisive factor for assessing the abusiveness of *Facebook's* terms of use was not whether the processing of user data was in compliance with the provisions of the GDPR, but rather the fact that *Facebook* users were left with no choice but to accept *Facebook*´s data policy. Hence, the Federal Court of Justice highlighted the importance that consumers as market participants must be independent and free in their decisions – which makes particularly sense when rephrased with Podszun´s words: *"The demand side decides on success in competition, so this referee must also be able to make free and independent decisions."*[294]

The FCJ sees *Facebook's* approach as an imposed extension of services (*"aufgedrängte Leistungserweiterung"*). According to the FCJ, that is a competition law concern, because private users could only receive a service that is indispensable for them – the social network itself – in combination with another undesirable service – a highly personalized user experience that uses various kinds of off-Facebook data.[295] Thus, users are forced to accept *Facebook*´s service in a way that goes beyond what they actually wanted. According to the FCJ, *Facebook* would impose its functionalities using off-Facebook data by taking advantage of its dominant position. Users would have to accept *Facebook*´s access to their off-Facebook data even if they would not consider the enhanced service to be worth the consideration – i.e. their user data.[296] This, on the other hand, automatically enables *Facebook* to collect as much user data as possible. The FCJ highlights in that context that the quality and quantity of user-related data would constitute a decisive factor for the monetarization of the network through advertising revenues.[297] The more the network knows about its users, the more attractive it becomes for advertisers. Consequently, the competition law concern would not only come from the exploitation of users due to

---

293 German Federal Court of Justice, decision of June 23rd, 2020, KVR 69/19, *Facebook*, GRUR-RS 2020, 20737, marginal no. 53.
294 Podszun, D'Kart Antitrust Blog, "Facebook @ BGH", June 23rd, 2020, available on the internet under https://www.d-kart.de/en/blog/2020/06/23/facebook-bgh/ (last accessed: 24/10/20).
295 German Federal Court of Justice, decision of June 23rd, 2020, KVR 69/19, *Facebook*, GRUR-RS 2020, 20737, marginal no. 58.
296 German Federal Court of Justice, decision of June 23rd, 2020, KVR 69/19, *Facebook*, GRUR-RS 2020, 20737, marginal no. 97.
297 German Federal Court of Justice, decision of June 23rd, 2020, KVR 69/19, *Facebook*, GRUR-RS 2020, 20737, marginal no. 62.

the imposed extension of services but especially from the resulting obstacle to competition within the advertising market.[298] According to the Court, there is the risk that (potential) competitors could lose the competition for advertising contracts which, on the other hand, would be necessary to profitably monetize the network.[299] The Court therefore stated that the possibility of an impairment of the market for online advertising could not be ruled out, given the negative impact on competition for advertising contracts.[300] Contrary to the opinion of the Higher Regional Court of Düsseldorf, there would also be no need to establish that there is a separate market for online advertising for social media and that *Facebook* holds a dominant position in this market.[301] The Court stated that the impairment does not have to occur in the dominated market, but could also occur in a non-dominated third market.[302]

The Federal Court of Justice also addressed the issue of the required causality. The Higher Regional Court Düsseldorf took the view that there had to be a strict instrumental causality (behavioural causality or *"Verhaltenskausalität"*) between market dominance and exploitation. The FCJ, on the other hand, stated that a causality of results (*"Ergebniskausalität"*) would be sufficient, meaning that a causal link between the dominant position and the abuse is even presumed when the conduct is in principle possible for any company, but the specific harmful effects for competition only occur in the case of dominant companies.[303]

At the end of its reasoning, the Federal Court of Justice states another interesting point: According to the FCJ, the Higher Regional Court Düsseldorf had failed to recognize that for some users, access to the social network would be decisive for participating in social life, so that they cannot be expected to refrain from joining the social network.[304] In addition, the Court stated that *Facebook* as a communication platform would be also be of essential importance for the public discourse on political,

---

298 See German Federal Court of Justice, decision of June 23rd, 2020, KVR 69/19, *Facebook*, GRUR-RS 2020, 20737, marginal no. 62.

299 German Federal Court of Justice, decision of June 23rd, 2020, KVR 69/19, *Facebook*, GRUR-RS 2020, 20737, marginal no. 94.

300 Loc. cit.

301 Loc. cit.

302 Loc. cit.

303 German Federal Court of Justice, decision of June 23rd, 2020, KVR 69/19, *Facebook*, GRUR-RS 2020, 20737, marginal nos. 71 et seq.

304 German Federal Court of Justice, decision of June 23rd, 2020, KVR 69/19, *Facebook*, GRUR-RS 2020, 20737, marginal no 102.

social, cultural and economic issues, so that the social network would also be important for the purpose of mutual exchange and the expression of opinions in general.[305] Accordingly, the company would have a special legal responsibility when it comes to determining the conditions for the use of the platform.[306] With such a reasoning, the FCJ brings *Facebook* close to a public utility like gas, water or telephone service providers, which would result in far-reaching legal obligations for *Facebook*.

The Court specifically states that both the right to informational self-determination and the values of the GDPR can be important aspects with regard to the balancing of interests required under Sec. 19 ARC – the German equivalent to Art. 102 TFEU.[307] Especially fundamental rights such as the right to informational self-determination would have an impact on the legal relationship under private law and must be taken into account in the interpretation of general clauses in civil law – which also include Sec. 19 ARC.[308]

Above all, the decision of the FCJ did not specifically affirm the theory of harm presented by the German Bundeskartellamt and thus, neither did it affirm the interdisciplinary approach that the present work is focused on. As exciting as the decision is, it therefore also has a disappointing aspect: The FCJ did not really deal with either the Bundeskartellamt's argumentation which – over more than 100 pages – was based on a violation of data protection regulations, or the several arguments of the Higher Regional Court Düsseldorf. Rather, the FCJ deviated from the theory of harm presented by the Bundeskartellamt and saw the abuse of *Facebook*'s dominant position not in the exploitation of consumers based on the violation of the GDPR but in the "*aufgedrängte Leistungserweiterung*" and both the lack of choice for consumers as well as the resulting barriers to entry/expansion for competitors. However, the decision did not put an end to the discussion about the relationship between competition and data protection law either – on the contrary, in fact. In the main proceedings before the Higher Regional Court Düsseldorf, after the FCJ had rendered its decision in the interim proceedings, the Higher Regional Court referred the case to the ECJ under the preliminary ruling procedure

---

305 See German Federal Court of Justice, decision of June 23rd, 2020, KVR 69/19, *Facebook*, GRUR-RS 2020, 20737, marginal no 124.

306 Loc. cit.

307 See German Federal Court of Justice, decision of June 23rd, 2020, KVR 69/19, *Facebook*, GRUR-RS 2020, 20737, marginal no 109.

308 See German Federal Court of Justice, decision of June 23rd, 2020, KVR 69/19, *Facebook*, GRUR-RS 2020, 20737, marginal no 105.

of Art. 267 TFEU.[309] The ECJ shall now clarify whether a violation of data protection law can be a matter for a (national) competition authority and if the competition authority has the competence to sanction a violation of data protection law in cases like the one at hand.

Hence, even if the Bundeskartellamt`s decision in the *Facebook* case had very little prospects of success after the first decision of the Higher Regional Court Düsseldorf in the interim proceedings, the approach to combine data protection considerations with competition law assessments in the digital (platform) economy is by no means dead yet. The case has fuelled the debate further. According to Caspar, the previous decision of the Higher Regional Court Düsseldorf was merely an artificial attempt to shield competition law from data protection law.[310] Caspar is of the opinion that the Higher Regional Court ignored the reciprocity that exists in the digital world between a company`s power over vast amounts of data and its market dominance – as was to some extent affirmed by the FCJ in its decision.[311] Podszun even described the decision of the Higher Regional Court Düsseldorf as a wake-up call for the German legislator.[312] According to Podszun, the legislator now has to create the means by which *Google, Facebook, Amazon* and co. can be regulated properly.[313] A first attempt for such a regulation can be seen in the European Commission`s proposal for a "Digital Markets Act",[314] and the 10th Amendment to the German ARC – the so-called "GWB Digitalization Act".[315] The latter entered into force on the 19th January 2021 and intends in particular to adjust the control of abusive practices by dominant undertakings. More

---

309 1st Cartel Senate of the Higher Regional Court Düsseldorf, decision of March 24th, 2021, Kart 2/19 (V) – "Facebook".

310 See Holzki/Neuerer, "OLG Düsseldorf kassiert Vorwürfe des Kartellamts gegen Facebook", August 26th, 2019, available on the internet under https://www.handelsblatt.com/technik/it-internet/datenschutz-olg-duesseldorf-kassiert-vorwuerfe-des-kartellamts-gegen-facebook/24943100.html?ticket=ST-10780336-fQe2mQy0vL0ak5RT1F5e-ap4 (last accessed: 10/09/19).

311 See loc. cit.

312 See loc. cit.

313 See loc. cit.

314 See "Proposal for a Regulation of the European Parliament and of the Council on contestable and fair markets in the digital sector (Digital Markets Act)", COM/2020/842 final.

315 "Act Amending the Act against Restraints of Competition for a focused, proactive and digital competition law 4.0 and amending other competition law provisions" ("GWB-Digitalisierungsgesetz" – GWB Digitalisation Act) of 18 January 2021, Federal Law Gazette 2021 I, pp. 2 et seqq.

precisely, the amendment aims to provide a remedy for the challenges that (German) competition law has to face when dealing with such dominant undertakings in the digital economy.[316] The question on whether there is also a need for the European legislator to adapt the relevant "core provision" of European competition law – meaning Art. 102 TFEU – will be discussed next.

---

316 See Monopolkommission, Policy Brief, Ausgabe 4 – Januar 2020, p. 1, available on the internet under https://www.monopolkommission.de/images/Policy_Brief/MK_Policy_Brief_4.pdf (last accessed: 27/03/20); see also Paal/Kumkar, NJW 2021, 809 (809, 811).

F. The interplay between big data and data protection considerations and Art. 102 TFEU in order to regulate "platform power" – the Bundeskartellamt`s *Facebook* case in the context of European competition law

Regardless of the doubts expressed by the Higher Regional Court Düsseldorf, the Bundeskartellamt`s *Facebook* case and its pioneer approach could have far-reaching consequences – also for European competition law. More precisely, the *Facebook* case might lead to a rethinking of the application of competition law provisions in the digital (platform) economy. It has to be mentioned that this would not be the first time the German competition law system has influenced European competition law. When European competition law was first being drafted, the German ARC served as a pioneer and inspiration.[317] Admittedly, the circumstances back then were different in so far as there was no real alternative for inspirations other than the German ARC and the US American Sherman Act, but the influence of the German system might repeat itself in today`s context, nonetheless. The Bundeskartellamt applied an approach in its *Facebook* case that might likewise serve as a pioneer. In the course of this, European competition and data protection law in the form of the GDPR could fur-

---

317 The formation of the European Community was strongly influenced by ordoliberal ideas and people affiliated to ordoliberalism such as the German Walter Hallstein, who also happened to be the first president of the European Commission (Gerber, in: Großfeld et. al., 1998, 654 (666)). Ordoliberalism and the ideas behind it were particularly suited to the idea of a common market leading to a unified European community (loc. cit.). Due to the ordoliberal background, according to which competition law was a central element in the creation of the common market, Germany had a particular influence since the idea of ordoliberalism was predominantly developed by the Freiburg School and people such as Franz Böhm and Walter Eucken. Additionally, the German Act against Restraints of Competition did not only embody many of the ordoliberal ideas but was also the best-developed and most respected competition law in Europe at that time (Gerber, in: Großfeld et. al., 1998, 654 (668 et seq.)). Thus, Germany had a leading role regarding the drafting of a European competition law and functioned as an example with its own system (loc. cit.). Hence, the European competition law is heavily influenced by the German system (Gerber, in: Großfeld et. al., 1998, 654 (666 et seqq.); see also Schmoeckel/Maetschke, 2016, p. 308).

ther converge in a way that data protection considerations could become a normative yardstick, especially for Art. 102 TFEU. In the following section, this possibility as seen in the *Facebook* case shall be discussed in the context of European competition law, thereby providing an answer to the aspect of the research question raised in the introduction: Can data protection considerations be internalized by or incorporated within Art. 102 TFEU and is such an approach – by which data protection and competition law considerations are bridged – desirable?

The following part will first elaborate on the possible influence of big data as well as the influence of the GDPR and its data protection considerations as a normative yardstick for Art. 102 TFEU (more under I.). This part itself will then be further subdivided into two sections. Firstly, the influence of big data and data protection considerations as criteria for the establishment of dominance will be discussed (more under I. 1.). Next, the possibility to use the GDPR as a normative yardstick for abusive conduct under Art. 102 TFEU will be examined (more under I. 2.). Lastly, the arguments for and against such an interdisciplinary approach will
be discussed (more under II.).

I. Big data and the General Data Protection Regulation as a normative yardstick for Art. 102 TFEU

As mentioned above,[318] big data and the way such data is handled by the relevant undertaking constitutes an important parameter of competition in today`s digital economy. Therefore, it is only consistent when data protection law in the form of the GDPR and its considerations are taken into account as normative guidance to competition law regarding examinations of data-driven business models.[319] The following part will show the way such data protection considerations can be internalized by or incorporated within Art. 102 TFEU. As mentioned in the introduction, the focus will lie in this context on the establishment of dominance and the abuse of such a dominant position.

---

318 See pp. 20 et seqq.; B. I. "Big data and its importance for the digital economy".
319 See Podszun/de Toma, NJW 2016, 2987 (2992).

1. Big data and data protection considerations as criteria for the establishment of dominance under Art. 102 TFEU

It was explained above that Art. 102 TFEU is used to address undertakings that abuse their dominant position.[320] This, in turn, is characterized by an undertaking`s ability *"to behave to an appreciable extent independently of [...] competitors, customers and ultimately [...] consumers."*[321] In *AstraZeneca* on the other hand, the General Court equates this concept of independence with a certain degree of market power.[322] Therefore, the term "dominance" within the meaning of Art. 102 TFEU relies on an interpretation that captures undertakings with such market power.[323]

Against this background, it can be explained why and how big data and privacy considerations should and could constitute criteria for market power and thus for the establishment of dominance under Art. 102 TFEU. Predominantly, the claim for such a need is based on the fact that big data constitutes a key asset in the digital (platform) economy and the market positions of undertakings can be greatly dependent on it.[324] Big data and access to data can create a significant competitive advantage which creates market power. The market power, in return, fosters the dominant position of an undertaking.[325] Additionally, as substantiated above,[326] high market shares are considerably less significant in the digital economy than in other industries for a finding of dominance under Art. 102 TFEU.[327] Hence, they do not constitute a reliable indicator and the establishment of dominance cannot be based solely on them. Therefore, the above-mentioned "plus factors"[328] have an increased relevance here, and the way data and

---

320 See p. 41; C. I. "Article 102 of the Treaty on the Functioning of the European Union".
321 ECJ in case C-27/76, *United Brands* v Commission, ECLI:EU:C:1978:22, para. 65.; ECJ in case C-85/76, *Hoffmann-La Roche v Commission*, ECLI:EU:C:1979:36, para. 38; see p. 41, C. I. "Article 102 of the Treaty on the Functioning of the European Union".
322 See GC in case T-321/05, *AstraZeneca v Commission*, ECLI:EU:T:2010:266, para. 267; ECJ in case C-457/10 P, *AstraZeneca v Commission*, ECLI:EU:C:2012:770, paras. 177–181; see also Odudu, in: Arnull/Chalmers, 2015, p. 621.
323 Odudu, in: Arnull/Chalmers, 2015, p. 620.
324 See pp. 20 et seqq.; B. I. "Big data and its importance for the digital economy".
325 See Stucke/Grunes, 2016, p. 41.
326 See p. 25; B. II. 2. "Characteristics of the digital platform economy".
327 Körber, ZUM 2017, 93 (95); see Jones/Sufrin, 2016, pp. 344 et seq.
328 See p. 42; C. I. 1. "The establishment of dominance and the resulting "special responsibility".

privacy considerations can be incorporated into these plus factors will be explained below.

In Germany, for instance, by means of the 9th Amendment to the German Competition Act,[329] and the resulting adjustment of said act to the digital economy, this thought has already found its way into § 18 para. 3a no. 4 ARC. There, it is explicitly stated that *"in the case of multi-sided markets and networks, in assessing the market position of an undertaking, account shall also be taken of the undertaking's access to data relevant for competition"*. Bearing in mind that the drafting of the European competition law was heavily influenced by the German competition law system,[330] the question arises whether such influence should repeat itself so that Art. 102 TFEU undergoes an adjustment similar to that of the 9th Amendment to the German Competition Act? However, due to the rather flexible wording of Art. 102 TFEU, it might be the case that big data and access to it could already be considered a criterion for dominance under the present form of Art. 102 TFEU.

In order to find an answer to this question, which forms an aspect of the overall research question of this dissertation, the extensive case law of the EU Courts has to be taken into account. This is based on the fact that it is the EU Courts that, according to Art. 19 (1) of the Treaty on European Union, ensure that the law is observed in the interpretation and application of the Treaties. This includes the EU Courts filling gaps through the development of the law by their judicial decisions that might otherwise exist in the legal system of the EU.[331] Hence, the Court's decisions are of particular importance here and can make an amendment irrelevant.

a) The extent of data collection and the level of data protection as a criterion for market power

In *Hoffmann-La Roche*, one of the leading cases on dominance within the meaning of Art. 102 TFEU, the ECJ stated rather broadly that *"the existence of a dominant position may derive from several factors"*.[332] This statement

---

329 See Ninth Amendment of the Act against Restraints of Competition (Neuntes Gesetz zur Änderung des Gesetzes gegen Wettbewerbsbeschränkungen) of June 1st, 2017 (Federal Law Gazette 2017 I, pp. 1416 et seqq.).
330 See footnote 317.
331 See Streinz, 2016, p. 143.
332 ECJ in case C-85/76, *Hoffmann-La Roche v Commission*, ECLI:EU:C:1979:36, para. 39.

illustrates that there is no exhaustive list as to whether or not a certain criterion can be taken into account in the assessment of dominance. Thus, data-related considerations can in principle constitute such criteria, too. Additionally, the Court's statement in the *AstraZeneca* case can be applied to data as well in order to illustrate its relevance as a criterion for market power. As mentioned earlier in this section,[333] in *AstraZeneca*, the Court equates dominance with a certain degree of market power that is sufficient to maintain higher prices than competitors without losing market shares or sufficient to maintain market shares whilst lowering quality.[334] It was also mentioned earlier that data is often considered to be the new currency of the digital (platform) economy.[335] Part III of chapter B of this dissertation proved that this colloquial terminology is not too far-fetched from a German legal perspective.[336] More precisely, it was substantiated that data can indeed be considered a method of payment in return for access to the platform's IT infrastructure. Therefore, principles of competition law that apply to monetary prices as traditional currency can also be applied to data as payment in kind sui generis. Data, as the modern method of payment in the digital economy, functions as consideration alike. Hence, undertakings that collect vast amounts of data from their customers and/or users to the detriment of the user's privacy can be considered as demanding a higher price (in kind) than competitors that collect less data in return for their product/service. If the relevant undertaking can maintain those high prices in form of the collection of vast amounts of user data and still does not lose any market shares, this can be considered – in the light of *AstraZeneca* – to indicate market power and thus dominance within the meaning of Art. 102 TFEU.

Likewise, maintaining market shares whilst lowering quality, as indicated by the ECJ as a criterion for market power, can be applied in a data protection law context, too. Lowering quality can be equated with a lower degree of data protection since this can be a quality criterion for

---

333 See p. 88; F. I. 1. "Big data and data protection considerations as criteria for the establishment of dominance under Art. 102 TFEU".

334 See GC in case T-321/05, *AstraZeneca v Commission*, ECLI:EU:T:2010:266, para. 267; ECJ in case C-457/10 P, *AstraZeneca v Commission*, ECLI:EU:C:2012:770, paras. 177–181; see also Odudu, in: Arnull/Chalmers, 2015, p. 621.

335 See p. 20; B. I. "Big data and its importance for the digital economy".

336 See pp. 29 et seqq.; B. III. "Personal data as consideration in the digital platform economy".

which undertakings compete in the digital economy.[337] Additionally, in *TomTom/Tele Atlas*, the Commission explicitly stated that *"confidentiality concerns can be considered as similar to product degradation"*,[338] and even though this case did not concern personal data but customers' information on possible future business activities, the rationale behind this statement remains the same. The Commission explicitly recognizes that the way by which an undertaking makes use of certain customer information can lead to a decrease in the product value. In this context, the level of data protection must not be falsely equated with the extent of data collection, which was explained above and which was used in order to illustrate that a parallel can be drawn between an excessive collection of data and the notion of excessive pricing under Art. 102 TFEU. In contrast, the level of data protection is not solely defined by the mere extent to which data is being collected but also particularly by the manner in which the data collected is handled afterwards.[339] Hence, privacy aspects such as the level of transparency in the undertaking's data policy, the level of actual data protection mechanisms against any kind of data theft, or the fact whether or not the data collected will be transferred to third parties plays a prominent role here, too. Therefore, with regard to the level of data protection, several aspects need to be taken into account. Consequently, should an undertaking offer lower protection regarding the personal data of its customers/users due to the fact that it neglects one or more of the aforementioned aspects, it can be considered as offering a product and/or service in a market that is of lower quality and likewise of lower value than those of its competitors. However, should the undertaking in question be nonetheless able to maintain its market shares or, as the case may be, even gain market shares, it could indicate market power and thus dominance within the meaning of Art. 102 TFEU. On the other hand, one has to

---

337 See European Commission in case no. COMP/M.7217, *Facebook/Whatsapp*, para. 87 where it is stated that *"consumer communications apps compete for customers by attempting to offer the best communication experience"*, which includes, inter alia, *"privacy and security, the importance of which varies from user to user but which are becoming increasingly valued, as shown by the introduction of consumer communications apps* (such as Threema) *specifically addressing privacy and security issues"*; see also European Commission, press release on the approval of case M.8124 Microsoft/LinkedIn, published 06/12/2016, where it was stated that consumers see data privacy *"as a significant factor of quality"*, available on the internet under http://europa.eu/rapid/press-release_IP-16-4284_en.htm (last accessed: 27/03/20).

338 European Commission in case no. COMP/M.4854, C(2008) 1859,*TomTom/Tele Atlas*, para. 274.

339 Alpmann/Krüger/Wüstenbecker, 2014, p. 267; Weber, 2017, p. 286.

emphasize that treating the level of data protection as a quality criterion can lead to difficulties in so far as the relationship between data protection and quality is often shaped by a subjective perception of the users.[340] The fact that their data will be transferred to a third party, maybe even outside the EU, can constitute much more of a concern for people than the fact that the undertaking`s data protection policy is not fully transparent, or vice versa. Hence, as long as the preferences differ, it is difficult to rely on this second aspect in a competition law analysis. In addition, the level of data protection is difficult to measure anyway, which presents another practical problem.

b) Access to (big) data as a barrier to expansion

Within the assessment of an undertaking`s possibly dominant position, a special emphasis lies on the impact that could come from an expansion by actual competitors or the market entry of potential competitors.[341] This is based on the fact that the easier it is for a new competitor to enter the market or for an existing competitor to expand, the more likely it is for the strong position of an undertaking to be weakened.[342] Consequently, in assessing the market position of an undertaking, it is important to look at obstacles which could make such a market entry or expansion more difficult or ultimately even impossible. These obstacles are categorized as so-called "barriers to entry or expansion".

The Commission`s *Guidelines* on the enforcement priorities in applying Article 82 of the EC Treaty (Art. 102 TFEU) explicitly state that these barriers to entry or expansion can take various forms. This illustrates that there is no exclusive list defining such barriers.[343] Additionally, the *Guidelines* explicitly state that "*advantages specifically enjoyed by the dominant*

---

340 See Cooper, "Privacy and Antitrust: Underpants Gnomes, the First Amendment, and Subjectivity", George Mason Law Review 2013, 1129 (1138), available on the internet under http://www.georgemasonlawreview.org/wp-content/uploads/2014/03/Cooper_Website.pdf (last accessed: 24/01/20).

341 Eilmansberger/Bien, in: MüKoEuWettbR, Art. 102 AEUV, marginal no. 103; Bergmann/Fiedler, in: Loewenheim et al., Art. 102 TFEU, marginal no. 132.

342 Bergmann/Fiedler, in: Loewenheim et al., Art. 102 TFEU, marginal no. 132.

343 See European Commission, Communication from the Commission — Guidance on the Commission's enforcement priorities in applying Article 82 of the EC Treaty to abusive exclusionary conduct by dominant undertakings, OJ 2009 C 45, 7 (9), marginal no. 17.

undertaking, such as [...] *privileged access to essential inputs*" can constitute a barrier to entry and/or expansion.[344] Hence, access to certain key inputs that are particularly important in order to run a successful business within a given market can especially constitute a barrier.[345] In the context of the digital (platform) economy, personal data presents itself as a key input for many of the data-driven businesses.[346] Consequently, big data and access to data can constitute a barrier to entry or expansion for other (potential) competitors that lack such access.[347] Eventually, this can foster market power.[348] The rationale behind this thought is that big data and access to data often results in a competitive advantage for the undertaking having this access. Especially when the data is not available elsewhere and can only be gained by collecting it from users directly, it presents an immense challenge for undertakings in the digital platform economy to nonetheless successfully launch and maintain a business. This is even more true because transferring data from one undertaking to another is often very difficult, which fosters lock-in-effects, regardless of the fact that the GDPR explicitly stipulates the right to data portability in Art. 20 GDPR.[349] Hence, this also forms a criterion for market power and has to be considered within the assessment of dominance under Art. 102 TFEU.[350]

---

344 Loc. cit.
345 See Jones/Sufrin, 2016, p. 338.
346 See OECD, "Data-driven Innovation for Growth and Well-being – Interim Synthesis Report", October 2014, p. 11, available on the internet under https://www.oecd.org/sti/inno/data-driven-innovation-interim-synthesis.pdf (last accessed: 22/05/19); see also See N. Pantlin, et al., "Data Use – Protecting a Critical Resource", PLC Magazine, January/ February 2018, 19–27, who refer to data as the "new oil", thereby illustrating its status as a key input; in that context, see also Consumer Commissioner Meglena Kuneva, Keynote Speech at the Roundtable on Online Data Collection, Targeting and Profiling, Brussels, 31 March 2009, available on the internet under http://europa.eu/rapid/press-release_SPEECH-09-156_en.htm (last accessed: 01/05/19).
347 See Bundeskartellamt, "Big Data und Wettbewerb", October 2017, p. 7, available on the internet under https://www.bundeskartellamt.de/SharedDocs/Publikation/DE/Schriftenreihe_Digitales/Schriftenreihe_Digitales_1.pdf?__blob=publicationFile&v=3 (last accessed: 23/01/20); see also Mohr, EuZW 2019, 265 (270).
348 See Jones/Sufrin, 2016, p. 337.
349 See footnote 286.
350 See with regard to the relevant provision in the ARC Bosch, in: Bechtold/Bosch, GWB Kommentar, § 18 GWB, marginal no. 58; See also Körber, NZKart 2016, 303 (305 et seq.).

However, this statement has to be put into perspective in order to avoid wrongly generalizing the thought raised at the beginning of this paragraph. There is no suggestion that insufficient access to data always constitutes a barrier to entry or expansion in the digital economy. In public discussions, it is often falsely assumed that the amount of data would be decisive in itself in facilitating network effects and thus also market power, which could then constitute a barrier to entry or expansion.[351] This is a gross misconception, though. In their joint paper *Competition Law and Data*,[352] the French and German competition authorities focus, in addition to the amount of data, particularly on the availability of such data in order to assess whether it can constitute a barrier to entry.[353] However, such an approach is also insufficient since there are other aspects that are decisive, too. Firstly, one must in particular also take account of the competitive value of the data that is included in the data set of the undertaking in question. Not every personal datum is of the same significance for product enhancements, personalized advertisements or other methods of use and therefore is not of the same competitive or economic significance. For instance, the names of users will be less attractive to advertisers that are active in the sports equipment industry than information about users' hobbies in order to place matching advertisements. Secondly, both the size and depth of a dataset are of course important for modern data science but whether or not access to big data constitutes a barrier to entry and/or expansion depends also very much on the business model itself. Besides that, the undertaking`s ability to analyze the data must be taken into account as well. Even the biggest data pools will be worthless without the relevant business strategies and means by which the economic value of data can be "extracted". Additionally, it will only constitute a barrier in cases where the undertaking is dependent on access to as much data as possible in order to enhance its products or to monetize its business.

---

351 See Nuys, WuW 2016, 512 (515).
352 Autorité de la concurrence and Bundeskartellamt, "Competition Law and Data", May 10th, 2016, available on the internet under https://www.bundeskartellamt.de/SharedDocs/Publikation/DE/Berichte/Big%20Data%20Papier.pdf?__blob=publicationFile&v=2 (last accessed: 26/01/20).
353 See Autorité de la concurrence and Bundeskartellamt, "Competition Law and Data", May 10th, 2016, pp. 26 and 36 et seqq., available on the internet under https://www.bundeskartellamt.de/SharedDocs/Publikation/DE/Berichte/Big%20Data%20Papier.pdf?__blob=publicationFile&v=2 (last accessed: 26/01/20).

The latter is specifically the case with regard to two-sided online platforms in the digital economy like *Facebook* or *Google*. Their data-driven business models are predominantly monetized through the placement of personalized advertisements according to each user`s data. Therefore, the more data these undertakings can access, the more those advertisements can be personalized in accordance with the user`s preferences and/or needs. In turn, the more likely it is that the user will eventually click on the advertisement. This, on the other hand, increases the value for companies buying the spaces where their ads can be placed. Ultimately, this also attracts more companies that are willing to pay for such spaces, which will in return raise the overall profits made by the undertaking with its data-driven business model. Therefore, access to big data regarding one side of the platform – the user side – will affect the growth of the "money-making" side of the platform – the advertising side. Consequently, an undertaking lacking such access will struggle considerably more to expand its business. This is based on the fact that the advertisements placed will be less matched to the users and, therefore, are also less likely to lead to a conclusion of a contract between the user and the company behind the advertisement. As a result, the placement of advertisements is of less interest to companies as potential customers on the advertising side of the platform. Overall, an undertaking that does not have sufficient access to big data will have difficulties in attracting customers on the advertising side. Due to the fact that placing such advertisements is of a lower economic value for the companies in question, there will be a smaller number of companies that are actually willing to pay for advertisements on the undertaking`s website. The undertaking, with a limited access to relevant data or even no access at all, will therefore make a lower overall profit. However, making lower profits in general also means that less money is available for business divisions like marketing and innovation. As described above, though,[354] innovation is crucial in the digital economy and constitutes an important parameter of competition.[355] Thus, one can see that lacking

---

354 See p. 23; B. II. "The digital (platform) economy and its characteristics".

355 See Graef, "Stretching EU Competition Law Tools for Search Engines and Social Networks", Internet Policy Review 2015, pp. 2 et seq., available on the internet under https://papers.ssrn.com/sol3/papers.cfm?abstract_id=2655555 (last accessed: 23/07/19); see also Bundeskartellamt, B6–113/15, "Arbeitspapier Marktmacht von Plattformen und Netzwerken", June 2016, p. 80, available on the internet under https://www.bundeskartellamt.de/SharedDocs/Publikation/DE/Berichte/Think-Tank-Bericht.pdf?__blob=publicationFile&v=2 (last accessed: 23/08/19).

access to big data will ultimately negatively affect the expansion on both sides of a multi-sided platform and can therefore constitute a barrier to expansion or a barrier to entry in the first place.

As a conclusion, one can say that it is crucial to sufficiently address the interaction between the volume, quality and availability of the data as well as the company's ability to analyze it. Additionally, the relevant business model has to be taken into account, which will ultimately lead to the fact that it is very much a detailed case-by-case decision whether or not access to data can constitute a barrier to entry or expansion.

c) Interim conclusion

As seen from the elaborations above, big data and data protection considerations can already be integrated into the present form of Art. 102 TFEU with regard to the assessment of the possibly dominant position of an undertaking. This can be done in a twofold way. On the one hand, access to big data can be taken into account as a barrier to entry and/or expansion since access to such data constitutes an essential input for the data-driven business models in the digital platform economy. Competitors lacking such access might be prevented from entering into competition with undertakings that do have big data pools. On the other hand, the extent of data collection and the level of data protection can be treated as criteria for market power. An excessive extent of data collection can be equated with excessive pricing. The notion of excessive pricing known from competition law can be applied here as well. Moreover, the level of data protection can constitute a quality criterion for products and services of online platforms. Hence, retaining or even gaining market shares whilst collecting significantly more user data or whilst offering a lower level of data protection than competitors can indicate market power and thus dominance.

Generally, it is irrelevant that neither the notion of access to data as a barrier to entry/expansion nor the extent of data collection and the level of data protection are yet explicitly recognized in European competition law as criteria for the establishment of dominance under Art. 102 TFEU. As shown, they can be read into it, nonetheless. This is not least due to the case law of the CJEU, which makes an amendment to the competition law provisions – as seen in Germany – unnecessary. Thus, the aspect of the overall research question, whether big data and data protection considerations can be internalized by or incorporated within Art. 102 TFEU with regard to the establishment of dominance, must be answered in the affirmative. Nonetheless, for reasons of legal certainty, these factors for the assessment of an undertaking`s dominant position should be explicitly acknowledged – e.g. within the Commission`s *Guidelines* on the enforcement of Art. 102 TFEU.

2. The GDPR as a normative yardstick for abusive conduct under Art. 102 TFEU

It was shown above that big data and privacy considerations can be taken into account in the assessment of dominance under Art. 102 TFEU. Within the next pages, the influence of data-related considerations on the notion of abuse under Art. 102 TFEU shall be discussed. From the explanation of Art. 102 TFEU at the beginning as part of the legal framework, it became clear that differentiating between legitimate and illegitimate conduct is already rather difficult. It took several decisions of the CJEU in order to provide some clarity as to which conduct might trigger Art. 102 TFEU.[356] However, with the emergence of new data-driven business strategies in the digital (platform) economy, identifying abusive conduct has again become a challenge. The underlying assumption of this dissertation is that difficulties in identifying abusive data-related conduct could be avoided to a large extent by taking data protection consideration into account as a normative yardstick. Thus, the GDPR, as Europe`s uniform data protection law, might provide a remedy for the challenges that cases such as the German Bundeskartellamt case against *Facebook* cause. The following part shall therefore assess if and how data protection considerations can constitute a key parameter in establishing exclusionary and exploitative conduct under Art. 102 TFEU.

a) Exclusionary abuses in the light of the GDPR

As mentioned above,[357] the notion of exclusionary abuse refers to an undertaking`s conduct, which has a negative impact on the competition structure in a market by foreclosing competitors in an anti-competitive way. In the context of data-related practices that might classify as such

---

356 See p. 45; C. I. 2. "The abuse of a dominant position".
357 See p. 45; C. I. 2. "The abuse of a dominant position".

exclusionary conduct, the most prominent form appears to be the refusal to supply a so-called "essential facility" (more under aa)). Another aspect where data protection considerations can constitute a key parameter in establishing exclusionary conduct is to be seen in the context of a dominant undertaking`s "special responsibility" not to (further) impair genuine competition in the market (more under bb)).

aa) The essential facilities doctrine in a data-related context

The essential facilities doctrine deals with situations in which competitors can claim, under Art. 102 TFEU, access to a certain input that is *"objectively necessary"* for competition.[358] In its cases, the Commission has defined an essential facility as *"a facility or infrastructure without access to which competitors cannot provide services to their customers"*.[359] The CJEU, on the other hand, has never explicitly recognized the doctrine of an "essential facility" as such.[360] The ECJ instead preferred the term *"indispensable"*.[361] In the case of *Bronner*,[362] the ECJ listed four criteria which would have to be fulfilled in order to classify the refusal to an indispensable facility as abusive under Art. 102 TFEU: The refusal would have to be likely to eliminate all competition in the market; it would have to be impossible to justify the refusal objectively; access to the essential facility must be indispensable for the other undertaking`s business; and lastly, there must be no

---

358 See European Commission, Communication from the Commission — Guidance on the Commission's enforcement priorities in applying Article 82 of the EC Treaty to abusive exclusionary conduct by dominant undertakings, OJ 2009 C 45, 7 (9), marginal no. 83.

359 See European Commission in interim measures decision IV/34.174, *Sealink/B&I Holyhead*, para. 41.

360 See Jones/Sufrin, 2016, p. 500; the term essential facility can be found in two judgements of the GC. However, there it is only repeated within the part "Arguments of the parties" but not named within the actual "Findings of the Court" (see GC in joined cases T-374, 375, 384 and 388/94, *European Night Services and Others v Commission*, ECLI:EU:T:1998:198, para. 191; GC in case T-52/00, *Coe Clerici Logistics SpA v Commission*, ECLI:EU:T:2003:168, para. 62).

361 See ECJ in case C-7/97, *Oscar Bronner GmbH & Co KG v Mediaprint*, ECLI:EU:C:1998:569, para. 38.

362 ECJ in case C-7/97, *Oscar Bronner GmbH & Co KG v Mediaprint*, ECLI:EU:C:1998:569.

actual or potential substitute for the facility/infrastructure in question.[363] The latter requirement not only refers to the fact that there is no substitute to the facility but also means that the facility cannot be replicated.[364]

In the context of big data, it is already highly doubtful whether vast amounts of data can be classified as a facility in the sense of the doctrine. This is based on the fact that the essential facility doctrine has been applied in cases where ports,[365] intellectual property rights,[366] or certain distribution networks[367] were regarded as such facilities/infrastructures. These facilities are all characterized by the fact that they were owned by the dominant undertaking and therefore under its exclusive control. However, the personal data of users and/or customers is not owned by the data controller and the controller will thus lack the characteristic exclusive control due to opposing rights by the data subjects. Additionally, it is hard to argue that the data pools of *Google, Facebook* and co. cannot be replicated since there are various "data brokers" that could help incumbents to build their own data pools.[368] The aforementioned aspects can already in themselves contradict an application of the doctrine with regard to big data. What is more though, a refusal to provide access to big data can be objectively justified since principles stipulated by the GDPR, such as the above-mentioned principle of purpose limitation,[369] would legitimately prevent the undertaking from sharing its dataset with competitors. The relevant undertaking will hardly ever collect data for the purpose of sharing it with others but rather for its own purposes, by which it aims at monetizing its business model. Therefore, a transfer to a competitor would be in breach of the original purpose and would thus infringe Art. 5 (1) (b) GDPR. Additionally, a transfer of personal data to another undertaking,

---

363 See ECJ in case C-7/97, *Oscar Bronner GmbH & Co KG v Mediaprint*, ECLI:EU:C:1998:569, para. 41.
364 See Bruc, European Competition Journal 2019, 177 (196).
365 See European Commission in interim measures decision IV/34.689, *Sea Containers v. Stena Sealink*, OJ 1994 L 15/8.
366 See inter alia ECJ in joined cases C-241–242/91 P, *RTE & ITP v Commission*, ECLI:EU:C:1995:98.
367 See ECJ in case C-7/97, *Oscar Bronner GmbH & Co KG v Mediaprint*, ECLI:EU:C:1998:569.
368 See also European Commission in case no. COMP/M.4731, C(2008) 927 final, *Google/DoubleClick*, paras. 364 et seqq., where the Commission is rather reluctant with regard to the assumption that data could not be replicated; see also Körber, NZKart 2016, 303 (308).
369 See p. 54; C. II. 2. b) "The principles of purpose limitation and data minimization".

i.e. a competitor, would also classify as a processing of data. As a result, a legal base is required for the transfer of data according to Art. 5 (1) (a) GDPR. Art. 5 (1) (a) GDPR states, inter alia, that personal data shall be processed lawfully – meaning on a valid legal base.[370] Without such a legal base, the undertaking`s refusal to give access to its data pools would be objectively justified because otherwise, the undertaking could be held liable for an infringement of the GDPR. Consequently, data protection considerations do not lead to an abusive conduct here but rather prevent certain conduct from being found abusive under Art. 102 TFEU since a refusal to grant access to data pools can be based on Art. 5 GDPR as objective justification.[371]

---

370 See Frenzel, in: Paal/Pauly, DSGVO/BDSG Kommentar, Art. 5 DSGVO, marginal no. 14.

371 Against this background, it is surprising that the 10th and newest Amendment to the (German) Act against Restraints of Competition explicitly adds "to refuse the portability of data" to § 19 para. 2 no. 5 ARC – the provision for the essential facility doctrine in the ARC. As a result, the refusal to provide access to an undertaking`s own data pool could – in principle – constitute an abuse of a dominant position – provided that there is no objective justification for the refusal. As shown, however, in such cases the transfer of personal data would require a legal base. The mere duty under competition law cannot constitute a legal base, as it would bypass the GDPR. Hence, the provisions of the GDPR do indeed often provide an objective justification for the refusal to grant access to certain data. The Federal Ministry for Economic Affairs and Energy, which was responsible for the very first ministerial draft bill, seemed to have known that problem, which is why already the draft bill stated that one would have to take into account whether, and with what level of anonymization, the data concerned can be released in accordance with data protection law. Additionally, it stated that the release of the data must be permissible irrespective of a possible claim for access under competition law; the latter should not create a new legal basis for the lawfulness of the processing (see Federal Ministry of Economics and Energy, Ministerial Draft of the Federal Ministry of Economics and Energy for a Tenth Act to amend the Act against Restraints of Competition for a focused, proactive and digital competition law 4.0 (GWB Digitization Act), p. 84, available on the internet under https://www.bmwi.de/Redaktion/DE/Downloads/G/gwb-digitalisierungsgesetz-referentenentwurf.pdf?__blob=publicationFile&v=10 (last accessed: 25/03/20)); see for the same considerations the final "Beschlussempfehlung" of the bill, Bundestag document 19/25868, Beschlussempfehlung und Bericht des Ausschusses für Wirtschaft und Energie zu dem Regierungsentwurf des GWB-Digitalisierungsgesetzes, p. 113 et seqq., available on the internet under https://dip21.bundestag.de/dip21/btd/19/258/1925868.pdf (last accessed: 27/03/2021). The practical relevance of § 19 para. 2 no. 5 ARC will therefore be extremely limited.

bb) The General Data Protection Regulation as an indicator for infringements of the undertaking`s "special responsibility"

Data protection and competition law considerations can also be linked under the special responsibility doctrine. A dominant undertaking has a special responsibility, according to which it must not *"allow its conduct to impair genuine and undistorted competition on the common market"*.[372] Consequently, the dominant undertaking must only resort to "competition on the merits".[373] The Bundeskartellamt referred in its initial press release with regard to its investigation into *Facebook* to a similar "special obligation" of dominant undertakings like *Facebook*.[374] Accordingly, the infringement of data protection law could constitute a departure from such competition on the merits, which would lead to an infringement of the undertaking`s special responsibility as a form of exclusionary abuse.[375] In *CMB* and *Tetra Pak II*, the Court explicitly stated that *"the actual scope of the special responsibility imposed on a dominant undertaking must be considered in the light of the specific circumstances of each case"*.[376] Thus, data protection law can indeed be considered crucial in a data-related context. The special responsibility of dominant undertakings in the digital (platform) economy must result in the fact that they have the obligation to refrain from certain infringements of data protection law such as the GDPR.

Körber objects to an extension of the special responsibility doctrine because the special responsibility would only exist regarding competition as such and not (beyond the obligations of other undertakings) with regard

---

372 ECJ in case C-322/81, *NV Nederlandsche Banden Industrie Michelin v Commission of the European Communities*, ECLI:EU:C:1983:313, para. 57.

373 See p. 45; C. I. 2. "The abuse of a dominant position".

374 See Bundeskartellamt, press release "Bundeskartellamt initiates proceeding against Facebook on suspicion of having abused its market power by infringing data protection rules", March 2nd, 2016, available on the internet under https://www.bundeskartellamt.de/SharedDocs/Meldung/EN/Pressemitteilungen/2016/02_03_2016_Facebook.html?nn=3591568 (last accessed: 27/03/20).

375 See Costa-Cabral/Lynskey, CML Rev. 2017, 11 (35).

376 ECJ in joined cases C-395 and 396/96 P, *Compagnie Maritime Belge Transport SA v Commission*, ECLI:EU:C:2000:132, para. 114; ECJ in case C-333/94 P, *Tetra Pak International SA v Commission of the European Communities*, ECLI:EU:C:1996:436, para 24.

to the legal system as a whole.[377] On the one hand, Körber is indeed right in stating that the special responsibility would only exist with regard to the process of competition and not regarding the legal order in general. On the other hand, Körber neglects a decisive fact: As highlighted above,[378] an infringement of data protection law can result – in the data-driven digital economy – in a competitive advantage. If the requirements of the GDPR are circumvented, which limit the undertaking`s access to personal data as its key input, a competitive advantage is created by the resulting illegal and unfair processing of data. This is against the principle of competition on the merits and distorts competition, which is incompatible with the special responsibility a dominant undertaking has. Therefore, such an infringement can definitely affect the process of competition and the special responsibility would not be broadened to an undue extent.

A question that comes up in this context is whether this conclusion leads to the fact that any infringement of data protection law would automatically trigger Art. 102 TFEU? The answer is no. A broadening of the special responsibility to an extent where infringements of data protection law by dominant undertakings would automatically result in infringements of Art. 102 TFEU is highly unlikely. It is rather necessary to assess the circumstances of each case since it is important to ascertain whether or not there is an actual and plausible possibility that the conduct could distort effective competition.[379] Such a distortion of competition will in most cases only be likely in the course of infringements of the above-mentioned decisive cornerstones of the GDPR.[380] This is based on the fact that those provisions and principles in particular are meant to secure the rights of data subjects and particularly the control over their data, which could limit the data pools of undertakings. Infringements of other provisions – for instance, those about mere documentation obligations (e.g. Art. 30 GDPR) – will not cause harm to consumers, will not result in a competitive advantage for the dominant undertaking and will thus not constitute a competition law concern, either. Moreover, it could provide a filter to assess whether it was particularly the dominant position of the

---

377 Körber, NZKart 2019, 187 (191); with a similar misconception regarding the importance of data protection violations for competition in the digital (platform) economy also Ellger, WUW 2019, 493 (493).

378 See p. 106; F. I. 2. b) aa) "The influence of data protection considerations on the notion of abuse under Art. 102 (1) TFEU".

379 See Eilmansberger/Bien, in: MüKo KartellR Kommentar, Art. 102 AEUV, marginal no. 181.

380 See pp. 52 et seqq.; C. II. 2. "The decisive cornerstones of the GDPR".

undertaking in question that provided the conditions for the infringement of data protection law. Hence, the question of the causal link between the undertaking`s dominant position and the infringement of data protection law would be suitable to prevent Art. 102 from being deprived of any limitation.

Generally speaking, a strict causal link between the dominant position and its abuse is not required under European competition law – meaning the dominant position does not have to constitute the base for the abuse.[381] There is only a link of causality required between the abusive behaviour and the harmful effect as an alleged result from the abuse.[382] However, in order to prevent an excessive application of Art. 102 TFEU to general violations of the law, a dual link of causality should be required if one wants to sanction infringements of provisions from other fields of law – e.g. data protection law infringements. More precisely, if it was clearly the dominant position that, on the one hand, paved the way for an infringement of data protection law and, on the other hand, had customers not reacting negatively to such an infringement, it should be a matter for competition law. If there is no causal link to the dominant position, the matter should be handled on a mere data protection law basis in order to prevent an undue overlap between the two fields of law. The same should apply if there is no causal link between the infringement of data protection law and the competitive advantage resulting in a foreclosure of the market. This dual causal link would prevent Art. 102 TFEU from being deprived of any limitation.

In practice, it will be particularly the infringement of Art. 6 (1) (b), the processing of personal data that cannot be based on a valid consent, which lets a violation of the undertaking`s "special responsibility" overlap with the infringement of data protection law. In order to rely on the data subject`s consent as a legal base for the processing of data, the consent must be, inter alia, freely given according to the definition of consent in Art. 4 No. 11 GDPR. However, dominant undertakings like *Facebook* often make

---

381 See Weiß, in: Calliess/Ruffert, AEUV, Art. 102, marginal no. 44; Eilmansberger/Bien, in: MüKoEuWettbR, Art. 102 AEUV, marginal nos. 131 et seqq.; Paal, in: BeckOK InfoMedienR, AEUV, Art. 102, marginal no. 28 (effective 01/05/19); ECJ in case C-6/72, *Europemballage Corporation and Continental Can Company v Commission*, ECLI:EU:C:1973:22, para. 27.

382 Fuchs, in: Immenga/Mestmäcker, KartellR Kommentar, Art. 102 TFEU, marginal no. 137; ECJ in case C-6/72, *Europemballage Corporation and Continental Can Company v Commission*, ECLI:EU:C:1973:22, para. 27.

use of their market power and leave the user (= data supplier)[383] with no real choice but to give their consent, if they want to get access to the platform. Additionally, dominant online platforms often make the use of their services conditional upon the consent to the processing of personal data. However, the extent to which dominant platforms collect personal data is often not even necessary for the performance of the contract. According to Art. 7 (4) GDPR, these circumstances have to be taken into account when assessing whether or not the consent was freely given. Additionally, a consent can only be freely given when there is an alternative option to choose, and there is only an alternative when the market is characterized by a healthy competitive structure that prevents dominant undertakings from imposing their excessive data processing terms by virtue of their market power.[384] Therefore, particularly these cases create a link between data protection (the right to informational self-determination) and competition law (securing healthy competition).

Overall, it will be vital to ascertain whether the way for the infringements of data protection provisions, such as the ones of the GDPR, was paved by the dominant position of the undertaking in question and whether the infringement will lead to (i) an enhanced access of the undertaking to the personal data of its customers, (ii) the undertaking being able to reinforce its dominant position with this data and whether it will lead to (iii) an undue impairment of genuine and undistorted competition. If those conditions are fulfilled, it would be by no means an excessive broadening of the special responsibilities doctrine. On the contrary, the aforementioned requirements rather mirror the case law of the ECJ stating that *"the actual scope of the special responsibility imposed on a dominant undertaking must be considered in the light of the specific circumstances of each case".*[385]

---

383 See p. 64; D. II. 1. b) "The objectives of the GDPR and data protection law in general"; Buchner, WRP 2019, 1243 (1245).

384 See also Buchner, WRP 2019, 1243 (1245).

385 ECJ in joined cases C-395 and 396/96 P, *Compagnie Maritime Belge Transport SA v Commission*, ECLI:EU:C:2000:132, para. 114; ECJ in case C-333/94 P, *Tetra Pak International SA v Commission of the European Communities*, ECLI:EU:C:1996:436, para 24.

b) Exploitative abuses in the light of the General Data Protection
   Regulation

Besides the fact that the GDPR and its underlying data protection considerations could affect the establishment of an exclusionary abusive conduct
under the special responsibilities doctrine, they could also provide guidance on the finding of exploitative conduct. The German Monopolies
Commission (Monopolkommission) has affirmed this general possibility
in a special report called *Competition Policy: The Challenge of Digital Markets*.[386] In this report, the Monopolies Commission stated that *"the unbalanced nature of the service provided by the internet provider (in this case, for
instance facilitating social interaction opportunities) and the service provided
by the users in turn (facilitating access to personal data)"* could be classed
as an exploitative abuse.[387] As part of the elaborations of Art. 102 TFEU,
it was explained that the second category of abuse, exploitative abuse,
refers to conduct by which a dominant undertaking takes advantage of
its market power in order to exploit its business partners. Due to the
fact that undertakings in the digital (platform) economy have a strong
incentive to gain access to as much user data as possible, the focus of this
paragraph will lie on exploitative conduct aimed at acquiring personal data
from users. In this regard, data protection law could provide a normative
indicator for such conduct in so far as it could classify a certain behaviour
as abusive when data protection rights are infringed. The rationale behind
this approach lies in the fact that certain data protection rights are solely
infringed by undertakings with the intention of circumventing limitations
regarding the collection of personal data. The fact that companies pursue
such a circumventive practice was shown by the Bundeskartellamt's *Facebook* case. In that case, not only was the way in which the users' consent
as obtained by *Facebook* highly questionable from a data protection point
of view, but principles such as transparency, purpose limitation and data
minimization were also neglected by the undertaking in order to collect
more user data. The following part shall therefore assess, in a European
dimension, whether the use of data contrary to data protection law, as

---

386 Monopolkommission, "Competition Policy: The challenge of digital markets",
   Special Report 68, available on the Internet under https://www.monopolkom-
   mission.de/images/PDF/SG/s68_fulltext_eng.pdf (last accessed: 28/01/20).
387 Monopolkommission, "Competition Policy: The challenge of digital markets", Special Report 68, para. 329, available on the Internet under
   https://www.monopolkommission.de/images/PDF/SG/s68_fulltext_eng.pdf (last
   accessed: 28/01/20).

was seen in the *Facebook* case, can lead to abusive conduct relevant for Art. 102 TFEU. The assessment will be structured according to the wording of Art. 102 TFEU. Hence, the general clause of Art. 102 (1) TFEU will be discussed first.[388] Afterwards, the examples of abusive conduct named in Art. 102 (2) TFEU will be elaborated. More precisely, the examples named in Art. 102 (2) lit. a) TFEU will be investigated since the remaining examples of lit. b) – d) are already, due to their wording, less likely to be triggered in a data-related context.

aa) The influence of data protection considerations on the notion of abuse under Art. 102 (1) TFEU

The notion of abuse can be found in its most unspecific form in the general clause of Art. 102 (1) TFEU, according to which the abuse of a dominant position is prohibited. As stated above, there is no exact definition of the notion of abuse which requires its interpretation.[389] The definition of an (exclusionary) abuse that the ECJ gave in *Hoffmann-La Roche* does not provide a clear orientation, either. Essentially, in that case the ECJ merely stated that the notion of abuse is to be regarded as an objective concept relating to the behaviour of an undertaking by which the structure of competition is weakened.[390] The actual significance and added value of that judgement for the definition of the term "abuse" in a context of consumer exploitation is limited though. However, taking a look at the case law of the ECJ, it becomes clear that the Court orientates itself in its interpretation of Art. 102 TFEU on the objectives of the Treaties.[391] Hence,

---

388 In its German version, Art. 102 (1) TFEU speaks of an "abusive exploitation" (missbräuchliche Ausnutzung). The English version simply uses the word "abuse" and it is indeed correct that the general clause of Art. 102 (1) TFEU does not only prohibit exploitative abuses but likewise exclusionary abuses. However, due to the focus on the personal data of users, the general clause of Art. 102 (1) TFEU will be discussed with a focus on exploitative abuses here, which is why it is elaborated under F. I. 2. b) "Exploitative abuses in the light of the GDPR" instead of forming its own section before the differentiation between exploitative and exclusionary abuses in the light of the GDPR.

389 See p. 45; C. I. 2. "The abuse of a dominant position".

390 See also Eilmansberger/Bien, in: MüKo KartellR Kommentar, Art. 102 AEUV, marginal no. 157.

391 See for instance ECJ in case C-6/72, *Europemballage Corporation and Continental Can Company v Commission*, ECLI:EU:C:1973:22, para. 25, where it is stated that *"with a view to safeguarding the principles and attaining the objectives set out in*

the conduct of an undertaking can be considered as abusive within the meaning of Art. 102 (1) TFEU, when it must be regarded as an objective misconduct in the light of the objectives pursued by the Treaties.[392]

Against this background, it becomes clear that reference can be made to European data protection law and the underlying valuation in order to assess an allegedly abusive data-related conduct under Art. 102 (1) TFEU. The establishment of the link between data protection and competition law is based on the fact that European law often applies a teleological and systematic method, by which the provisions are interpreted in the light of the other provisions in the Treaties. Especially because EU law is regarded as a closed and independent legal system,[393] the so-called "principle of the unity of the legal order" ("Einheit der Rechtsordnung") allows for such an approach. The right to data protection is explicitly recognized in Art. 16 (1) TFEU and (as mentioned) likewise in Art 8 CFREU. According to Art. 6 (1) TEU, the CFREU has the same legal value as the Treaties. Therefore, it must have an influence on the interpretation of other primary Union law such as Art. 102 TFEU. As mentioned above,[394] it is even explicitly required by Art. 51 (1) CFREU that Union bodies such as the Commission or the CJEU take the rights of the CFREU into account in all their actions and promote the application thereof. Consequently, this must affect the interpretation of Art. 102 TFEU alike. Additionally, since Art. 51 (1) CFREU stipulates that the institutions shall not only observe the principles but shall also promote the application thereof, it cannot be sufficient to merely take data protection considerations into account only to subsequently reject them as part of the competition appraisal – as was done in *Asnef-Equifax*[395] and *Facebook/WhatsApp*.[396] On the contrary, promoting the application thereof contradicts an approach by which it is held that *"any possible issues relating to the sensitivity of personal data are* [in general] *not, as such, a matter for competition law".*[397] Hence, the valuation behind provisions about data protection and privacy, such as

---

Articles 2 and 3 of the Treaty, Articles 85 to 90 (nowadays Art. 101 to 106 TFEU) *have laid down general rules applicable to undertakings."*

392 See Bulst, in: Langen/Bunte, EU KartellR Kommentar, Art. 102 AEUV, marginal no. 84.

393 Frenz, Handbuch Europarecht, § 4, marginal no. 405.

394 See p. 66; D. II. 2. "Other links between data protection and competition law".

395 ECJ in case C-238/05, *Asnef-Equifax v Ausbanc*, ECLI:EU:C:2006:734.

396 European Commission in case no. COMP/M.7217, C(2014) 7239 final, *Facebook/Whatsapp*.

397 ECJ in case C-238/05, *Asnef-Equifax v Ausbanc*, ECLI:EU:C:2006:734, para. 63.

Art. 8 CFREU, can indeed be referred to in order to assess the abusive conduct of an undertaking in a data-related context. Admittedly, there are a few such cross-section clauses (so-called "Querschnittsklauseln") in EU law which lay down that certain principles are to be taken into account in the implementation of Union policies and activities.[398] The relation between these cross-section clauses and Art. 102 TFEU has been rarely discussed so far,[399] so that one may question the legal significance of provisions like Art. 51 (1) CFREU. However, the fact that these Querschnittsklauseln are not sufficiently observed in some areas of law does not legitimatize that they should be disregarded in all areas of law. Moreover, this dissertation aims to show if and how data protection considerations can be integrated into a European competition law context. It is not an objective to assess whether future practice will sufficiently follow such an approach. In fact, whether or not it will be promoted by the EU institutions is speculative and only time will tell.

Additionally, the underlying principle of the present approach, by which one links the valuation of fundamental rights to the interpretation of other fields of EU law, was affirmed by the ECJ in *Johnston*.[400] In that case, it was stated that fundamental rights *"must be taken into consideration in Community law"*.[401] Admittedly, the case dealt with rights of the European Convention for the Protection of Human Rights and Fundamental Freedoms, but this statement must be applied even more to fundamental rights explicitly secured under the CFREU as a primary source of EU law. This is even more true since Art. 3 TEU explicitly states that it is, inter alia, the *"Union's aim [...] to promote [...] its values"*.[402] The term "values", on the other hand, refers to Art. 2 TEU, which names, inter alia, *"respect for human rights"* as one of those values. This creates a link to the CFREU,[403] and

---

398 See for instance Art. 8 et seqq. TFEU.
399 Eilmansberger/Bien, in: MüKo EuWettbR, Art. 102 AEUV, marginal no. 23.
400 ECJ in case C-222/84, *Johnston v Chief Constable of the Royal Ulster Constabulary*, ECLI:EU:C:1986:206.
401 See ECJ in case C-222/84, *Johnston v Chief Constable of the Royal Ulster Constabulary*, ECLI:EU:C:1986:206, para. 18.
402 The term "values" obviously refers to Art. 2 TEU, which names, inter alia, "respect for human rights" as one of those values. This creates a link to the CFREU (Calliess, in: Calliess/Ruffert, Art. 2 EUV, marginal no. 27) and includes thus also the right to privacy or the right to data protection (see Hilf/Schorkopf, in: Grabitz/Hilf/Nettesheim, Das Recht der Europäischen Union, Art. 2 EUV, marginal no. 37).
403 Calliess, in: Calliess/Ruffert, Art. 2 EUV, marginal no. 27.

thus likewise to the right to privacy and the right to data protection.[404] Provisions about the objectives of EU law, such as Art. 2 respectively Art. 3 TFEU, function as an important yardstick not only for the interpretation of secondary law but also for the interpretation of provisions of primary law – i.e. Art. 102 TFEU.[405] As mentioned before in this section, the Court also interprets Art. 102 TFEU in the light of the objectives of the Treaties.[406] Therefore, whether or not a data-related conduct is to be regarded as abusive under Art. 102 (1) TFEU is to be assessed, inter alia, in the light of Art. 8 (2) CFREU.

Consequently, should the behaviour of a dominant undertaking infringe or, at least to a large extent, contradict Art. 8 (2) CFREU, namely the right that one's personal data must be processed fairly for specified purposes and on the basis of consent or some other legitimate basis laid down by law (e.g. Art. 6 (1) (b) – (f) GDPR), this behaviour can be seen as an abuse within the meaning of Art. 102 (1) TFEU. In a case like that, the harm to consumers would lie in the infringement of their fundamental rights. A prime example for such a scenario is again *Facebook*. The platform deprives its users of any informational self-determination by granting itself, de facto, a general authorization for a comprehensive processing of user data.[407]

This approach is also in line with the decision practice of the European Commission. As mentioned earlier, the Commission explicitly stated in its *1998 Football World Cup* decision that *"Article 82 [102 TFEU] can properly be applied, where appropriate, to situations in which a dominant undertaking's behaviour direct prejudices the interests of consumers. notwithstanding* [sic!] *the absence of any effect on the structure of competition"*.[408] The Commission specifically rejected the argument that conduct in breach of Art. 102 TFEU must negatively affect the process of competition, given that the provision

---

404　See Hilf/Schorkopf, in: Grabitz/Hilf/Nettesheim, Das Recht der Europäischen Union, Art. 2 EUV, marginal no. 37.

405　See ECJ in case C-6/72, *Europemballage Corporation and Continental Can Company v Commission*, ECLI:EU:C:1973:22, para. 25; see also Schröter, in: Schröter/Jakob/Klotz/Mederer, Europäisches WettbewerbsR, p. 60, marginal no. 43.

406　See for instance ECJ in case C-6/72, *Europemballage Corporation and Continental Can Company v Commission*, ECLI:EU:C:1973:22, para. 25, where it is stated that "with a view to safeguarding the principles and attaining the objectives set out in Articles 2 and 3 of the Treaty, Articles 85 to 90 (nowadays Art. 101 to 106 TFEU) have laid down general rules applicable to undertakings".

407　See also Buchner, WRP 2019, 1243 (1246).

408　European Commission, case no. IV/36.888 – *1998 Football World Cup*, para. 100.

would not be intended to protect the interests of consumers in a direct manner.[409]

However, infringements of data protection rights would also lead to a harm for the process of competition so that it is not only the afore-mentioned aspects that link data protection and competition law. The GDPR forms the legal framework in the data-driven digital economy and imposes requirements that limit access to the undertaking`s key input: personal user data. Therefore, particularly the type, range and content of the services on the profitable advertising side of an online platform are determined by conflicting data protection rights of users. This is due to the fact that principles such as purpose limitation and data minimization and the corresponding user rights will lead to a limited data pool of the under-taking. Less user data, however, will affect the accuracy of the personalized advertisements offered by undertakings such as *Facebook*. This, in turn, will limit the platform`s ability to match users and advertisers. Ultimately, companies will pay less for the spaces where advertisements can be placed. Consequently, if these requirements of the GDPR are circumvented, bear-ing in mind that access to personal data can have a "dominance-promoting effect", a competitive advantage is created. As a result, infringements of data protection law overlap with competition law concerns.

The approach just presented is by and large congruent with the afore-mentioned approach the Bundeskartellamt applied in its *Facebook* case.[410] Especially the ECJ`s case of *Johnston*[411] and the *Pechstein* case of the FCJ[412] – one of the bases for the Bundeskartellamt`s reasoning – show similarities in their reasoning. This illustrates that a case like the Bundeskartellamt`s *Facebook* case could be pursued in a European competition law context as well. However, this does not constitute the only way in which data protection considerations can be integrated into the assessment of abusive conduct under Art. 102 TFEU, as the following elaborations will show.

---

409 European Commission, case no. IV/36.888 – *998 Football World Cup*, para. 99.

410 See p. 70; E. "The Facebook case of the German Competition Authority (Bun-deskartellamt)".

411 ECJ in case C-222/84, *Johnston v Chief Constable of the Royal Ulster Constabulary*, ECLI:EU:C:1986:206.

412 German Federal Court of Justice, judgement of June 6th, 2016, KZR 6/15, *Pechstein*, NJW 2016, 2266 (2271 et seq.).

bb) Excessive collection of data as a form of excessive pricing

Article 102 (2) TFEU describes in lit. a) the imposition of unfair purchase prices as a first example of abusive conduct. In *United Brands*, the ECJ has stated that the imposition of unfair purchase prices as a form of abusive conduct would be fulfilled when an undertaking charges "*a price which is excessive because it has no reasonable relation to the economic value of the product supplied*" (so-called excessive pricing).[413]

It was highlighted above that the provision of personal data can be considered a method of payment in the digital (platform) economy.[414] Therefore, a parallel can be drawn between the excessive collection of data as excessive pricing in kind sui generis and excessive monetary pricing. However, the question arises as to what point should the collection of data i be regarded as excessive or, in the words of the Monopolies Commission, "unbalanced" compared to the service provided in return by the undertaking. In *United Brands*, the ECJ answered this question by focusing on the difference between the costs actually incurred and the price charged. Additionally, the ECJ focused in that case on the difference between the price charged by the undertaking in question and the prices charged by competitors.[415]

At least the latter requirement could be applied in a data-related context by taking account of competitors and the extent to which they collect data from their users. It has to be emphasized, though, that such a comparison might be suitable in theory but it would cause several difficulties in practice. Predominantly, this is due to the fact that the extent to which competitors collect data from their customers will be much harder to evaluate without a detailed insight into the competitors` businesses than the monetary prices that competitors charge for their product/service on a given market. Monetary prices are publicly available but reliable information about the exact extent to which a certain undertaking collects data is much harder to obtain. In addition, the first criterion, namely the difference between the costs incurred for the service and the price charged for it, is not suitable within a data-related context, either. There is an obvious difference between the monetary costs incurred on the one hand and the personal

---

413 ECJ in case C-27/76, *United Brands v Commission*, ECLI:EU:C:1978:22, para. 249.
414 See pp. 29 et seqq.; B. III. "Personal data as consideration in the digital platform economy".
415 ECJ in case C-27/76, *United Brands v Commission*, ECLI:EU:C:1978:22, paras. 252 et seqq.

data as payment in kind for the product/service on the other hand. A comparison between two monetary sums, namely costs in comparison to monetary prices, does allow for a conclusion. However, monetary costs incurred in comparison to a certain level of data collected will not lead to any statement about the excessiveness of the data collection.

As an alternative criterion, one can take the principles of the GDPR into account. Accordingly, an infringement of the aforementioned principles of purpose limitation and data minimization of Art. 5 (1) (b) respectively (c) GDPR can constitute an excessive collection of data.[416] These principles stipulate three requirements regarding the processing of data: it must be (i) proportionate, (ii) relevant for the purpose and (iii) limited to what is necessary in order to achieve the purpose.[417] The purpose, on the other hand, must be specific, explicit and legitimate according to Art. 5 (1) (b) GDPR.

A purpose is legitimate particularly in cases where the data subject has given its consent.[418] This, however, requires not only that the data subject be aware of the extent to which consent is given, but also that the data subject has a genuine and free choice and is able to refuse or withdraw consent without detriment.[419] However, the exact extent to which consent was given is often not clear and not transparent to the data subject under the general terms and conditions. Additionally, neither is there a free choice when consent is required under the general terms and conditions of the dominant undertaking in a way that there is an "all-or-nothing approach", as illustrated by the *Facebook* case. The validity of consent is therefore highly doubtful and so is the legitimacy of the purpose. What is more, though, the purpose has to be specific and explicit. The Article 29 Working Party, the predecessor to today`s European Data Protection Board, has clearly stated with regard to these requirements that it is insufficient to simply name a broad "umbrella purpose" under which various further remotely related processing activities would be summarized.[420] Hence, purposes like "advertisement" or "product enhancement", for which personal data is

---

416 See p. 54; C. II. 2. b) "The principles of purpose limitation and data minimization".
417 Frenzel, in: Paal/Pauly, DSGVO/BDSG Kommentar, Art. 5 DSGVO, marginal nos. 34 et seqq.
418 Frenzel, in: Paal/Pauly, DSGVO/BDSG Kommentar, Art. 5 DSGVO, marginal no. 28.
419 See recital 42 of the GDPR.
420 See Art. 29 Data Protection Working Party, Working Paper 203, Opinion 03/2013 on purpose limitation, pp. 16 et seqq., available on the internet

ultimately collected, are of such generality that they cannot be seen as specific and explicit.[421] However, an undertaking will have a strong incentive to formulate the purpose as broadly as possible since the data collected can only be processed for the relevant purpose. It is exactly the nature of a broad purpose though that will pave the way for a disproportionate collection of data and which will give rise to concerns not only under data protection but also under competition law.

Overall, it becomes clear that the principles of data minimization and purpose limitation can be referred to in order to identify an excessive collection of data, which can be seen as an excessive and thus abusive pricing under Art. 102 TFEU. The question as to whether or not such conduct must be based on the dominant position in order to fall under the prohibition of Art. 102 TFEU, meaning whether a causal link between the conduct on the one hand and the market position on the other is necessary, can be left undecided if there is an undue strengthening of the dominant position anyway. In the literature, causal link is still discussed, even though it is to a large extent already acknowledged that it does not constitute a requirement of Art. 102 TFEU.[422] However, dominant online platforms will predominantly only be able to impose excessive prices in the form of an extensive data collection due to their dominant position anyway. Thus, under the circumstances elaborated above, an excessive collection of data can indeed lead to an abuse under Art. 102 (2) (a) TFEU.

cc) Unfair contractual terms and conditions in the light of the General Data Protection Regulation

Another form of abusive conduct named by Art. 102 (2) (a) TFEU is the imposition of *"other unfair contractual terms and conditions"*. However, the question arises as to what point such contractual clauses are to be considered *"unfair"* within the meaning of Art. 102 TFEU. According to case law

---

under https://ec.europa.eu/justice/article-29/documentation/opinion-recommendation/files/2013/wp203_en.pdf (last accessed: 28/01/20).

421 See Schantz, in: BeckOK DatenschutzR, Art. 5 DSGVO, marginal nos. 15 et seqq. (effective 01/02/19).

422 See Eilmansberger/Bien, in: MüKoEuWettbR, Art. 102 AEUV, marginal nos. 131 et seqq.; Fuchs, in: Immenga/Mestmäcker, KartellR Kommentar, Art. 102 TFEU, marginal no. 136; Paal, in: BeckOK InfoMedienR, AEUV, Art. 102, marginal no. 28 (effective 01/05/19); ECJ in case C-6/72, *Europemballage Corporation and Continental Can Company v Commission*, ECLI:EU:C:1973:22, para. 27.

of the ECJ, it is vital in that regard to balance the interests of the parties concerned and the principle of proportionality can provide an orientation in that context.[423]

In the case of *Belgische Radio en Televisie,* which dealt with the imposition of unfair trading conditions by an authors' royalties collecting society onto its members, the ECJ was particularly concerned with the weighing of the parties` interests against the limitation of the authors`, composers` and publishers` freedom to dispose of their works.[424] In a data-related context, it is especially the informational self-determination that constitutes a legitimate interest of the users. Thus, the limitation of the users` freedom to control the use of their personal data has to be especially taken into account within the weighing of interests. This interest of the users then has to be weighed against the interest of the undertaking to collect as much data as possible. The actual problem, however, arises in this context from the fact that the data policies of undertakings like *Facebook* often lack the required transparency with regard to the actual extent of the data processing and collection. Therefore, users are often oblivious as to what data is being processed and how. Consequently, users give their consent to data policies, the extent of which they do not even fully understand, thereby limiting their freedom to dispose of their personal data to an equally unknown extent. It is particularly such misleading terms and conditions which will pave the way for a disproportionate processing of personal data.[425] Additionally, in cases where the dominant undertaking makes the use of its service dependent on the user`s consent to the contractual terms, one cannot assume that the consent was freely given, either. Such an "all-or-nothing" approach makes use of the market power of the dominant undertaking and leaves the user with no real choice. Ultimately, contractual terms as seen in the *Facebook* case infringe two essential principles of Art. 5 (1) GDPR: the principle that personal data must always be processed lawfully on a legal base and that it must be processed in a transparent manner. The infringements of those principles and the resulting infringement of the rights of the data subjects must be taken into account within the weighing of interests. From this perspective, it is thus the lawfulness

---

423 See ECJ in case C-127/73, *Belgische Radio en Televisie v SV SABAM,* ECLI:EU:C:1974:25, paras. 8 – 12; Fuchs, in: Immenga/Mestmäcker, KartellR Kommentar, Art. 102 TFEU, marginal no. 186.

424 See ECJ in case C-127/73, *Belgische Radio en Televisie v SV SABAM,* ECLI:EU:C:1974:25, para. 8.

425 See Schneider, Journal of European Competition Law and Practice 2018, 213 (223).

and transparency in particular that is not only decisive under the GDPR but also under Art. 102 (2) (a) TFEU in order to assess whether or not contractual terms are to be seen as "unfair" in a data-related context.[426] The "unfairness" will be underpinned if the dominant undertaking uses, directly or indirectly, its market power to impose the contractual terms so that they could not be imposed by an undertaking without the relevant market power.[427]

In its *Facebook* decision, the Higher Regional Court Düsseldorf offered the criticism that it would not in itself indicate a threat to the interests protected under competition law (freedom of competition and openness of the market access) when the use of a certain contractual condition is inadmissible according to a legal act like the GDPR.[428] However, the Court failed to take two things into account: Firstly, even though the freedom of competition and openness of the market are the prime concerns of competition law, they are not the only ones.[429] Secondly, unfair contractual terms by which the dominant undertaking gets undue access to vast amounts of personal data does indeed endanger both the freedom of competition and openness of the market. The link between gaining access to greater amounts of personal data on the one hand and the competitive advantage resulting from it on the other has been elaborated above.[430] The Higher Regional Court Düsseldorf did not sufficiently consider the potential market foreclosure resulting from such undue access to personal user data.

c) Interim conclusion

The above analysis shows that the excessive and non-transparent collection of personal user data, as was done by *Facebook*, can indeed lead to an abusive conduct under Art. 102 TFEU. It was shown that data-related considerations and especially privacy and data protection concerns can be included, not only with regard to the establishment of dominance but also with

---

426 The fact that a lack of transparency can lead to abusive conduct was also illustrated by the ECJ in *AstraZeneca* (*see* ECJ in case C-457/10 P, *AstraZeneca AB and AstraZeneca plc v European Commission*, ECLI:EU:C:2012:770).

427 See O'Donoghue/Padilla, 2006, p. 195.

428 1st Cartel Senate of the Higher Regional Court Düsseldorf, decision of August 26th, 2019, VI-Kart 1/19 (V) – "Facebook", marginal no. 46.

429 See pp. 60 et seqq.; D. II. 1. a) "The objectives of European competition law".

430 See pp. 100 et seqq.; F. I. 2. a) bb) "The General Data Protection Regulation as an indicator for infringements of the undertaking's "special responsibility".

regard to the assessment of abusive conduct. This provides an affirmative answer to the aspect of the overall research question as to whether big data and data protection considerations can be internalized by or incorporated within Art. 102 TFEU with regard to the assessment of abusive conduct.

Infringements of the crucial cornerstones of the GDPR can especially be taken into account in order to assess whether or not a certain conduct must be seen as abusive under Art. 102 TFEU. It was shown that this argument is based on the fact that the GDPR forms the legal framework in the data-driven digital economy and imposes requirements that limit access to the undertaking`s key input: personal user data. Undertakings that circumvent these crucial provisions of the GDPR in order to collect more user data obtain an undue competitive advantage. In turn, this becomes a competition law issue. Less user data will affect the accuracy of the personalized advertisements, which are offered by undertakings like *Facebook* in order to monetize their businesses. Limited accuracy, on the other hand, would lead to a limited ability of the platform to match users and advertisers. Ultimately, companies would pay less for the spaces where advertisements can be placed. Consequently, if these requirements of the GDPR are circumvented, bearing in mind that access to personal data can have a "dominance-promoting effect", a competitive advantage is created by an illegal and unfair processing of data. This is against the principle of competition on the merits and distorts competition. Consequently, not only do certain infringements of data protection provisions by dominant undertakings infringe the fundamental rights of consumers but they also distort the process of competition. This "theory of harm" should be taken into account by courts and competition authorities throughout Europe.

Additionally, an undue overlap of the two fields of law, by which the competition authorities might mutate to a data protection authority sui generis, could be prevented by establishing a dual causal link when competition authorities want to sanction infringements of data protection law under the competition law regime. Data protection infringements would then only become a competition law matter if (i) there is a causal link between the infringement and the dominant position and (ii) if there is a causal link between the infringement and the competitive advantage.[431]

---

431 In Germany, the legislator has started to adjust the German competition law (the ARC) to the peculiarities of the digital economy by means of the 9th Amendment to the Act against Restraints of Competition and the changes to the Act that came with the amendment. On the 24th of January 2020, the Federal Ministry of Economics and Energy published its ministerial draft bill for

One way or another, there is no actual need for an adjustment of Art. 102 TFEU and a case such as that of the German Bundeskartellamt could also arise in a European competition law context. Predominantly, this possibility is based on the broad wording of Art. 102 TFEU and the constant and sometimes even somewhat excessive judicial development of the law by the European Court of Justice.[432] The case law closes gaps in the law that may otherwise arise. However, even though there is no real need for an adjustment of Art. 102 TFEU, at least a clarification and explicit affirmation of the presented approach would be desirable nonetheless – e.g. through an adjustment of the Commission`s *Guidelines* on the enforcement of Art. 102 TFEU.

II. Arguments for and against the approach of linking data protection considerations to competition law concerns

As shown above, there is no real need for an amendment of Art. 102 TFEU. Admittedly, such an amendment would have been complicated to realize anyway due to the principle of unanimity that applies according to Art. 48 (1), (4) TEU to changes to the Treaties. Nonetheless, an explicit affirmation of the approach illustrated above would still be desirable. A way by which this could be done is an amendment of the Commission`s *Guidelines*, which play an important role with regard to the application of European competition law provisions. Thus, a clarification regarding the interplay between provisions of data protection law and competition law in the *Guidelines* would be a way by which one could enhance legal certainty and provide dominant undertakings with the chance to anticipate

---

the newest, the 10th Amendment to the Act against Restraints of Competition, which was approved by the Federal Cabinet on 9 September 2020 and which entered into force on 19 January 2021. The newest amendment with the name "ARC Digitalization Act" intents to adjust the control of abusive practices to the peculiarities of the digital economy. The "correction" in the wording of § 19 para. 1 ARC looses the requirement of causality between an undertaking`s market power and the abusive practice in question. However, as discussed above with regard to Art. 102 TFEU, such an adjustment could result in an excessive application of competition law to general violations of the law (see also Polley/Kaup, NZKart 2020, 113 (114)). As a result, the 10th Amendment to the German ARC should not constitute an inspiration for an adjustment of European competition law similar to the adjustment of the German ARC.

432 See Pechstein/Kubicki, in: Pechstein/Nowak/Häde, Frankfurter Kommentar EUV/GRC/AEUV, Art. 19 EUV, marginal nos. 27 et seq.

whether or not certain business practices could be seen as abusive. However, such a clarification would also mean that one generally affirms the possibility of such an interdisciplinary approach and that in turn provokes counterarguments. These arguments for and against an affirmation and clarification of the approach respectively will be elaborated next.

1. Arguments in favour of the approach

The approach of linking data protection considerations to competition law assessments is backed by several legal arguments. Firstly, it has been explained above that EU law is regarded as a closed and unified legal system.[433] Therefore, the principle of the unity of the legal order ("Einheit der Rechtsordnung") can be applied, according to which provisions of the unified legal system should not contradict each other. However, such a contradiction would arise as, on the one hand, Art. 2 and 3 TEU state that the values of the EU, such as human rights, shall be promoted but, on the other hand, Art. 102 TFEU does not take them into account and even neglects them in a competition law assessment. Additionally, Art. 51 (1) CFREU specifically demands that the institutions of the Union promote the application of rights included in the Charter in all their actions. As mentioned above,[434] this must, inter alia, also apply to actions such as the application or interpretation of competition law rules.

A further, yet unmentioned, argument in favour of the approach can be found in the principle of "effet utile" (so-called principle of effectiveness). This principle is of central importance for the interpretation of provisions of EU law.[435] It is understood as a substantive guiding principle according to which the most effective possible implementation of the Treaty objectives is to be achieved.[436] Consequently, a provision must be interpreted in such a way that it achieves the best possible benefit for the integration objective. As stated at the beginning,[437] both the GDPR and

---

433 See p. 106; F. I. 2. b) aa) "The influence of data protection considerations on the notion of abuse under Art. 102 (1) TFEU.

434 See pp. 106 et seqq.; F. I. 2. b) aa) "The influence of data protection considerations on the notion of abuse under Art. 102 (1) TFEU.

435 Frenz, Handbuch Europarecht, § 6, marginal no. 419.

436 See for instance ECJ in case C-53/81, *Levin v Staatssecretaris van Justitie*, ECLI:EU:C:1982:105, para. 15.

437 See pp. 59 et seqq.; D. II. 1. "The objectives of data protection and competition law".

Art. 102 TFEU also aim to promote the integration process. Additionally, as previously stated, one of the Treaty's objectives is to promote the values of the EU which include, inter alia, the protection of human rights such as the ones of the CFREU. On the basis of these two arguments, namely the achievement of the Treaty objectives, i.e. the promotion of human rights, and the integration objective, the principle of effet utile requires that data protection and competition law considerations be linked in the digital (platform) economy in order to secure the most effective possible implementation of the Treaty objectives.

In addition, another argument can be found in the legal principle of "ne bis in dem", according to which one cannot institute any legal actions twice for the same cause of actions. Thus, undertakings could have an incentive to be fined under the regime of the GDPR in order to not fear any record fines under the competition law regime, as previously observed in the cases of *Google*[438] and *Intel*.[439]

Due to the fact that the approach itself can be regarded as reasonable compared to an approach that would treat data protection and competition law concerns separately in all scenarios, it would also be desirable to explicitly acknowledge this approach within the Commission's *Guidelines*. As mentioned, this would in particular enhance legal certainty. Derived from the principle of legal certainty, the principle of certainty known in the field of constitutional law would also call for such a clarification. According to this latter principle, legal consequences that may result from a certain conduct must be foreseeable for the public. However, undertakings may currently not anticipate that infringements of data protection law could trigger Art. 102 TFEU. Hence, it is not only the approach itself which is backed by various legal arguments in favour of it, but also the call for an explicit clarification.

2. Arguments against the approach

Despite the fact that there are several reasons in favour of the approach by which data protection and competition law considerations are bridged, there are also arguments against it. In scholarly literature and amongst

---

438 European Commission in case no. AT.39740, C(2017) 4444 final – *Google Search (Shopping)*.
439 European Commission in case no. COMP/C-3 /37.990, D(2009) 3726final – *Intel*.

practitioners, it is the threat to the autonomy and self-sufficiency of competition law that is especially emphasized as a counterargument.[440] However, as elaborated above, competition law cannot be regarded as wholly autonomous in a unified European legal system. Additionally, it is often mentioned that an "interdisciplinary" approach would cause analytical challenges.[441] Admittedly, as (for example) the elaborations with regard to excessive pricing have shown, it can be challenging to analyze whether or not data protection law has been infringed to such an extent that it constitutes an abuse under competition law. However, challenges like that lie in the nature of competition law itself rather than in the bridging of the legal matters. Besides, it cannot constitute a valid counterargument to state that it would be simply too challenging and difficult to apply this interdisciplinary approach. That is all the more true if the consequence was endangerment not only to effective competition but also to the interests and rights of consumers.

Moreover, it is argued that if it were only sufficient for a company to be dominant for an application of competition law to determine that the company had violated a provision (e.g. one of data protection law) and derived competitive advantages from it, the scope of application of competition law would be practically limitless.[442] However, it is precisely the similarity in the objectives of competition and data protection law and the status of a fundamental right that constitutes a crucial difference to areas like environmental law, labour law, or similar. The "interdisciplinary" approach is to a large extent based on these aspects. Moreover, it was shown above that not every infringement of data protection law is able to trigger Art. 102 TFEU. On the contrary, in fact: Only an infringement of the fundamental cornerstones such as Art. 5 or Art. 6 GDPR might also result in an infringement of Art. 102 TFEU. Thus, the scope of competition law becomes by no means limitless.

---

440 See for instance Körber, NZKart 2019, 187 (195 et seqq.); see also Schneider, Journal of European Competition Law and Practice 2018, 213 (215).

441 See Schneider, Journal of European Competition Law and Practice 2018, 213 (215).

442 Körber, NZKart 2019, 187 (195).

3. Interim conclusion

When balancing the above-mentioned arguments in favour of the approach with the arguments against it, it becomes clear that data protection law and competition law considerations should be bridged in competition law assessments dealing with data-driven business models and their possibly abusive business practices. Contrary to what is argued in the literature, competition law cannot be regarded as wholly autonomous in a unified European legal system. Moreover, important legal principles, like the principle of the unity of the legal order or the European principle of effet utile, require that data protection and competition law considerations be linked in the digital (platform) economy. Only that way, can the most effective implementation of the Treaty objectives – integration of an efficient internal market and promotion of the EU`s values -be secured.[443] In order to enhance legal certainty, this approach should also be explicitly affirmed and clarified – for instance, within the Commission`s *Guidance* on the enforcement of Art. 102 TFEU. This would also be important in order to avoid any contradictions between the provisions of the Treaties. Lastly, such a clarification could also provide guidance for the relevant authorities, the interplay of which will be discussed next.

---

443 As stated before (see footnote 361), the term "values" obviously refers to Art. 2 TEU, which names, inter alia, "respect for human rights" as one of those values. This creates a link to the CFREU (Calliess, in: Calliess/Ruffert, Art. 2 EUV, marginal no. 27) and includes thus also the right to privacy or the right to data protection (see Hilf/Schorkopf, in: Grabitz/Hilf/Nettesheim, Das Recht der Europäischen Union, Art. 2 EUV, marginal no. 37).

G. Competence and expertise of competition authorities to enforce compliance with data protection law through competition law sanctions

As mentioned previously, one could fear that the competition authority mutates into a data protection authority sui generis. Thereby, it might exceed both its competence and expertise.[444] The fact that it is in principle necessary and theoretically also possible to include data protection considerations in competition law assessments was illustrated throughout the chapters above. This chapter now deals with another question: Does the competition authority have the competence (more under I.) as well as expertise (more under II.) to enforce data protection law by means of competition law sanctions? This query is of relevance for the overall research question in so far as a lack of competence or expertise could contradict the bridging of competition and data protection law in competition law cases.

I. Formal competence to sanction data-related behaviours via completion law

By considering a certain infringement of a provision from a field of law other than competition law itself, official enforcement competences might as a consequence overlap.[445] This is particularly likely for the approach presented above, by which data protection law functions as a normative yardstick for competition law. The problem resulting from such overlapping competences is the fact that different (enforcement) authorities might interpret and apply the same rule differently. This would endanger legal certainty and could even constitute a disincentive for innovation. Ultimately, instead of benefitting the process of competition, it could be harmed by the approach if the enforcement competences are not clearly allocated.

---

444 See p. 115; F. I. 2. c) "Interim conclusion".

445 See Monopolkommission, Wettbewerb 2018 – XXII. Hauptgutachten der Monopolkommission gemäß § 44 Abs. 1 Satz 1 GWB, July 3rd, 2018, p. 260, available on the internet under https://www.monopolkommission.de/images/HG22/HGXXII_Gesamt.pdf (last accessed: 24/08/19).

Therefore, it is important to avoid overlapping enforcement competences in the first place.

With regard to the GDPR, Art. 55 specifically stipulates that only the data protection authorities of each member state shall be competent to exercise the powers conferred on them in accordance with the Regulation. According to Art. 58 GDPR, these powers include, inter alia, the imposition of administrative fines for infringements of the GDPR or the imposition of limitations on the processing of data. Hence, sanctioning a certain data-related behaviour with a fine according to Art. 23 (2) (a) of Council Regulation (EC) No. 1/2003,[446] based on its abusive character in the sense of Art. 102 TFEU, could in principle contradict the competence allocation in Art. 55 GDPR. The same applies to the measure taken by the German Bundeskartellamt in its *Facebook* case. In that case, the Bundeskartellamt carried out what was called *"an internal divestiture of Facebook's data"*.[447] Such a limitation on processing is mentioned as one of the powers of the data protection authorities according to Art. 55 (1), 58 (2) (f) GDPR. Thus, the German Bundeskartellamt took measures that seem to be within the exclusive competence of the data protection authorities. Additionally, the mere fact that an infringement of the law was committed by a dominant undertaking in the sense of Art. 102 TFEU cannot in itself be sufficient to sanction the behaviour under the competition law regime.[448]

However, as was shown above,[449] the infringement of data protection law provisions by dominant undertakings within the digital (platform) economy can result in a relevant harm to competition. This fact constitutes a significant difference to other fields of law. According to Art. 4 et seqq. of Council Regulation (EC) No. 1/2003, the national competition authorities and the European Commission shall have the power to bring infringements of Art. 101 and 102 TFEU to an end. Hence, once a certain

---

446 Council Regulation (EC) No 1/2003 of 16 December 2002 on the implementation of the rules on competition laid down in Articles 81 and 82 of the Treaty, Official Journal L 001, 04/01/2003, pp. 1–25.

447 See Bundeskartellamt, press release "Bundeskartellamt prohibits Facebook from combining user data from different sources", February 7th, 2019, available on the internet under https://www.bundeskartellamt.de/Shared-Docs/Meldung/EN/Pressemitteilungen/2019/07_02_2019_Facebook.html;jsessionid=832649993354525E65A66B820BEC5711.1_cid378?nn=3591568 (last accessed: 27/03/20).

448 See 1st Cartel Senate of the Higher Regional Court Düsseldorf, decision of August 26th, 2019, VI-Kart 1/19 (V) – "Facebook", p. 17.

449 See p. 115; F. I. 2. c) "Interim conclusion".

behaviour of an undertaking triggers Art. 102 TFEU, it is the Commission or the national competition authorities that have the exclusive competence. In order to bring infringements of Art. 101 or 102 TFEU to an end, national competition authorities might impose fines or order interim measures (Art. 5 Reg. 1/2003). In addition, the Commission may also impose behavioural or structural remedies (Art. 7 Reg. 1/2003) on undertakings. A behavioural remedy can consist in the imposition of a positive duty to do something or a negative duty to refrain from doing something.[450] Thus, the competence for the measures taken by the German Bundeskartellamt can also be derived from Reg. 1/2003.

The aforementioned discussion illustrates that in cases where Art. 102 TFEU is triggered by an undertaking's data-related behaviour, the competences of data protection and competition authorities do overlap. As pointed out by the Monopolkommission in one of its reports, it could be argued, however, that the focus of an examination by a competition authority and a data protection authority differs.[451] An independent prosecution and sanction of data protection law violations are not sought by the competition authorities and would indeed exceed the authority's competence.[452] Instead, the competition authority has to prove the abuse of a dominant position through the unlawful processing of personal data. In that context, the competition authority only incidentally examines a norm of data protection law which is intended to serve as a normative yardstick for the abusiveness of the business practice in question. The fact that sanctioning a competition-relevant behaviour under the regime of competition law may en passant lead to a correction of deficits in other fields of law, too, is not a problem.[453] Therefore, the competition law sanction may, incidentally, also correct problems in the field of consumer protection.[454]

However, as shown throughout previous chapters, this incidental examination is the core of the competition law examination in cases like the Bundeskartellamt's *Facebook* case. Consequently, overlapping compe-

---

450 Ritter/Wirtz, in: Immenga/Mestmäcker, KartellR Kommentar, Art. 7 VO 1/2003, marginal nos. 44 et seq.
451 Monopolkommission, Wettbewerb 2018 – XXII. Hauptgutachten der Monopolkommission gemäß § 44 Abs. 1 Satz 1 GWB, July 3rd, 2018, p. 261, available on the internet under https://www.monopolkommission.de/images/H G22/HGXXII_Gesamt.pdf (last accessed: 24/08/19).
452 See footnote 451.
453 See Franck, ZWeR 2016, 137 (141).
454 Franck, ZWeR 2016, 137 (141).

tences can hardly be avoided in the end.[455] Nonetheless, due to the fact that infringements of data protection law by dominant undertakings can cause a harm not only to consumers but also to the process of competition,[456] the matter cannot fall within the exclusive competence of the data protection authorities. Otherwise, one could argue that the competition authorities will be restricted in their competence as well – just as is argued with regard to the competence of data protection authorities in the present context.[457] As a result, the competence of competition authorities is indeed (also) given with regard to the sanctioning of infringements of data protection law, provided that such infringements can be classified as an abuse of a dominant undertaking's position with harm to consumers and competition.

II. Lacking expertise with regard to data protection law

As stated earlier, a problem resulting from the dual competence is the danger that the same rules might be interpreted differently by the two authorities. Amongst others, this fact can result from a lack of expertise on the part of one of the authorities with regard to the field of law they are less familiar with. Generally speaking, competition authorities are deemed to be experts regarding competition law but not with regard to data protection law. Hence, they might come to conclusions in their interpretation of a certain provision in the field of data protection law that are different to those of the data protection authorities of the member states.[458] This endangers not only legal certainty but it also contradicts one of the objectives of the GDPR – securing a uniform standard of data protection law.

---

455 Monopolkommission, Wettbewerb 2018 – XXII. Hauptgutachten der Monopolkommission gemäß § 44 Abs. 1 Satz 1 GWB, July 3rd, 2018, p. 261, available on the internet under https://www.monopolkommission.de/images/HG22/HGXXII_Gesamt.pdf (last accessed: 24/08/19).
456 See p. 20; B. I. "Big data and ist importance for the digital economy".
457 See for instance Körber, NZKart 2019, 187 (194); Dietrich, "Will das Kartellamt zur Superbehörde werden?", March 11th, 2019, available on the internet under https://www.lto.de/recht/kanzleien-unternehmen/k/facebook-entscheidung-bundeskartellamt-wettbewerbsrecht-datenschutzverstoss-superbehoerde-zustaendigkeit-rechtsbereiche/ (last accessed: 01/09/19); Schreiber, GRUR-Prax 2019, 266 (266).
458 See also Ellger, WUW 2019, 446 (454 et seq.), who is also of the opinion that the various authorities might interpret provisions of the GDPR differently.

In order to avoid such contradictory decisions, a close coordination between the competent competition and data protection authorities would be necessary. Such a close coordination could consist in a shared approach, according to which the data protection authority would assess whether or not data protection law has been infringed and the competition authority would assess the impact of an alleged infringement on the process of competition or as harm for consumers. That way, both authorities would work within their field of expertise. What is more, though, contradictory decisions would be prevented as well.

In Germany, by means of the 9th Amendment to the ARC, a legal base for such a cooperation has already been created. The 9th Amendment altered the wording of § 50c ("Cooperation of Authorities") of the German Competition Act[459] so that the competition authorities may work together with, inter alia, the data protection authorities of the states. More precisely, the competition and data protection authorities of each state may exchange information – including undertakings' business secrets – to the extent that this is necessary for the performance of their respective functions. They may subsequently use such information in their proceedings, too. The German legislator thereby acknowledged that in the digital economy in particular, data and access to data can have a significant impact on the market position of companies.[460] Hence, competition law and data protection law become intertwined.[461] The German legislator has acknowledged this and stated in the legislative reasons for the 9th Amendment that in order *"to fulfil their tasks, the competition authorities and the data protection officers of the federal and state governments are [...] dependent on the possibility of a comprehensive exchange"*.[462] Therefore, the data protection authorities can support the Bundeskartellamt when it comes to the interpretation and assessment of data protection law in competition law cases.

Such a legal base for cooperation between the relevant authorities would be important on a European level as well – e.g. by means of an EU regulation. Art. 57 (1) (g) GDPR does state that each supervisory authority shall cooperate with other supervisory authorities with a view to ensuring the consistency of application and enforcement of the GDPR. It has to be

---

459 § 50c became § 50f due to the recent 10th Amendment to the ARC.
460 Government draft, Parliamentary Publication (BT-Drucksache) 18/10207, p. 81.
461 Paal/Hennemann, "Big Data as an Asset", p. 78, available on the internet under http://www.abida.de/sites/default/files/Gutachten_ABIDA_Big_Data_as_an_Asset.pdf (last accessed: 02/09/19).
462 Government draft, Parliamentary Publication (BT-Drucksache) 18/10207, pp. 81 et seq.

noted, though, that the provision refers only to supervisory authorities in the sense of Art. 4 (21) GDPR. Article 4 (21) GDPR, on the other hand, refers to the data protection authorities of the member states. Hence, a co-operation with the competition authorities is not intended by Art. 57 (1) (g) GDPR. However, provision for the cooperation would not only help to avoid contradictory decisions and thus also help secure a uniform level of data protection law as intended by the GDPR, but it would also enhance legal certainty. Therefore, the European legislator should become active in this context in order to also prevent competition authorities exceeding their level of expertise.

III. Interim conclusion

As stated at the beginning of this chapter, one could fear that the competition authority mutates into a data protection authority sui generis when pursuing a case under Art. 102 TFEU for an infringement of data protection law. Thereby, the competition authority in question might exceed both its competence and expertise. However, it was shown that the competition authorities could indeed derive their competence in such cases from Council Regulation (EC) No. 1/2003. This is based on the fact that the competition authority's main focus in these cases would lie on Art. 102 TFEU. The relevant provisions of data protection law would only be assessed incidentally in order to examine whether or not Art. 102 TFEU has been infringed as well. One has to take into account, though, that the incidental assessment of the relevant provision of data protection law does constitute the main examination point. Therefore, cases involving the sanctioning of a data-related behaviour fall (also) within the competence of the data protection authorities. In order to prevent contradictory decisions as a result of the dual competence, a shared approach between the relevant authorities would be desirable. Additionally, a shared approach would also help avoid the competition authority becoming active in a field of law that might go beyond their actual expertise. In order to create a legal base for the cooperation between competition and data protection authorities, the European legislator should become active – e.g. by means of a European regulation.

Such a legal base would not only enhance the legal certainty amongst the official authorities but would also strengthen the effective protection of consumer interests. Additionally, strengthening the cooperation between the official authorities in order to secure an effective enforcement of both data protection and competition law in the digital platform economy would also be in the interest of the many companies which comply with the applicable rules – otherwise, competitors could have a competitive advantage from the infringements of the relevant provisions.[463]

---

463 See Mundt, WUW 2019, 181 (186).

H. The immanence of data processing by online platforms – an extension of the so-called "Immanenztheorie" to Art. 102 TFEU

The previous chapter has shown that the competition authorities have both the competence and means to regulate dominant data-driven undertakings in the digital (platform) economy. In the following section, it shall be assessed whether the practice of extensive data processing by online platforms like *Facebook* might escape the application of Art. 102 TFEU, nonetheless. More precisely, it shall be examined whether *Facebook* could evade the application of competition law by considering the fact that an extensive processing of data is immanent in most online platforms. A way by which this thought could be realized is an extension of the so-called immanence theory ("Immanenztheorie") to Art. 102 TFEU.[464]

I. Background of the idea

Generally speaking, Art. 102 TFEU does not provide an explicit statutory exemption for abusive behaviour similar to Art. 101 (3) TFEU. However, as previously mentioned,[465] the ECJ acknowledges in its case law the possibility that a prima facie abusive practice may be objectively justified, nonetheless. The Court applies in that context what can be described as a two-stage approach.[466] Firstly, the Court assesses whether or not a certain behaviour is to be considered abusive. Next, the Court examines whether the abusive behaviour in the sense of Art. 102 TFEU might be justified in

---

464 Generally speaking, the so-called "Immanenztheorie" permits (under certain requirements) restrictions of competition necessary for the contractual success of certain types of contract. According to the Immanenztheorie, certain restrictions are inherent in some agreements that actually intend to achieve a legitimate aim. In such cases, necessary restrictions of competition are therefore accepted (Dück/Maschemer, WRP 2013, 167 (170)).

465 See p. 47; C. I. 3. "The possibility of an objective justification for abusive conduct".

466 Case C-53/03, *Synetairismos Farmakopoion Aitolias & Akarnanias (Syfait) and Others v GlaxoSmithKline plc and GlaxoSmithKline AEVE*, ECLI:EU:C:2004:673, opinion of AG Jacobs, para. 72.

the given case. AG Jacobs, on the other hand, goes one step further and is of the opinion that it would be *"more accurate to say that certain types of conduct on the part of a dominant undertaking do not fall within the category of abuse at all"*.[467] Such an approach is known with regard to collusive agreements under the immanence theory. According to said theory, certain collusive agreements do not fall within the scope of Art. 101 TFEU in the first place.[468] This is based on the fact that a restriction of competition is immanent in some agreements that are, however, generally recognized by the legal system.[469] Therefore, certain necessary restrictions of competition are accepted in such cases. The approach can be described as a teleological reduction based on the spirit and purpose of European competition law.[470] It was highlighted above that European competition law is to a large extent aimed at ensuring a "healthy" system of competition.[471] In the case of Article 101 TFEU, it must therefore be examined whether the undertaking that makes use of the restriction of competition ultimately contributes to the intensification of competition.[472] If that is the case and if the restriction is objectively necessary for that purpose, the restriction does not fall under Art. 101 TFEU according to the immanence theory. The immanence theory is so far identical to the "ancillary restraints doctrine".[473] According to the latter doctrine, restraints that are objectively necessary to a pro-competitive objective do not fall within the scope of Art. 101 (1) TFEU.[474]

Due to the fact that there is no explicit provision about possible reasons for a justification under Art. 102 TFEU there is, in principle, no exhaustive

---

467 Case C-53/03, *Synetairismos Farmakopoion Aitolias & Akarnanias (Syfait) and Others v GlaxoSmithKline plc and GlaxoSmithKline AEVE*, ECLI:EU:C:2004:673, opinion of AG Jacobs, para. 72.

468 Zimmer, in: Immenga/Mestmäcker, Art. 101 AEUV, marginal no. 145; with regard to § 1 ARC but with the same reasoning see also Nordemann, in: Loewenheim/Meessen/Riesenkampff, GWB Kommentar, § 1, marginal no. 149.

469 See for instance Zimmer, in: Immenga/Mestmäcker, Art. 101 AEUV, marginal no. 145; Dück/Maschemer, WRP 2013, 167 (170).

470 Weiß, in: Callies/Ruffert, Art. 101 AEUV, marginal nos. 114 et seq.; see also Rudersdorf, RNotZ 2011, 509 (520).

471 See pp. 60 et seqq.; D. II. 1. a) "The objectives of European competition law".

472 Zimmer, in: Immenga/Mestmäcker, Art. 101 AEUV, marginal no. 151.

473 See Müller/Thiede, EuZW 2017, 246 (246).

474 ECJ in case C-382/12 P, *Master Card Inc. and others v* Commission, ECLI:EU:C:2014:2201, para. 91; ECJ in case C-42/84, *Remia BV and others v Commission of the European Communities*, ECLI:EU:C:1985:327, para. 20; Jones/Sufrin, 2016, p. 238; Bellamy/Child, 2013, marginal no. 2.147.

list either.[475] Hence, one could take up the idea behind the immanence theory and argue that an extensive processing of user data is immanent in certain online platforms. Prime examples are social networks and search engines like *Facebook* and *Google*. Social networks and search engines, on the other hand, constitute businesses that provide a useful product to people that is generally accepted by the legal system. Besides their purposes as actual search engines and social networks, these online platforms can lead, in their function as intermediate, to a broadening of the offers in terms of the target group, to lower transaction costs and to more transparency due to the possibility of online product reviews.[476] Therefore, the question comes up as to whether – in accordance with the opinion of AG Jacobs – their data-related business practices constitute types of conduct that do not fall within the category of abuse at all. This approach could be seen as an extension of the immanence theory to Art. 102 TFEU.

In its *Facebook* case, the Bundeskartellamt likewise referred to the immanent processing of data by social networks. More precisely, the Bundeskartellamt stated that it took *"into account that an advertising-funded social network generally needs to process a large amount of personal data"*.[477] Moreover, the Bundeskartellamt specifically acknowledged that the product of a social network is driven precisely by this personal data.[478] The fact that the processing of vast amounts of data is immanent in such advertising-funded social networks is also mirrored in *Facebook*`s annual report. *Facebook*`s revenue in 2018 was almost 56 billion US dollars, 98 % of which were generated by (personalized) advertisements.[479] These numbers

---

475 See Huttenlauch/Lübbig, in: Loewenheim et al., Art. 102 TFEU, marginal no. 294; Jung, in: Grabitz/Hilf/Nettesheim, Das Recht der Europäischen Union, Art. 102 AEUV, marginal no. 145; Fuchs, in: Immenga/Mestmäcker, Art. 102 AEUV, marginal no. 152.

476 Mundt, WUW 2019, 181 (182).

477 Bundeskartellamt, case summary of case no. B6–22/16 – *Facebook*, published February 15th, 2019, p. 1, available on the internet under https://www.bundeskartellamt.de/SharedDocs/Entscheidung/EN/Fallberichte/Missbrauchsaufsicht/2019/B6-22-16.pdf?__blob=publicationFile&v=3 (last accessed: 27/03/20).

478 Bundeskartellamt, decision of February 6th, 2019, case no. B6–22/16 – *Facebook*, p. 156, marginal no. 488, available on the internet under https://www.bundeskartellamt.de/SharedDocs/Entscheidung/DE/Entscheidungen/Missbrauchsaufsicht/2019/B6-22-16.pdf?__blob=publicationFile&v=8 (last accessed: 03/09/19).

479 Facebook, Facebook Reports Fourth Quarter and Full Year 2018 Results, p. 1, available on the internet under https://s21.q4cdn.com/399680738/files/doc_financials/2018/Q4/Q4-2018-Earnings-Release.pdf (last accessed: 03/09/19).

illustrate that advertising-funded platforms like *Facebook* would not exist without the processing of vast amounts of data.

II. Legal appraisal of the idea

As illustrated above, one could adopt the idea behind the immanence theory and argue that without the processing of vast amounts of data, social networks or search engines would not exist at all. As a result, one could argue further that business practices like the one used by *Facebook* do not constitute a harm to the process of competition. On the contrary, one might say they rather create new competition and new markets as they allow for social networks or search engines to exist. Therefore, one might have to apply a teleological reduction to Art. 102 TFEU as well.

However, if the idea of extending the immanence theory to Art. 102 TFEU is consistently thought through, the existence of social networks would have to be impossible without business practices that infringe data protection law. This results from the fact that the immanence theory likewise requires that an operation has to be impossible to carry out in the absence of the restriction in question.[480] Only if this requirement is fulfilled, does the restriction escape the scope of Art. 101 (1) TFEU.[481] The fact that the operation is simply more difficult to implement or less profitable without the practice concerned cannot give the practice in question the "objective necessity" required in order for it to fall outside the scope of Art. 101 TFEU.[482] The same requirements have to apply regarding Art. 102 TFEU.

With regard to *Facebook*`s extensive collection of user data without the users' valid consent, it is the objective necessity in particular that is lacking. The extensive collection of user data without the explicit consent of users rather falls within the latter category of practices, that make it simply less difficult or more profitable to operate a business like a social network. *Facebook* could still run their social network if they were complying with European data protection law. It is not the extensive collection of user

---

480 See with regard GC in case T-112/99, M6 and Others v Commission, ECLI:EU:T:2001:215, para. 104.

481 Nordemann, in: Loewenheim/Meessen/Riesenkampff, GWB Kommentar, § 1, marginal no. 149.

482 See ECJ in case C-382/12 P, *Master Card Inc. and others v* Commission, ECLI:EU:C:2014:2201, para. 91.

data in itself that is a competition law concern. Neither is the extensive collection of user data in itself abusive. It is rather the fact that *Facebook* neglects the provisions of the GDPR in order to collect and process as much data as possible. In return, that data makes it simply easier for *Facebook* to enhance their services and to generate more profit. However, it is not impossible for *Facebook* to get access to the data by legitimate means. Not complying with the GDPR is merely more convenient for *Facebook*. This, on the other hand, is where the competition law concern derives from. By circumventing the corner stones of the GDPR and the unlawful processing of data, *Facebook* has an undue competitive advantage. As a result, one can no longer speak of competition on the merits.

The fact that the circumvention of the essential provisions of the GDPR is the actual problem of the case is reflected in the report by the German Bundeskartellamt. There, it was predominantly criticized that *"users have insufficient control over the processing of their data and its allocation to their* Facebook *accounts"*.[483] Moreover, the Bundeskartellamt stated that *"the data protection boundaries set forth in the GDPR were clearly overstepped, also in view of* Facebook's *dominant position"*.[484] Hence, it was not the extensive processing in itself that constituted the competition law problem but rather the infringement of the GDPR.

Consequently, the idea of an extension of the immanence theory to such abusive practices under Art. 102 TFEU fails because of the fact that it is not immanent in online platforms that they process vast amounts of user data in an illegal manner. However, that is precisely the problem from where the competition law concerns derive. The mere processing of vast amounts of data is indeed immanent in social networks (as well as in search engines) but that is not a competition law concern.

---

483 Bundeskartellamt, case summary of case no. B6–22/16 – *Facebook*, published February 15th, 2019, p. 1, available on the internet under https://www.bundeskartellamt.de/SharedDocs/Entscheidung/EN/Fall-berichte/Missbrauchsaufsicht/2019/B6-22-16.pdf?__blob=publicationFile&v=3 (last accessed: 27/03/20).

484 Bundeskartellamt, case summary of case no. B6–22/16 – *Facebook*, published February 15th, 2019, p. 2, available on the internet under https://www.bundeskartellamt.de/SharedDocs/Entscheidung/EN/Fall-berichte/Missbrauchsaufsicht/2019/B6-22-16.pdf?__blob=publicationFile&v=3 (last accessed: 27/03/20).

I. The classification of online platforms like *Facebook* as a natural monopoly sui generis and the problems arising from it

The last chapter has shown that abusive data-related business practices, as known from the *Facebook* case, do not escape the application of competition law by extending the immanence theory to Art. 102 TFEU. However, besides regulating dominant internet platforms through an "interdisciplinary approach" by which data protection and competition law considerations are being bridged, one could even go a step further. More precisely, some suggest making online platforms like *Facebook* the subject of direct regulations.[485] This discussion is connected to the overall research question in so far as it could provide an alternative way of dealing with the competition law challenges that these platforms raise. If dominant platforms such as *Facebook*, *Google* and co. can be classified as natural monopolies, one would have to think about a direct regulation instead of regulating the data-related business practices on a case-by-case assessment with an interdisciplinary approach of competition and data protection law. Especially in the digital (platform) economy, monopoly tendencies are a common phenomenon. Therefore, directly regulating these (de facto) monopolies might be a sensible idea. Timothy Wu, Professor at Columbia Law School, pointed out in this context: *"Most of the major sectors today are controlled by one dominant company or an oligopoly. Google "owns" search;* Facebook, *social networking;* eBay *rules auctions;* Amazon, *retail; and so on."*[486] This list of undertakings illustrates the rationale behind the

---

485 See for instance Graw, "Facebook – Ein Monopol, das zerschlagen gehört", April 4th, 2018, available on the internet under https://www.welt.de/debatte/kommentare/article175369044/Mark-Zuckerbergs-Werk-Facebook-ein-Monopol-das-zerschlagen-gehoert.html (last accessed: 13/09/19); see also Kühl, "Zerschlagt, was euch kaputt macht", May 21st, 2019, available on the internet under https://www.zeit.de/digital/internet/2019-05/facebook-zerschlagung-wahlkampf-monopol-soziale-medien-digitalkonzerne/komplettansicht (last accessed: 13/09/19), referring to these tendencies in the public as well.
486 Tim Wu, "In the Grip of the Internet Monopolists", November 13th, 2010, available on the internet under https://www.wsj.com/articles/SB10001424052748704635704575604993311538482 (last accessed 02/09/19).

claims that seem to get stronger in public: It is argued that companies like *Facebook* and *Google* constitute natural monopolies so that they should be regulated accordingly.[487]

In the following section, it will be assessed whether *Facebook* and the like can indeed be considered natural monopolies (more under I.). Following this, the problems resulting from natural monopolies in the digital (platform) economy will be elaborated (more under II.), before discussing the best suitable regulatory approach for such a scenario (more under III.). Lastly, an interim conclusion will be given (more under IV.).

I. The parallels between natural monopolies and online platforms like *Facebook*

Monopolies endanger the process of competition by their very existence. If a firm is not constrained by competitors, it is likely that prices will be raised above the competitive market price.[488] Additionally, the dynamic development of the market could be negatively affected by the lack of competition.[489] The process of innovation is especially fuelled by competition and might be substantially slowed down. These consequences can be seen not only with regard to monopolies but also in the case of the related but less familiar "natural monopolies".[490] In the following section, the term "natural monopoly" will first be elaborated. Following this, it will be examined whether online platforms such as *Facebook* could be classified as natural monopolies.

---

487 See for instance Gersemann, "Zerschlagt Facebook nicht!", April 4th, 2018, available on the internet under https://www.welt.de/print/die_welt/debatte/article175406752/Leitartikel-Zerschlagt-Facebook-nicht.html (last accessed: 13/09/19); see also Kühl, "Zerschlagt, was euch kaputt macht", May 21st, 2019, available on the internet under https://www.zeit.de/digital/internet/2019-05/facebook-zerschlagung-wahlkampf-monopol-soziale-medien-digitalkonzerne/komplettansicht (last accessed: 13/09/19); Graw, "Facebook – Ein Monopol, das zerschlagen gehört", April 4th, 2018, available on the internet under https://www.welt.de/debatte/kommentare/article175369044/Mark-Zuckerbergs-Werk-Facebook-ein-Monopol-das-zerschlagen-gehoert.html (last accessed: 13/09/19).
488 Jones/Sufrin, 2016, p. 8.
489 See Kerber/Schwalbe, in: MüKoEUWettbR, Einl., marginal no. 602.
490 See Gersdorf, in: Spindler/Schuster, Recht der elektronischen Medien, § 9 TKG, marginal no. 26.

1. The term "natural monopoly"

Generally speaking, the term "natural monopoly" describes a market in which a single undertaking can serve the market at lower cost than two or more undertakings could.[491] This so-called "subadditivity of the costs" is present if the fixed costs of the operation of the business are very high but the costs for each additional production unit are low.[492] If one undertaking serves the market, the fixed costs can be spread over larger production quantities so that the costs of each additional unit decrease.[493] Therefore, growing economies of scale and increasing returns to scale are a characteristic of natural monopolies.[494] Prime examples for natural monopolies are the markets for electricity, gas or water supply.[495] Here, the costs of the operation of the business and the establishment of the pipe or cable systems are significant. However, the costs of transporting an additional "unit" are low. Consequently, it is sensible to have the market served by only one undertaking. If these conditions are fulfilled, the market is to be regarded as a natural monopoly. It is important to mention in this context that there is a crucial difference between monopolies and natural monopolies. The term "natural monopoly" does not refer to the actual number of suppliers in a market.[496] One could be forgiven for thinking that the term refers to an actual monopoly, i.e. a market where there is only one seller. In fact, however, the term refers only to the relationship between demand and the technology of supply.[497] If the entire demand within a relevant market can be satisfied at lowest cost by one firm rather than by two or more, the market presents itself to be a natural monopoly – regardless of the actual number of undertakings in it.[498] Over the course of time, though, a consolidation process will most likely take place in the course of which the natural monopolist will have forced its competitors to exit the market. Additionally, it has to be mentioned that natural monopolies are often

---

491 Ewald, in: Wiedemann, Handbuch des Kartellrechts, § 7, marginal no. 68; Kerber/Schwalbe, in: MüKoEUWettbR, Einl., marginal no. 600; Posner, Stanford Law Review 1969, 548 (548).
492 See footnote 491.
493 Kerber/Schwalbe, in: MüKoEUWettbR, Einl., marginal no. 600.
494 Ewald, in: Wiedemann, Handbuch des Kartellrechts, § 7, marginal no. 68.
495 Kerber/Schwalbe, in: MüKoEUWettbR, Einl., marginal no. 600.
496 Posner, Stanford Law Review 1969, 548 (548).
497 Posner, Stanford Law Review 1969, 548 (548).
498 Posner, Stanford Law Review 1969, 548 (548).

characterized by high sunk costs.[499] These sunk costs derive their name from the fact that they are irrecoverable once incurred – especially if the market entry turns out to have been a failure. Prime examples for sunk costs are costs of research and development, highly-specialized equipment or marketing.[500] These irreversible sunk costs are also a barrier to entry and thus a reason for the invulnerability of a (natural) monopoly.[501]

2. The classification of *Facebook* as a natural monopoly

The aforementioned characteristics apply to online platforms like *Facebook* as well. *Facebook* invested several billion US dollars into its algorithm and its infrastructure.[502] For instance, *Facebook* operates 15 massive data centres and has already announced several more in order to cope with the increase in demand.[503] This digital infrastructure that is necessary for *Facebook*`s business as a globally available social network shows parallels with the physical infrastructure that classic natural monopolies such as utility companies need in order to provide their services. Without the massive data centres which host *Facebook*`s servers, the company could not provide access to the platform to so many people from all around the world. Each individual user, however, hardly costs the company any additional costs once the platform is online and running.[504] Additional users

---

499 Spelthahn, 1994, p. 222; Ewald, in: Wiedemann, Handbuch des Kartellrechts, § 7, marginal no. 68; Schmidt/Haucap, 2012, p. 45.

500 Jones/Sufrin, 2016, p. 82.

501 Ewald, in: Wiedemann, Handbuch des Kartellrechts, § 7, marginal no. 68.

502 Miller, "Facebook's $1 Billion Data Center Network", February 2nd, 2012, available on the internet under https://www.datacenterknowledge.com/archives/2012/02/02/facebooks-1-billion-data-center-network (last accessed: 01/10/19); see also Huang, "Facebook's US$1b data centre in Singapore to open in 2022", October 29th, 2018, available on the internet under https://www.edb.gov.sg/en/news-and-events/insights/innovation/facebook-s-us-1b-data-centre-in-singapore-to-open-in-2022.html (last accessed 01/10/19), where the Singapore Economic Development Board (EDB), a government agency under the Ministry of Trade and Industry, says that the Singapore data center, that Facebook started to build in September 2018, will cost more than 1 billion US$ alone.

503 See Peterson, "Data centers year in review", January 1st, 2019, available on the internet under https://engineering.fb.com/data-center-engineering/data-centers-2018/ (last accessed: 16/09/19).

504 See for a more general argumentation also Paal, GRUR 2013, 873 (873 et seq.); see also Yang/Ji, "The Platform Economy and Natural Monopoly: reg-

only increase the platform's value for other users based on the network effects. Therefore, due to the extremely high initial costs but the low costs of each additional "unit" – i.e. another user – there are strong economies of scale and increasing returns to scale.[505] As a result, the characteristic subadditivity of costs is also given.[506]

Thierer, however, argues that the digital infrastructure is importantly different from the physical infrastructure of more traditional natural monopolies like water or electricity suppliers.[507] According to Thierer, the digital infrastructure of *Facebook* and co. does not entail the same fixed costs as required by pipe/cable systems or similar physical infrastructures.[508] However, Thierer does not even compare the costs required for the digital infrastructures of *Facebook*, *Google* and others with the costs required for physical infrastructures such as pipe or cable systems. Additionally, even if the costs of physical infrastructures were considerably higher than those of *Facebook*'s digital infrastructure, the question arises as to whether physical and digital infrastructures can even be compared. Arguably, it is rather a comparison between apples and oranges – as the saying goes. It is obvious that the development of a nationwide or even international physical infrastructure requires more manpower and resources

---

ulating or laissez-faire?", available on the internet under https://pdfs.semantic-scholar.org/b270/28b47b26656356b08115d52cb981b61e6358.pdf (last accessed: 01/10/19).

505 See also Kimmelman, "The Right Way to Regulate Digital Platforms", Harvard Kennedy School – Shorenstein Center on Media, Politics and Public Policy, September 18th, 2019, available on the internet under https://shorensteincenter.org/the-right-way-to-regulate-digital-platforms/ (last accessed: 11/11/19); see also with regard to this phenomenon in the platform economy in general: European Commission, Competition policy for the digital era – A report by Jacques Crémer, Yves-Alexandre de Montjoye and Heike Schweitzer, p. 20, available on the internet under https://ec.europa.eu/competition/publications/reports/kd0419345enn.pdf (last accessed: 01/04/20).

506 See also the argumentation of Sasse, " A Micro-Economic Perspective on Social Media in Context of the New Economy", Microeconomics and Macroeconomics 2016, p. 57, available on the internet under http://article.sapub.org/10.5923.j.m2economics.20160402.03.html (last accessed: 01/10/19).

507 Thierer, "The Perils of Classifying Social Media Platforms as Public Utilities", Journal of Communications Law and Technology Policy 2013, 249 (249 et seqq.), available on the internet under https://scholarship.law.edu/commlaw/vol21/iss2/2/ (last accessed: 13/09/19).

508 Thierer, "The Perils of Classifying Social Media Platforms as Public Utilities", Journal of Communications Law and Technology Policy 2013, 249 (249 et seqq.), available on the internet under https://scholarship.law.edu/commlaw/vol21/iss2/2/ (last accessed: 13/09/19).

than a digital infrastructure. Obviously, this difference makes it more expensive as well. However, Thierer's argumentation is misleading in so far as it seems to suggest that a certain minimum amount is required with regard to the fixed costs. In fact, though, it is rather the subadditivity of the costs that is crucial and not a specific threshold of fixed costs.

Moreover, another argument for *Facebook*'s classification as a natural monopoly is the fact that it is immanent of social networks that they fulfil their function best when as many people as possible make use of them. Hence, the unique strong network effects of social networks also suggest that it would be most sensible to have the market served by one company – as is characteristic for natural monopolies.[509] What is more, due to the network effects, *Facebook* and co. will gather more and more valuable user data. As discussed throughout this work, data is a crucial resource in the digital platform economy, which makes access to data a central driver of natural monopoly tendencies.[510] Overall, one should consider the strong network effects that characterize online platforms as also pertinent to the application of the natural monopoly doctrine to *Facebook* and co.[511] The strong network effects are also to be taken into account with regard to *Facebook*'s huge digital infrastructure. Based on the network effects, it is often required to develop a large infrastructure that is able to cope with billions of active users. Only then, will the platform be attractive to users.[512] Consequently, another fact that has to be considered when speaking of *Facebook* as a natural monopoly is the fact that it is not profitable for competitors to build a similar infrastructure due to the network effects. People want to use only one social network, one which is also used by all their friends. In addition, there are so-called "positive feedback effects" between the economies of scale and network effects.[513]

---

509 See also European Commission, Competition policy for the digital era – A report by Jacques Crémer, Yves-Alexandre de Montjoye and Heike Schweitzer, p. 23, available on the internet under https://ec.europa.eu/competition/publications/reports/kd0419345enn.pdf (last accessed: 01/04/20).

510 See also Ducci, 2020, p. 47.

511 See also Ducci, 2020, p. 26 et seq.

512 Monopolkommission, "Competition Policy: The challenge of digital markets", Special Report 68, marginal no. 43, available on the Internet under https://www.monopolkommission.de/images/PDF/SG/s68_fulltext_eng.pdf (last accessed: 28/01/20).

513 See Paal, GRUR 2013, 873 (873 et seq.); see also Stelzer, "Digitale Güter und ihre Bedeutung in der Internet-Ökonomie", p. 14, available on the internet under https://www.tu-ilmenau.de/fileadmin/public/iwm/diggut.pdf (last accessed: 01/10/19).

Essentially, this means they constantly reinforce each other like an upward spiral. Furthermore, the high costs that occur in order to develop the necessary algorithms are prime examples for high sunk costs that are often to be found in natural monopolies as well.

Ultimately, based on the network effects and the technological advantage that *Facebook* has, a consolidation process took place in the course of which competitors such as *StudiVZ* have exited the market. As a result, one could indeed argue that *Facebook* constitutes a natural monopoly itself.

However, a crucial point that seems to be neglected in the discussions about *Facebook*`s classification as a natural monopoly is the market definition. As stated earlier, the term "natural monopoly" describes a market in which a single undertaking can serve the market at a lower cost than two or more undertakings could.[514] By referring to *"the market"*, it becomes clear that the term "natural monopoly" refers to the economic circumstances in a particular market. In that context, it is important to take into account the two-sided nature of digital online platforms like *Facebook*. Their business model is aimed at two different customer groups: In the case at hand, the private *Facebook* user on the one side and the advertising companies on the other side. Consequently, these platforms serve in principle two markets.[515] Therefore, it seems appropriate to draw a parallel to multi-product companies. Platforms such as *Facebook* provide two products themselves: On the one hand, the platform itself for its actual use (here a social network for socializing with friends) and on the other

---

514 Ewald, in: Wiedemann, Handbuch des Kartellrechts, § 7, marginal no. 68; Kerber/Schwalbe, in: MüKoEUWettbR, Einl., marginal no. 600.

515 See Bundeskartellamt, B6–113/15, Arbeitspapier Marktmacht von Plattformen und Netzwerken, June 2016, p. 33, available on the internet under https://www.bundeskartellamt.de/SharedDocs/Publikation/DE/Berichte/Think-Tank-Bericht.pdf?__blob=publicationFile&v=2 (last accessed: 23/08/19), stating that at least with regard to advertising-funded platforms such as Facebook, one should consider two distinct markets; also 1st Cartel Senate of the Higher Regional Court Düsseldorf, decision of August 26th, 2019, VI-Kart 1/19 (V) – "Facebook", where the Court assumes a distinct market for social networks as well; Volmar, ZWeR 2017, 386 (391); European Commission in case no. COMP/M.7217, C(2014) 7239 final, *Facebook/Whatsapp*, paras. 13 et seqq.; in contrast to that: Monopolkommission, "Competition Policy: The challenge of digital markets", Special Report 68, marginal no. 58, stating that *"from an economic perspective, one side of the platform cannot be defined as a separate market when one delineates the market"*, available on the Internet under https://www.monopolkommission.de/images/PDF/SG/s68_fulltext_eng.pdf (last accessed: 28/01/20); also Dewenter et al., NZKart 2014, 387 (390).

hand, spaces for advertisements on that platform (online advertising).[516] In order to classify a multi-product company as a natural monopoly, both products not only need to be characterized by growing economies of scale and a resulting subadditivity of costs but economies of scope have to be present as well.[517] With regard to *Facebook*, however, the aforementioned characteristics that render the platform a natural monopoly only apply to the market for social networks but not to the market for online advertising. Predominantly, this is based on the fact that the market for online advertising does not require the investment of high fixed costs as is necessary for the digital infrastructure of social networks. Additionally, companies want to place their advertisements not just on one website but want to make use of several online mediums in order to enhance the scope of their advertisements.[518] Hence, there will always be room for competitors to exist. Contrary to the scenario of a natural monopoly, there will therefore always be more than one company. As a result, one has to be precise when speaking of *Facebook* as a natural monopoly in so far as one can only classify the platform as a natural monopoly in the market for social networks.

II. The problems resulting from natural monopolies in the digital (platform) economy

At first glance, natural monopolies do not appear to be as bad for consumers as "normal" monopolies. In the case of a natural monopoly, a company can take over the supply of a given market at the lowest cost. This is actually desirable for consumers as it seems to suggest that the efficiency gains will be passed on to them. At the same time, however, the monopoly position of the supplier provides incentives to exploit this position to the detriment of consumers.[519] Due to the lack of competition, natural monopolies may in fact lead to inefficient market results.[520] First

---

516 See also Bundeskartellamt, B6–113/15, Arbeitspapier Marktmacht von Plattformen und Netzwerken, June 2016, p. 33, speaking of two products as well, available on the internet under https://www.bundeskartellamt.de/SharedDocs/Publikation/DE/Berichte/Think-Tank-Bericht.pdf?__blob=publicationFile&v=2 (last accessed: 23/08/19).

517 See Kerber/Schwalbe, in: MüKoEUWettbR, Einl., marginal no. 601.

518 See Volmar, ZWeR 2017, 386 (391).

519 Gersdorf, in: Spindler/Schuster, Recht der elektronischen Medien, §9 TKG, marginal no. 26.

520 See Kerber/Schwalbe, in: MüKoEUWettbR, Einl., marginal nos. 602 et seq.

and foremost, natural monopolies are likely to lead to excessive pricing.[521] Due to the fact that the monopolist does not have to fear the disciplinary effect of competing offers, it is essentially free in its choice of offers and prices.[522] In the present context, charging excessive monopoly prices would mean that online platforms like *Facebook* might require the user to provide even more data in return for access to the platform. Additionally, the lack of competition can result in a disincentive to innovate. As pointed out above,[523] competition is the main driver for innovation in the digital platform economy. Consequently, if there is a lack of competition, the incentive to innovate is to a large extent missing as well. This has also been expressed by Chris Hughes, co-founder of *Facebook*, who wrote in an essay for the New York Times in May 2019 that it was the pressure in the early days of *Facebook* to beat their former competitors such as *Myspace*, *Friendster* and co. that spurred innovation.[524] Consequently, if competitors are missing, innovation might stop or could at least be immensely slowed down.[525] Moreover, digital online platforms that classify as natural monopolies also raise substantial concerns about another way of harming the quality of their services. More precisely, these natural monopolists are able to manipulate – either on their own or at least by providing the means for other companies – the behaviour of users. The prominent example of *Cambridge Analytica* proved that with regard to *Facebook* in 2018. Due to their market power as a natural monopolist, companies like *Facebook* are able to obtain high-dimensional, large datasets by which they can analyze users' behaviour almost in real time. For instance, depending on the most recent "likes", search queries or posts, *Facebook* can analyze the users' emotional state and can target them with sales accordingly.[526] That way, *Facebook* and co. can influence users to make a choice which is most profitable to the platform.[527] However, *Facebook* and co. are not only able to

---

521 Posner, Stanford Law Review 1969, 548 (550 et seqq.).
522 Gersdorf, in: Spindler/Schuster, Recht der elektronischen Medien, §9 TKG, marginal no. 26.
523 See p. 25; B. II. 2. "Characteristics of the digital platform economy".
524 Hughes, "It`s time to break up Facebook", May 9th, 2019, available on the internet under https://www.nytimes.com/2019/05/09/opinion/sunday/chris-hughes-facebook-zuckerberg.html (last accessed: 20/09/19).
525 See also Krämer, Wirtschaftsdienst 2019, 47 (49).
526 See also Kimmelman, "The Right Way to Regulate Digital Platforms", Harvard Kennedy School – Shorenstein Center on Media, Politics and Public Policy, September 18th, 2019, available on the internet under https://shorensteincenter.org/the-right-way-to-regulate-digital-platforms/ (last accessed: 11/11/19).
527 Loc. cit.

manipulate users in their choices but they also have a strong influence on undertakings in other markets. Various businesses rely on these platforms to connect with their customers, which presents another critical aspect of their position as a natural monopolist.[528]

In more general terms: It is the function of competition to constantly improve market outcomes and if competition is lacking, market outcomes will not be improved either. Hence, this risk of market failure is particularly likely with regard to natural monopolies. Additionally, this danger is all the more present when there are significant barriers to entry – as is the case with regard to *Facebook*. The strong network effects and the lock-in effects constitute such barriers to entry. As a result, *Facebook* should not only be considered a natural monopoly but might even become a real monopolist in the market for social networks in the future.[529] Therefore, possible solutions in order to prevent such a scenario have to be developed. As discussed in the preceding chapters, problematic data-related business practices could be dealt with under competition law on a case-by-case basis and by bridging competition and data protection law. However, in the case of a (digital) natural monopoly, one might have to go one step further. Hence, the following section will discuss a possible regulatory approach to natural monopolies in the digital (platform) economy.

---

528 See Vestager, Speech "Building a positive digital world", Digital Summit, Dortmund (Germany), October 29th, 2019, available on the internet under https://wayback.archive-it.org/12090/20191130020041/https://ec.europa.eu/commission/commissioners/2014-2019/vestager/announcements/building-positive-digital-world_en (last accessed: 28/03/20), stating that *"the power of platforms doesn't just affect competition between those platforms. Their decisions can also influence dozens of other markets, where businesses rely on platforms to connect with their customers"*.

529 See also Bundeskartellamt, case summary of case no. B6–22/16 – *Facebook*, published February 15th, 2019, p. 6 where it was stated that there are indicators suggesting that Facebook becomes a monopolist in the market for social networks, available on the internet under https://www.bundeskartellamt.de/SharedDocs/Entscheidung/EN/Fallberichte/Missbrauchsaufsicht/2019/B6-22-16.pdf?__blob=publicationFile&v=3 (last accessed: 27/03/20).

III. The regulatory approach to natural monopolies such as *Facebook* in the digital (platform) economy

In order to deal with the problems raised by natural monopolies in the digital platform economy, one could think of three possibilities in particular. Firstly, platforms like *Facebook* could become the subject of direct regulation. Secondly, one could unbundle these tech giants and thirdly, one could consider nationalizing them. However, the latter two are particularly unsuitable for internationally integrated companies like *Facebook, Alphabet (Google), Amazon* and co. More precisely, nationalizing or unbundling a foreign company would contradict the sovereignty of the state in which they were founded.[530] Above that, these measures constitute extensive interventions regarding the companies` property rights. What is more, unbundling such companies could simply create even more problems due to a "hydra effect" – with regard to *Facebook,* for instance, it could ultimately create two *Facebooks.*[531] In addition, platforms like *Facebook* are nowadays not just social networks but also a medium for daily news. Therefore, nationalizing or unbundling a company like that could also raise substantial questions about the freedom of the press. Above all, however, both nationalizing and unbundling should be the ultima ratio in a market-oriented constitutional state. Therefore, if any measures were to be undertaken, the adequate regulatory approach would be to make *Facebook* the subject of direct regulation. Nicholas Clegg himself, former Deputy Prime Minister of the United Kingdom and since October 2018 *Facebook*`s Vice-President for Global Affairs and Communications, said *Facebook* does want to be regulated and it would be the legislator`s task to develop adequate regulations.[532]

This dissertation does not aim to develop a whole set of rules as a regulatory framework but shall rather encourage the debate on this issue

---

530 See also Eberl, in: Aderhold et al., 1994, pp. 39 et seqq.

531 See EU Competition Commissioner Vestager in an interview with the "Spiegel", Hülsen/Müller, "Haben sich die deutschen Autokonzerne abgesprochen, um Innovationen zu verhindern? Hier spricht EU-Wettbewerbskommissarin Vestager über ihre Ermittlungen und die Marktmacht von Facebook", April 12th, 2019, available on the internet under https://www.spiegel.de/plus/margrethe-vestager -daimler-vw-und-bmw-haben-nun-zehn-wochen-zeit-a-00000000-0002-0001-0000 -000163403870 (last accessed: 12/11/19).

532 Hanfeld, "Was erlauben Facebook?", June 26th, 2019, available on the internet under https://www.faz.net/aktuell/feuilleton/debatten/warum-facebook-wirklich-nach-regulierung-ruft-16253951.html (last accessed: 14/10/19).

– especially from a competition law point of view. Of course, measures of direct regulation of platforms like *Facebook* need to address not only matters of competition law interest but also social issues such as hate speech. However, this latter aspect does not fall within the framework of this dissertation, which is why no suggestions will be made for a regulatory solution in that regard.

Obviously, there is no magic pill that could easily provide a solution to the issues raised above. In fact, the legislator, regulatory institutions, economists and various other actors need to participate in the development of an adequate regulatory framework for natural monopolies in the digital (platform) industry. Therefore, the aim at this stage is rather to highlight important aspects that should be taken into account in this context. Above all, there are four aspects in particular which shall be highlighted by this dissertation as essential cornerstones for a regulatory framework from a competition law perspective.

1. Interoperability

The first keyword in this regard is "interoperability". The general problem with *Facebook*'s position as a natural monopolist in the market for social networks is the lack of competition. The strong network effects that are present in this market result in the fact that people often refrain from joining a competitor's social network as they would not be able to connect with the same number of friends. Consequently, competitors can generate neither the same user number nor the same data pools as *Facebook*. The competitive disadvantage resulting from this lack of data is obvious and was illustrated throughout the last chapters. Therefore, one has to think of mechanisms that could provide a remedy to that situation and which could lower such barriers to entry/expansion. A way by which this could be done is by establishing a requirement of interoperability for *Facebook*'s services.[533] By establishing a mandatory interoperability on *Facebook*'s ser-

---

533 See for the same idea under the American Sherman Act Kimmelman, "The Right Way to Regulate Digital Platforms", Harvard Kennedy School – Shorenstein Center on Media, Politics and Public Policy, September 18th, 2019, available on the internet under https://shorensteincenter.org/the-right-way-to-regulate-digital-platforms/ (last accessed: 23/03/20); see also Federal Ministry for Economic Affairs and Energy, "Ein neuer Wettbewerbsrahmen für die Digitalwirtschaft – Bericht der Kommission Wettbewerbsrecht 4.0" (= A New Competition Framework for the Digital Economy – Report by the Com-

vices, network effects could be weakened and barriers to entry would be lowered.

More precisely, the term "interoperability" shall describe the idea that users from other social networks can get connected to users from *Facebook*. That way, network effects would no longer have the same influence on the competitive structure in the market and smaller networks could actually compete with the incumbent. Additionally, competitors would be able to enhance their own data pools, which would also render them more competitive.

2. Merger regulation

Another regulatory cornerstone that is also connected to the aspect of enhancing the competitive structure is a stricter merger regulation applicable to such natural monopolists in the digital economy. In the last decade, *Facebook* has acquired numerous companies, amongst which have been potential competitors like *Instagram* and crucial tools such as *CTRL-Labs*,[534] that could have given competitors the upper hand.[535] In fact, *Facebook* made 76 high-profile acquisitions in total in the last ten years, amounting to a sum of widely more than 25 billion US dollars.[536] The need for a stricter merger regulation derives from the fact that several of these acquisitions were likely to harm the process of competition but did not meet the value thresholds for a mandatory pre-merger notification of the relevant competition authorities. The most prominent example that illustrated this deficit was the *Facebook/WhatsApp* merger. It is a common feature of the digital (platform) economy that companies like *Facebook* bring together a variety of data from different markets, thereby creating an immense

---

mission Competition Law 4.0), p. 39 et seqq., available on the internet under https://www.bmwi.de/Redaktion/DE/Publikationen/Wirtschaft/bericht-der-kommission-wettbewerbsrecht-4-0.html (last accessed 01/04/21).

534 CTRL-Labs is a technology startup based in New York which develops a software that aims to allow people to control a computer with their mind.

535 See also Höppner, WUW 2020, 71 (72), speaking of Facebook`s "killer-acquisitions".

536 See the full list of Facebook`s acquisitions on https://www.crunchbase.com/organization/facebook/acquisitions/acquisitions_list#section-acquisitions (last accessed: 11/11/19).

competitive advantage.[537] The conglomerate structures that enable this pooling of cross-market data can often be observed in the digital economy and usually trace back to numerous takeovers – regularly the takeovers of small, innovative start-ups which, as mentioned above, could also have given competitors an advantage over the incumbent. However, in order to not cause too many "false positives" (Type I errors), meaning mandatory pre-merger notifications that actually do not raise any competition law concerns, the merger regulation thresholds should not be lowered in general. With regard to (natural) monopolists like *Facebook*, though, the potential harm of too many "false negatives" (Type II errors), meaning mergers that do raise competition law concerns but did not meet the thresholds for a pre-merger notification, must be of much greater concern than Type I errors. As a result, at least natural monopolists in the digital (platform) economy should be subject to stronger merger regulations.

More precisely, certain value thresholds with regard to the transaction seem to be inappropriate no matter what the threshold is. Markets in the digital economy move so quickly that a company`s value can similarly skyrocket in a short period of time, whereas it would have failed to meet the thresholds before. This fact is also illustrated when looking at some of the world`s biggest tech companies that have gained their immense power in a relatively short timeframe. Vestager has pointed this out in one of her speeches, stating that *"many of the biggest tech companies in the world –* Google, Facebook *or* Alibaba – *didn't even exist 25 years ago. Now they have hundreds of millions, even billions of users."*[538] Combined with the fact that growing companies can quickly get to the point where the market is likely to tip in their favour,[539] it is exactly this fast-paced nature of the digital economy that endangers competition. Therefore, it is essential to prevent

---

537 See Federal Ministry for Economic Affairs and Energy, "Ein neuer Wettbewerb-srahmen für die Digitalwirtschaft – Bericht der Kommission Wettbewerbsrecht 4.0" (= A New Competition Framework for the Digital Economy – Report by the Commission Competition Law 4.0), p. 17 et seq., available on the internet under https://www.bmwi.de/Redaktion/DE/Publikationen/Wirtschaft/bericht-der-kommission-wettbewerbsrecht-4-0.html (last accessed 01/04/21).

538 Vestager, Speech "Keeping the EU competitive in a green and digitial world", College of Europe, Bruges, March 2nd, 2020, available on the internet under https://ec.europa.eu/commission/commissioners/2019-2024/vestager/announcements/keeping-eu-competitive-green-and-digital-world_en (last accessed: 28/03/20).

539 Loc. cit.

natural monopolists from following a strategy of "killer-acquisitions",[540] which lives up to its name by the early acquisition of potential competitors or start-ups with competition-relevant technologies. Otherwise, natural monopolists will quickly reach the point where they become a real monopolist.

In the light of the aforementioned aspects, any acquisition by digital online platforms with natural monopoly power should be subject to a mandatory assessment regarding its competitive impact prior to the actual merger and irrespective of any value thresholds. Obviously, such an approach results in an enormous workload for the official authorities but keeping the European internal market competitive and free of obstacles to competition has been one of the major goals of the EU. Consequently, one should not be afraid to take more drastic measures where necessary. Otherwise, competition will falter and the competitiveness throughout the whole EU will suffer.[541] The merger regulation aspects of the regulatory framework must also take account of the peculiarities that characterize digital platform markets. For example, non-horizontal mergers may be particularly harmful due to the importance of interoperability between complementary products and due to the efficiency gains data-driven platforms enjoy by collecting a variety of user data on different levels.[542]

The European Commission seems to be aware of the general problem that there is an enforcement gap in the digital (platform) economy with regard to killer acquisitions by incumbents that fail to meet the turnover-based thresholds. As a corrective measure, the Commission revised its *Guidance on the application of the referral*

---

540 See Höppner, WUW 2020, 71 (72); see also see also with regard to this phenomenon in the platform economy in general: European Commission, Competition policy for the digital era – A report by Jacques Crémer, Yves-Alexandre de Montjoye and Heike Schweitzer, p. 117, available on the internet under https://ec.europa.eu/competition/publications/reports/kd0419345enn.pdf (last accessed: 01/04/20).

541 See Vestager, Speech "Keeping the EU competitive in a green and digitial world", College of Europe, Bruges, March 2nd, 2020, available on the internet under https://ec.europa.eu/commission/commissioners/2019-2024/vestager/announcements/keeping-eu-competitive-green-and-digital-world_en (last accessed: 28/03/20).

542 See Kimmelman, "The Right Way to Regulate Digital Platforms", Harvard Kennedy School – Shorenstein Center on Media, Politics and Public Policy, September 18th, 2019, available on the internet under https://shorensteincenter.org/the-right-way-to-regulate-digital-platforms/ (last accessed: 11/11/19).

mechanism set out in Article 22 of the Merger Regulation.[543] Article 22 of the EU Merger Regulation (EUMR) allows for one or more member states to request the Commission to examine any concentration that does not have an EU dimension but affects trade between member states and threatens to significantly affect competition within the territory of the member state(s) making the request.[544] Article 22 EUMR is applicable to all concentrations as defined in Art. 3 EUMR – hence, in principle, irrespective of any thresholds.[545] The wording of Art. 22 EUMR has not changed as a result of the revised Commission Guidance but the European Commission has had a long-standing approach to ignore Art. 22 referrals – this shall not be the case anymore according to the new guidance. Therefore, the new guidance, obviously, does not impose a notification obligation on transactions that would not meet the notification criteria of the EUMR. This would have required modifying the relevant provisions of the EUMR. However, the Commission`s new guidance does send a signal to member states that Art. 22 EUMR will have an actual practical relevance in the future. The only requirements for a referral under Art. 22 EUMR are that the concentration must (i) affect trade between member states and (ii) threaten to significantly affect competition within the territory of the member state(s) making the request.[546] However, there is a downside to this *"reappraisal of the application of Article 22"*, as the Commissions names it.[547] It lacks legal certainty. Prior to the revised guidance, the allocation of competences

---

543 See European Commission, Communication from the Commission – Commission Guidance on the application of the referral mechanism set out in Article 22 of the Merger Regulation to certain categories of cases, para 11, Brussels, 26/03/2021, C(2021) 1959 final.

544 European Commission, Communication from the Commission – Commission Guidance on the application of the referral mechanism set out in Article 22 of the Merger Regulation to certain categories of cases, para 6, Brussels, 26/03/2021, C(2021) 1959 final.

545 European Commission, Communication from the Commission – Commission Guidance on the application of the referral mechanism set out in Article 22 of the Merger Regulation to certain categories of cases, para 6, Brussels, 26/03/2021, C(2021) 1959 final.

546 European Commission, Communication from the Commission – Commission Guidance on the application of the referral mechanism set out in Article 22 of the Merger Regulation to certain categories of cases, para 13, Brussels, 26/03/2021, C(2021) 1959 final.

547 European Commission, Communication from the Commission – Commission Guidance on the application of the referral mechanism set out in Article 22 of the Merger Regulation to certain categories of cases, para 11, Brussels, 26/03/2021, C(2021) 1959 final.

between the member states and the European Commission was relatively clear. Consequently, undertakings not only knew if they had to notify a competent authority of the planned merger but also which authority was to be notified. Now, however, undertakings could be informed a day before the merger was meant to be completed that a member state has made a request under Art. 22 EUMR. This, in turn, would then result in the suspension obligation of Art. 7 EUMR being applicable. In contrast to such a scenario that neglects legal certainty as one of the guiding principles highlighted by the Commission before,[548] the approach suggested by this dissertation results in a high workload but also in a maximum of legal certainty. Consequently, when it comes to the regulation of mergers with the participation of natural monopolists, one should not rely on the Commission's new approach to Art. 22 EUMR in order to tighten merger regulation but the approach presented by this dissertation.

3. Transparency

The aforementioned regulatory aspects of interoperability and merger regulation are directly aimed at the competitive structure in the market, whereas the following aspects are much more connected to the interests of consumers. First and foremost, the aspect of transparency must be mentioned in that context as another primary goal for a regulatory framework. With regard to *Facebook*'s services, the lack of transparency is particularly obvious when it comes to the conclusion of the user agreements and with regard to the subsequent processing of user data. Even though enhancing transparency with regard to the processing of personal data has been a main objective of the GDPR, it seems there is still room for improvement. It is undisputed that people are widely unaware of the full extent to which *Facebook* processes user data in order to analyse people's (purchasing) behaviour. Therefore, it is crucial to improve people's awareness of the excessive collection of data in order to make sure that they have all the information necessary when deciding to use *Facebook, WhatsApp* and co. instead of a competitor's "product".

One way of doing that would be to constantly remind users of the fact that *Facebook* analyses their behaviour. More precisely, targeted advertisements should be clearly labelled as such and users should be provided

---

548 See European Commission, Commission Notice on Case Referral in respect of concentrations, OJ 2005 C 56/02, paras. 8, 13 and 14.

with the option to see where certain data came from. For instance, when *Facebook* shows a user an advertisement for running shoes because that user "liked" certain pictures on *Instagram* (e.g. a picture of a park and a picture of people doing sports), *Facebook* should be required to provide an info box that the user can click on in order to retrace the data flow leading to that advertisement. The info box would then inform the user about the fact that the advertisement for running shoes is connected to the pictures of the park and the sports group that the user "liked" on *Instagram*. This approach would create transparency and thus also awareness about the excessive processing of data. Ultimately, more transparency in that regard could cause users to switch to another "product" where less of their personal data is being processed.[549] This, in turn, would enhance competition.

4. Adjustment of the burden of proof

The last cornerstone for an effective regulatory framework consists in an adjustment of the burdens of proof. The problems that competition law has to face in the digital (platform) economy are often connected to challenges regarding the proof of anti-competitive and abusive behaviour.[550] Consequently, rebuttable presumptions could be established according to which the burden of proof would be placed on the natural monopolist as defendant. *Facebook*, in this case, would be subject to a more rigorous burden of proof regarding the demonstration of efficiencies in order to justify a potentially abusive behaviour.

However, the dangers are, again, type I errors[551] and a resulting disincentive for innovation. Therefore, one has to find a balance between less strict burdens of proof for the competition authorities on the one hand, and even reversed burdens of proof – i.e. rebuttable presumptions – on the other.[552] For instance, it would be sensible to apply a less strict bur-

---

549 The same scenario led to the success of „Threema" – the privacy friendly alternative to WhatsApp – that many user switched to when the excessive data policy of WhatsApp became a more prominent public topic (see for instance Knupfer, "Threema: Meistverkaufte App des Jahres", December 12th, 2014, available on the internet under https://www.handelszeitung.ch/unternehmen/technologie/threema-meistverkaufte-app-des-jahres-709810 (last accessed: 30/03/20)).
550 See also Höppner, WUW 2020, 71 (71 und 76).
551 See for an explanation p. 117; I. III. 2. "Merger regulation".
552 See also Kimmelman, "The Right Way to Regulate Digital Platforms", Harvard Kennedy School – Shorenstein Center on Media, Politics and Public Policy,

den of proof with regard to the harm for competition and/or consumers, which the competition authorities have to proof as a result of the abusive behaviour. A less strict burden of proof with regard to this aspect would not only fasten the whole procedure but would also help to overcome challenges that abusive data-related business practices cause, as was seen in the Bundeskartellamt`s *Facebook* case. In that case, the harm to competition and/or consumers was difficult to proof and a less stricter burden of proof would provide a remedy for that. A rebuttable presumption, on the other hand, would not be suitable for this aspect as it would lead to an immense overregulation. For the highly innovative digital economy, a strong overregulation would constitute a disincentive to innovate. Ultimately, this would slow down the technological progress in that industry.

However, rebuttable presumptions could be applied with regard to the requirement of causality. That way, the burden of proof could be placed on the natural monopolists, according to which they would have to disprove the causal link between the abusive behaviour and the exploitation of the dominant position. Such a presumption for a causal link between the abusive behaviour in question and the monopolists` dominant position would follow an approach similar to the one presented by the 10th Amendment of the ARC and the altered wording of § 19 para. 1 ARC.

IV. Interim conclusion

Based on the example of *Facebook*, it has been shown that certain platforms in the digital economy might indeed classify as natural monopolies. However, it is important to emphasize that one should not falsely generalize the discussion in so far as to state that every dominant platform can be regarded as a natural monopoly due to the often rather strong network effects in this industry. It is still necessary to assess each case individually in order to examine whether or not there is a subadditivity of the costs.

Additionally, even if *Facebook* can be regarded as a natural monopoly with regard to the market for social networks, *Facebook* has also been an important example in the discussion of a more general competition law problem: Abusive data-related business practices and the interplay between data protection and competition law in that context.

September 18th, 2019, available on the internet under https://shorensteincenter.org/the-right-way-to-regulate-digital-platforms/ (last accessed: 11/11/19).

J. Final conclusion and future prospects

The present dissertation has shown that European data protection and competition law considerations have become increasingly intertwined in the digital (platform) economy. Nonetheless, the case law of the CJEU and particularly the decisions of the European Commission seem to suggest that the favoured approach is not to include just yet data protection considerations in competition law cases.[553] Therefore, the *Facebook* case of the German Bundeskartellamt, that combined data protection considerations with competition law concerns and which formed an illustrative base for the present work, presented itself as even more revolutionary. However, it has also been shown that at least a rethinking has started to take place with regard to the relation between data protection and competition law in a European context. For instance, Margrethe Vestager, European Commissioner for Competition, has stated that she will keep a close eye on companies and how they use data.[554] The rationale behind this lies in the fact that not only does personal data constitute a key input in the digital economy for many companies and their data-driven business models but it also functions, de facto, as a method of payment. This is also recognized by the new European directive 2019/770. However, national law like German private law is still lacking the exact regulatory framework regarding the transferability of personal data. In order to enhance legal certainty, this legal framework needs to be developed by the legislators in the near future.

Another competition law aspect derived from big data is the fact that the awareness of users regarding the way companies handle their data has increased.[555] Hence, data and data-related matters such as the level of data

---

553 See p. 57; D. I. "The evolving opinion on the relation between data protection and competition law".

554 Vestager, Speech at the EDPS-BEUC Conference on Big Data, Brussels, September 29th, 2016, available on the internet under https://wayback.archive-it.org/12090/20191129222113/https://ec.europa.eu/commission/commissioners/2014-2019/vestager/announcements/big-data-and-competition_en (last accessed: 27/03/20).

555 See European Commission in case no. COMP/M.7217, *Facebook/Whatsapp*, marginal no. 87 where it is stated that "*consumer communications apps compete for customers by attempting to offer the best communication experience*", which includes, inter alia, "*privacy and security, the importance of which varies from user*

protection and the extent to which data is collected constitute important parameters of competition in the digital (platform) economy. This has to be taken into account in competition law assessments as well. As an overall consequence of the just mentioned aspects, both competition and data protection law are nowadays integral parts of the legal framework for handling data in the digital economy and can no longer be considered as clearly distinct. Quite the contrary: It has been shown that European data protection and competition law are in fact compatible with each other.[556] This is based not least on the similarities in their respective objectives since both competition and data protection law can be considered to be to some extent consumer-oriented – even though they pursue this aim in different areas. In addition, both legal acts also serve the internal market by securing its correct functioning. Moreover, securing the correct functioning of the internal market also means securing effective competition and this, in turn, will secure values for consumers in the long run. However, competition law and more precisely Art. 102 TFEU faces new challenges due to the data-driven business models in the digital economy. This is based on the fact that *"competition rules weren't written with big data in mind"*, as Vestager once said and as was stated at the very beginning of this dissertation.[557] Hence, the present work aimed to answer the question as to whether Art. 102 TFEU should receive normative guidance from rules such as those of the GDPR, which were indeed written with big data in mind.

As can be seen from the elaborations above, this question must be answered in the affirmative. Data-related and particularly data protection considerations can be integrated in both assessments of dominance and abusive conduct under Art. 102 TFEU. With regard to the assessment of dominance, access to big data can constitute a barrier to entry and/or expansion for (possible) competitors. Additionally, the extent to which data is collected and the level of data protection can constitute criteria for market power. More precisely, an excessive extent of data collection can be equated with the notion of excessive pricing. The level of data protection,

---

to user but which are becoming increasingly valued, as shown by the introduction of consumer communications apps (such as Threema) *specifically addressing privacy and security issues"*.

556 See p. 67; D. III. "Interim conclusion".

557 Vestager, Speech at the EDPS-BEUC Conference on Big Data, Brussels, September 29th, 2016, available on the internet under https://wayback.archive-it.org/12090/20191129222113/https://ec.europa.eu/commission/commissioners/2014-2019/vestager/announcements/big-data-and-competition_en (last accessed: 27/03/20).

on the other hand, can constitute a quality criterion – even though this criterion will indeed be rather difficult to measure in practice. Nonetheless, retaining or even gaining market shares whilst collecting significantly more user data or whilst offering a lower level of data protection than competitors can indicate market power and therefore also dominance.

With regard to the assessment of data-related conduct and its classification as abusive under Art. 102 TFEU, it is especially the excessive collection of data as well as the imposition of unfair contractual terms, by which user are obliged to give their consent to non-transparent data policies, that can constitute an abuse of a dominant position. To be exact, both these practices may fall under Art. 102 (2) (a) TFEU. In order to determine whether or not a certain collection of data is to be regarded as excessive, one should take the principles of purpose limitation and data minimization of Art. 5 (1) (b) respectively (c) GDPR into account. These principles stipulate a proportionality test according to which the collection of data must be seen as excessive if it is disproportionate in the light of the purposes for which it was collected. Additionally, infringements of other crucial cornerstones of the GDPR can also lead to the finding of an abuse. Particularly, infringements of provisions by which limitations regarding the processing of personal data are circumvented in order to collect more user data should be taken into account in order to assess whether or not a certain conduct must be seen as abusive under Art. 102 TFEU. As pointed out above, the undue collection of user data can lead to a significant advantage vis-à-vis competitors. Dominant undertakings must refrain from such infringements due to their special responsibility.[558] The special responsibility of dominant undertakings obliges them to refrain from methods other than those of normal competition on the merits. However, the undue collection of data by circumventing data protection provisions cannot be considered competition on the merits. Nonetheless, this does not mean that any infringement of data protection provisions by a dominant undertaking will result in an abuse of its position under Art. 102 TFEU. Such a scenario must be limited to infringements of crucial provisions like Art. 5 (1) GDPR or Art. 6 GDPR. Infringements of other provisions are not likely to affect inter-state trade and can therefore not fall under Art. 102 TFEU. This limitation of Art. 102 TFEU should not be weakened either. Hence, such matters should then be handled on a mere

---

558 See p. 42; C. I. 1. "The establishment of dominance and the resulting "special responsibility".

data protection law basis instead. That way, an undue overlap between the two fields of law can be prevented.

More importantly, however, not only is it possible to bridge data protection considerations with Art. 102 TFEU but competition authorities should also do so in order to secure a level playing field. The new challenges that competition law has to face in the digital (platform) economy can be best addressed by applying the competition law provisions under the normative guidance of data protection law. Introducing new and less flexible regulations to enable ex ante enforcement is not only unnecessary due to the broad wording of Art. 102 TFEU and the extensive case law of the ECJ, but it could also lead to fundamental disadvantages. Firstly, they might constitute disincentives for innovation and, secondly, stronger regulations could quickly become outdated again due to the dynamic nature of the digital economy. This would ultimately harm competition rather than protect it. As Vestager once said: *"Digital markets move fast. And we need to be able to keep up with them – or competition will falter, and our competitiveness will suffer."*[559]

In that context, one also has to bear in mind that competition law cannot be regarded as wholly autonomous in a unified European legal system. Therefore, legal principles like the principle of the unity of the legal order or the European principles of effet utile require that data protection and competition law considerations be linked in the digital (platform) economy. Only in this way, can the most effective possible implementation of the Treaty objectives be secured. Ultimately, such an approach is the best solution to prevent effective competition from being distorted due to abusive data-related business practices that might otherwise escape the application of competition law. The above-elaborated case law of the CJEU in cases like *Johnston*,[560] and the Querschnittsklausel of Art. 51 (1) CFREU, have shown that it is not actually really a matter of "can" and "should" in the first place. In fact, it is an actual obligation of the European Commission to take into account data protection considerations in its actions and thus also in competition law assessments. However, one has to prevent the competition authority from mutating to a data protection authority sui

---

559 Vestager, Speech "Keeping the EU competitive in a green and digitial world", College of Europe, Bruges, March 2nd, 2020, available on the internet under https://ec.europa.eu/commission/commissioners/2019-2024/vestager/announcements/keeping-eu-competitive-green-and-digital-world_en (last accessed: 28/03/20).

560 ECJ in case C-222/84, *Johnston v Chief Constable of the Royal Ulster Constabulary*, ECLI:EU:C:1986:206.

generis when pursuing a case under Art. 102 TFEU for an infringement of data protection law. Competition law cases that are about the sanctioning of a data-related behaviour fall (also) within the competence of the data protection authorities. In order to prevent contradictory decisions as a result of the dual competence, a shared approach between the relevant authorities would be desirable. Accordingly, the data protection authority would assess the alleged infringement of data protection law whereas the competition authority would assess the harm for competition deriving therefrom. Additionally, such a shared approach would also help to avoid the competition authority becoming active in a field of law that might go beyond their actual expertise. One way by which a shared approach could be established is a European regulation. It would serve as a legal base for the cooperation between the official authorities, as was done in Germany in the course of the 9th Amendment to the ARC.

The present dissertation has also shown that abusive data-related business practices, as known from the *Facebook* case, do not escape the application of competition law by extending the immanence theory to Art. 102 TFEU. However, besides regulating dominant internet platforms through an "interdisciplinary approach" by which data protection and competition law considerations are being linked, one could also make such platforms the subject of direct regulations should they classify as natural monopolies. This possibility was also discussed based on the example of *Facebook* and constitutes an alternative approach. It is important to emphasize, though, that one should not falsely generalize the discussion in so far as to state that every dominant platform can be regarded as a natural monopoly, thus justifying a direct regulation. Additionally, even if *Facebook* can be regarded as a natural monopoly with regard to the market for social networks, the example of *Facebook* was also important to discuss the more general competition law problem mentioned before: Abusive data-related business practices and the interplay between data protection and competition law in that context.

What will be interesting for the future in this regard is the fact that it has been shown that the GDPR has a broad territorial scope of application and can apply to companies outside the EU, too. The same applies to European competition law as last seen in the *Intel* case.[561] Hence, companies from countries outside the EU will not only have a strong incentive to comply with European competition law itself but will also have an even

---

561 European Commission in case no. COMP/C-3 /37.990, D(2009) 3726final – *Intel*.

bigger incentive to comply with European data protection law in order not to fear any of the record-breaking competition fines that have lately been imposed on companies within the digital economy. This could indeed strengthen the overall awareness of data protection rights and would enhance the digital single market. Additionally, people might gain more trust in data-related technologies, which is needed in order to promote these technologies and their immense potential.

Overall, the *Facebook* case of the Bundeskartellamt can serve as a pioneer for an approach in competition law assessments by which data protection and competition law considerations are linked. However, whether or not the European practice will follow such an approach will be shown in the years to come. In order to create a EU fit for the digital age,[562] it is obvious though that competition law assessments can no longer ignore the reciprocity that exists in the digital world between a company`s power over vast amounts of data and its market dominance. Additionally, if the potential of the highly innovative digital economy shall be fully exploited, not only is there a need to create a level playing field for a healthy competitive process, it is also necessary to gain people`s trust in the new technologies and preserve fundamental rights like the right to informational self-determination. For that reason, it is important that the interplay between data protection and competition law is acknowledged on a European level so that these two fields of law can develop their best possible degree of protection. It is now up to the European legislator, the Commission as the competent competition authority and the ECJ to ensure such acknowledgement. In that regard, this dissertation ends with the words of Competition Commissioner Margrethe Vestager: *"Technology can create new challenges for our values, like freedom and fairness and democracy. But it won't be technology that decides the future of those values. It will be us, as a society, with the choices we make, and the frameworks of rules we create for the digital future."*[563]

---

562 See Vestager, Speech "Shaping a digital future for Europe", Symposium on Digitalisation, The Hague, February 3rd, 2020, available on the internet under https://ec.europa.eu/commission/commissioners/2019-2024/vestager/announcements/shaping-digital-future-europe_en (last accessed: 27/03/20).

563 Vestager, Speech "Building a positive digital world", Digital Summit, Dortmund (Germany), October 29th, 2019, available on the internet under https://wayback.archive-it.org/12090/20191130020041/https://ec.europa.eu/commission/commissioners/2014-2019/vestager/announcements/building-positive-digital-world_en (last accessed: 28/03/20).

Bibliography

Alpmann, Josef A./Krüger, Rolf/Wüstenbecker, Horst, Alpmann Brockhaus Studienlexikon Recht, 4th edition, Munich 2014.

Andriychuk, Oles, The Normative Foundations of European Competition Law – Assessing the Goals of Antitrust through the Lens of Legal Philosophy, Cheltenham 2017.

Arnull, Anthony/Chalmers, Damian, The Oxford Handbook of European Union Law, Oxford 2015 (cited: author, in: Arnull/Chalmers).

Bamberger, Heinz Georg/Roth, Herbert/Hau, Wolfgang/Poseck, Roman, Beck'scher Onlinekommentar BGB, 50th edition, Munich 2019 (cited: author, in: BeckOK BGB).

Baumbach, Adolf/Hueck, Alfred, Beck'sche Kurzkommentare – Gesetz betreffend die Gesellschaften mit beschränkter Haftung, 21st edition, Munich 2017 (cited: author, in: Baumbach/Hueck).

Bechtold, Rainer/Bosch, Wolfgang, Gesetz gegen Wettbewerbsbeschränkungen Kommentar, 9th edition, Munich 2018, (cited: author, in: Bechtold/Bosch, GWB Kommentar).

Becker, Carsten, "Bundeskartellamt und Verbraucherschutz", Zeitschrift für Wettbewerbsrecht (ZWeR) 2018, 229–245.

Bellamy, Christopher/Child, Graham D., European Union Law of Competition, 7th edition, Oxford 2013.

Berg, Werner/Mäsch, Gerald, Deutsches und Europäisches Kartellrecht Kommentar, 3rd edition, Cologne 2018 (cited: author, in: Berg/Mäsch, KartellR Kommentar).

Bornkamm, Joachim/Montag, Frank/Säcker, Franz Jürgen, Münchener Kommentar Europäisches und Deutsches Wettbewerbsrecht, Volume 1, 2nd edition, Munich 2015 (cited: author, in: MüKoEuWettbR).

Bräutigam, Peter, Das Nutzungsverhältnis bei sozialen Netzwerken. Zivilrechtlicher Austausch von IT-Leistung gegen personenbezogene Daten, Multimedia und Recht (MMR) 2012, 635–641.

Brink, Stefan/Wolff, Heinrich Amadeus, Beck'scher Onlinekommentar Datenschutzrecht, 28th edition, Munich 2019 (cited: author, in: BeckOK DatenschutzR).

Bruc, Édouard, "Data as an essential facility in European law: how to define the "target" market and divert the data pipeline?", European Competition Journal 2019, 177–224.

Buchner, Benedikt, "Datenschutz und Kartellrecht", Wettbewerb in Recht und Praxis (WRP) 2019, 1243–1248.

Bunte, Hermann-Josef, Kartellrecht Kommentar, Volume 2, Europäisches Kartellrecht, 13th edition, Cologne 2018 (cited: author, in: Langen/Bunte, EU KartellR Kommentar).

Buttarelli, Giovanni, The EU GDPR as a clarion call for a new global digital gold standard, International Data Privacy Law 2016, 77–78.

Callies, Christian/Ruffert, Matthias, EUV/AEUV Kommentar – Das Verfassungsrecht der Europäischen Union mit Europäischer Grundrechtecharta, 5th edition, Munich 2016 (cited: author, in: Callies/Ruffert).

Cornelius, Kai, "Die „datenschutzrechtliche Einheit" als Grundlage des bußgeldrechtlichen Unternehmensbegriff nach der EU-DSGVO", Neue Zeitschrift für Wirtschafts-, Steuer- und Unternehmensstrafrecht (NZWiST) 2016, 421–426.

Costa-Cabral, Francisco/Lynskey, Orla, "Family Ties: The Intersection Between Data Protection and Competition in EU Law", Common Market Law Review (CML Rev.) 2017, 11–50.

Cseres, Kati J., "The Controversies of the Consumer Welfare Standard", Competition Law Review 2007, 121–173.

Daskalova, Victoria, "Consumer Welfare in EU Competition Law: What Is It (Not) About?", Competition Law Review 2017, 133–162.

Dewenter, Ralf/Rösch, Jürgen/Terschüren, Anna, "Abgrenzung zweiseitiger Märkte am Beispiel von Internetsuchmaschinen", Neue Zeitschrift für Kartellrecht (NZKart) 2014, 387–394.

Dowse, Melissa/Dück, Hermann, "Zwangseinwilligung zur Datenverarbeitung – zugleich Anmerkung zum Beschluss des OLG Düsseldorf in Sachen Facebook I", Neue Zeitschrift für Kartellrecht (NZKart) 2020, 80–83.

Dreier, Thomas/Schulze, Gernot, Urheberrechtsgesetz Kommentar, 6th edition, Munich 2018 (cited: author, in: Dreier/Schulze).

Ducci, Francesco, Natural Monopolies in Digital Platform Markets, Cambridge 2020.

Dück, Hermann/Maschemer, Andreas, Zwischen „Rule of reason" und Immanenztheorie – Zur dogmatischen Einordnung der Markenabgrenzungsvereinbarung, Wettbewerb in Recht und Praxis (WRP) 2013, 167–172.

Eberl, Christina, "Verstaatlichung international verflochtener Unternehmen", in: Aderhold, Eltje/Lipstein, Kurt/Schücking, Christoph/Stürner, Rolf, Festschrift für Hans Hanisch, Cologne, Berlin, Bonn, Munich 1994, pp. 39–57 (cited: Eberl, in: Aderhold et al.)

Ehmann, Eugen/ Selmayr, Martin, Beck'sche Kurzkommentare Datenschutzgrundverordnung, 2nd edition, Munich 2018 (cited: author, in: Ehmann/Selmayr, DS-GVO Kommentar).

Ellger, Reinhard, "Konditionenmissbrauch nach § 19 GWB durch Datenschutzverstoß – der Facebook-Fall des Bundeskartellamts", Wirtschaft und Wettbewerb (WUW) 2019, 446–454.

Ellger, Reinhard, "Facebook und das Kartellrecht – ein Drama in drei Akten", Wirtschaft und Wettbewerb (WUW) 2019, 493–493.

Eßer, Martin/Kramer, Philipp/von Lewinski, Kai, DSGVO BDSG Kommentar, 6th edition, Cologne 2018 (cited: author, in: Eßer/Kramer/von Lewinski, DSGVO/BDSG Kommentar).

Fleischer, Holger/Goette, Wulf, Münchener Kommentar zum GmbHG, Volume 1, §§ 1–34, 3rd edition, Munich 2018 (cited: author, in: MüKo GmbHG).

Forkel, Hans, "Lizenzen an Persönlichkeitsrechten durch gebundene Rechtsübertragung", Gewerblicher Rechtsschutz und Urheberrecht (GRUR) 1988, 491–501.

Franceschi, Alberto (de), "Digitale Inhalte gegen personenbezogene Daten: Unentgeltlichkeit oder Gegenleistung?", in: Schmidt-Kessel, Martin/Kramme, Malte, Geschäftsmodelle in der digitalen Wirtschaft, Jena 2017, pp. 115–138.

Franck, Jens-Uwe, "Eine Frage des Zusammenhangs: Marktbeherrschungsmissbrauch durch rechtswidrige Konditionen – Facebook im Visier des Bundeskartellamts", Zeitschrift für Wettbewerbsrecht (ZWeR) 2016, 137–164.

Frenz, Walter, Handbuch Europarecht, Volume 5 – Wirkung und Rechtsschutz, Heidelberg 2010.

Gerber, David J., "The European Competition Law Story: Some German Roles", in: Großfeld, Bernhard/Sack, Rolf/Möllers, Thomas M.J./Drexl, Josef/Heinemann, Andreas, Festschrift für Wolfgang Fikentscher, Tübingen 1998, pp 654–670.

Gersdorf, Hubertus/Paal, Boris P., Beck'scher Onlinekommentar Informations- und Medienrecht, 24th edition, Munich 2019 (cited: author, in: BeckOK InfoMedienR).

Gola, Peter, Datenschutz-Grundverordnung Kommentar, 2nd edition, Munich 2018 (cited: author, in: Gola, DSGVO Kommentar).

Grabitz, Eberhard/Hilf, Meinhard/Nettesheim, Martin, Das Recht der Europäischen Union, Volume II EUV/AEUV, 65th supplement delivery, Munich 2018 (cited: author, in: Grabitz/Hilf/Nettesheim).

Grabitz, Eberhard/Hilf, Meinhard/Nettesheim, Martin, Das Recht der Europäischen Union, Volume I, EUV/AEUV, 67th supplementary delivery, Munich 2019 (cited: author, in: Grabitz/Hilf/Nettesheim, Das Recht der Europäischen Union).

Grave, Carsten/Nyberg, Jenny, "Die Rolle von Big Data bei der Anwendung des Kartellrechts", Wirtschaft und Wettbewerb (WuW) 2017, 363–368.

Groeben, von der, Hans/Schwarze, Jürgen/Hatje, Armin, Europäisches Unionsrecht, 7th edition, Baden-Baden 2015 (cited: author, in: von der Groeben/Schwarze/Hatje).

Hacker, Philipp, "Daten als Gegenleistung: Rechtsgeschäfte im Spannungsfeld von DS-GVO und allgemeinem Vertragsrecht", Zeitschrift für die gesamte Privatrechtswissenschaft (ZfPW) 2019, 148–197.

Henssler, Martin, Münchener Kommentar zum Bürgerlichen Gesetzbuch, Volume 5/1, Schuldrecht – Besonderer Teil III/1, 7th edition, Munich 2018 (cited: author, in: MüKo BGB V).

Henssler, Martin/Krüger, Wolfgang, Münchener Kommentar zum Bürgerlichen Gesetzbuch, Volume 4, Schuldrecht – Besonderer Teil II, 7th edition, Munich 2016 (cited: author, in: MüKo BGB IV).

Höppner, Thomas, "Plattform-Regulierung light", Wirtschaft und Wettbewerb (WUW) 2020, 71–79.

Hoeren, Thomas/Sieber, Ulrich/Holznagel, Bernd, Handbuch Multimedia-Recht, 48th supplemantary edition, Munich 2019 (cited: author, in: Hoeren/Sieber/Holznagel, Handbuch MMR).

Hoffer, Raoul/Lehr, Leo Alexander, " Onlineplattformen und Big Data auf dem Prüfstand – Gemeinsame Betrachtung der Fälle Amazon, Google und Facebook", Neue Zeitschrift für Kartellrecht (NZKart) 2019, 10–20.

Hussain, Fatima, Internet of Things: Building Blocks and Business Models, Cham 2017.

Immenga, Ulrich/Mestmäcker, Ernst-Joachim, Wettbewerbsrecht – Kommentar zum Europäischen Kartellrecht, Volume 1, EU/Part 1, 6th edition, Munich 2019 (cited: author, in: Immenga/Mestmäcker, KartellR Kommentar).

Immenga, Ulrich/Mestmäcker, Ernst-Joachim, Wettbewerbsrecht – Kommentar zum Deutschen Kartellrecht, Volume 2, 5th edition, Munich 2014 (cited: author, in: Immenga/Mestmäcker, WettbewerbsR Kommentar).

Jandt, Silke/Roßnagel, Alexander, " Social Networks für Kinder und Jugendliche – Besteht ein ausreichender Datenschutz?", MultiMedia und Recht (MMR) 2011, 637–642.

Jarass, Hans D., Charta der Grundrechte der Europäischen Union Kommentar, 3rd edition, Munich 2016.

Jones, Alison/Brenda, Sufrin, EU Competition Law – Text, Cases, and Materials, 6th edition, Oxford 2016.

Kadar, Massimiliano, "European Union competition law in the digital era", Zeitschrift für Wettbewerbsrecht (ZWeR) 2015, 342–362.

Kamann, Hans-Georg/Miller, Robin Dominik, Kartellrecht und Datenschutzrecht – Verhältnis einer "Hass-Liebe"?, Neue Zeitschrift für Kartellrecht (NZKart) 2016, 405–412.

Kilian, Wolfgang, "Informationelle Selbstbestimmung und Marktprozesse – Zur Notwendigkeit der Modernisierung des Modernisierungsgutachtens zum Datenschutz", Computer und Recht (CR) 2002, 921–929.

Körber, Torsten, "Analoges Kartellrecht für digitale Märkte?", Wirtschaft und Wettbewerb (WuW) 2015, 120–133.

Körber, Torsten, "Die Facebook-Entscheidung des Bundeskartellamtes – Machtmissbrauch durch Verletzung des Datenschutzrechts?", Neue Zeitschrift für Kartellrecht (NZKart) 2019, 187–195.

Körber, Torsten, "Ist Wissen Marktmacht?" Überlegungen zum Verhältnis von Datenschutz, „Datenmacht" und Kartellrecht – Teil 1", Neue Zeitschrift Kartellrecht (NZKart) 2016, 303–310.

Körber, Torsten, "Konzeptionelle Erfassung digitaler Plattformen und adäquate Regulierungsstrategien", Zeitschrift für Urheber- und Medienrecht (ZUM) 2017, 93–101.

Krämer, Hagen, "Digitalisierung, Monopolbildung und wirtschaftliche Ungleichheit", Wirtschaftsdienst 2019, 47–52.

Kühling, Jürgen/Buchner, Benedikt, Datenschutz-Grundverordnung/BDSG Kommentar, 2nd edition, Munich 2018 (cited: author, in: Kühling/Buchner).

Kupik, Jan/ Mikeš, Stanislav, „Discussion on big data, online advertising and competition policy", European Competition Law Review (E.C.L.R.) 2018, 393–402.

Kutscher, Antonia, Der digitale Nachlass, Göttingen 2015.

Langhanke, Carmen/Schmidt-Kessel, Martin, "Consumer Data as Consideration", Journal of European Consumer and Market Law (EuCML) 2015, 218–223.

Loewenheim, Ulrich/Meessen, Karl M./Riesenkampff, Alexander, Kartellrecht, Volume 2 – GWB Kommentar, Munich 2006 (cited: author, in: Loewenheim/ Meessen/Riesenkampff).

Loewenheim, Ulrich/Meessen, Karl M./Riesenkampff, Alexander/Kersting, Christian/Meyer-Lindeman, Hans Jürgen, Kartellrecht Kommentar, 3rd edition, Munich 2016 (cited: author, in: Loewenheim et al.).

Mohr, Jochen, "Kartellrechtlicher Konditionenmissbrauch durch datenschutzwidrige Allgemeine Geschäftsbedingungen", Europäische Zeitschrift für Wirtschaftsrecht (EuZW) 2019, 265–273.

Müller, Christian H./Thiede, Thomas, "Kartellrechtliche Risiken durch Wettbewerbsverbote in Unternehmenskaufverträgen", Europäische Zeitschrift für Wirtschaftsrecht (EuZW) 2017, 246–249.

Mundt, Andreas, "Verbraucherschutz im Bundeskartellamt", Wirtschaft und Wettbewerb (WUW) 2019, 181–186.

Nuys, Marcel, "Big Data" – "Die Bedeutung von Daten im Kartellrecht", Wirtschaft und Wettbewerb (WuW) 2016, 512–520.

O'Donoghue, Robert/Padilla, Jorge A., The Law and Economics of Article 82 EC, Portland 2006.

Paal, Boris P., "Daten und Kartellrecht", Neue Zeitschrift für Kartellrecht (NZKart) 2018, 157–158.

Paal, Boris P., "Immaterialgüter, Internetmonopole und Kartellrecht", Gewerblicher Rechtsschutz und Urheberrecht (GRUR) 2013, 873–881.

Paal, Boris P./Kumkar, Lea Katharina, "Wettbewerbsschutz in der Digitalwirtschaft – Die wichtigsten Neuerungen der 10. GWB-Novelle im Überblick", Neue Juristische Wochenschrift (NJW) 2021, 809–815.

Paal, Boris P./Pauly, Daniel A., Beck'sche Kompaktkommentare – Datenschutz-Grundverordnung Bundesdatenschutzgesetz, 2nd edition, Munich 2018 (cited: author, in: Paal/Pauly, DSGVO/BDSG Kommentar).

Palandt, Otto, Beck'sche Kurz-Kommentare Bürgerliches Gesetzbuch, 78th edition, Munich 2019.

Pechstein, Matthias/Nowak, Carsten/Häde, Ulrich, Frankfurter Kommentar zu EUV, GRC und AEUV, Volume 1 – EUV und GRC, Tübingen 2017 (cited: author, in: Pechstein/Nowak/Häde, Frankfurter Kommentar EUV/GRC/AEUV).

Podszun, Rupprecht/de Toma, Michael, "Die Durchsetzung des Datenschutzes durch Verbraucherrechtm Lauterkeitsrecht und Kartellrecht", Neue Juristische Wochenschrift (NJW) 2016, 2987–2994.

Polley, Romina/Kaup, Rieke, "Paradigmenwechsel in der deutschen Missbrauchaufsicht – Der Referentenentwurf zur 10. GWB-Novelle", Neue Zeitschrift für Kartellrecht (NZKart) 2020, 113–119.

Posner, Richard A., "Natural Monopoly and Its Regulation", Stanford Law Review 1969, 548–643.

Prütting, Hanns/Wegen, Gerhard/Weinreich, Gerd, Bürgerliches Gesetzbuch Kommentar, 13th edition, Cologne 2018 (cited: author, in: Prütting/Wegen/Weinreich).

Rothmann, Robert/Buchner, Benedikt, "Der typische Facebook-Nutzer zwischen Recht und Realität – Zugleich eine Anmerkung zu LG Berlin v. 16.01.2018", Datenschutz und Datensicherheit (DuD) 2018, 342–346.

Rücker, Daniel/Kugler, Tobias, New European General Data Protection Regulation – A Practitioner`s Guide, Baden-Baden 2018.

Rudersdorf, Martin, "Wettbewerbsverbote in Gesellschafts- und Unternehmenskaufverträgen", Rheinische Notar-Zeitschrift (RNotZ) 2011, 509–530.

Säcker, Franz Jürgen/Rixecker, Roland/Oetker, Harmut/Limperg, Bettina, Münchener Kommentar zum Bürgerlichen Gesetzbuch, Volume 2 – §§ 241–310 BGB, 8th edition, Munich 2019 (cited: author, in: MüKo BGB II).

Schmidt-Kessel, Martin/Erler, Katharina/Grimm, Anna/Kramme, Malte, "Die Richtlinienvorschläge der Kommission zu Digitalen Inhalten und Online-Handel – Teil 2", Zeitschrift für das Privatrecht der Europäischen Union (GPR) 2016, 54–71.

Schmidt-Kessel, Martin/Grimm, Anna, "Unentgeltlich oder entgeltlich? – Der vertragliche Austausch von digitalen Inhalten gegen personenbezogene Daten", Zeitschrift für die gesamte Privatrechtswissenschaft (ZfPW) 2017, 84–108.

Schmidt, Ingo/Haucap, Justus, Wettbewerbspolitik und Kartellrecht – Eine interdisziplinäre Einführung, 9th edition, Munich 2012.

Schmoeckel, Mathias/Maetschke, Matthias, Rechtsgeschichte der Wirtschaft, 2nd edition, Tübingen 2016.

Schneider, Giulia, "Testing Art. 102 TFEU in the Digital Marketplace", Journal of European Competition Law and Practice 2018, 213–225.

Schreiber, Kristina, Facebook kombiniert Nutzerdaten missbräuchlich, da DSGVO-widrig, Gewerblicher Rechtsschutz und Urheberrecht, Praxis im Immaterialgüter und Wettbewerbsrecht (GRUR-Prax) 2019, 266.

Schulte, Josef L./Just, Christoph, Heymanns Kommentare zum gewerblichen Rechtsschutz, Kartellrecht Kommentar, 2nd edition, Cologne 2016 (cited: author, in: Schulte/Just, KartellR Kommentar).

Schwartmann, Rolf/Jaspers, Andreas/Thüsing, Gregor/Kugelmann, Dieter, Heidelberger Kommentar DS-GVO/BDSG, Heidelberg 2018 (cited: author, in: Schwartmann/Jaspers/Thüsing/Kugelmann, DSGVO/BDSG Kommentar).

Seidler, Katharina, Digitaler Nachlass – Das postmortale Schicksal elektronischer Kommunikation, Frankfurt/Main 2016.

Spelthahn, Sabine, Privatisierung natürlicher Monopole – Theorie und internationale Praxis am Beispiel Wasser und Abwasser, Wiesbaden 1994.

Spiecker genannt Döhmann, Indra, "Digitale Mobilität: Plattform Governance – IT-sicherheits- und datenschutzrechtliche Implikationen", Gewerblicher Rechtsschutz und Urheberrecht (GRUR) 2019, 341–352.

Spindler, Gerald/Schuster, Fabian, Recht der elektronischen Medien, 4th edition, Munich 2019 (cited: author, in: Spindler/Schuster, Recht der elektronischen Medien).

Steinrötter, Björn, Feuertaufe für die EU-Datenschutz-Grundverordnung – und das Kartellrecht steht Pate, Europäisches Wirtschafts- und Steuerrecht (EWS) 2018, 61–71.

Stern, Klaus/Sachs, Michael, Europäische Grundrechte-Charta Kommentar, Munich 2016 (cited: author, in: Stern/Sachs, GRCh Kommentar).

Streinz, Rudolf, Europarecht, 10th edition, Heidelberg 2016.

Stucke, Maurice E./Grunes, Allen P., Big Data and Competition Policy, Oxford 2016.

Tamke, Maren, "Big Data and Competition Law", Zeitschrift für Wettbewerbsrecht (ZWeR) 2017, 358–385.

Unseld, Florian, "Die Übertragbarkeit von Persönlichkeitsrechten", Gewerblicher Rechtsschutz und Urheberrecht (GRUR) 2011, 982–988.

Volmar, Maximilian, "Marktabgrenzung bei mehrseitigen Online-Plattformen", Zeitschrift für Wettbewerbsrecht (ZWeR) 2017, 386–408.

von Danwitz, Thomas, Die Grundrechte auf Achtung der Privatsphäre und auf Schutz personenbezogener Daten, Datenschutz und Datensicherheit (DuD) 2015, 581–585.

Weber, Klaus, Creifelds Rechtswörterbuch, 22nd edition, Munich 2017.

Weichert, Thilo, "Die Ökonomisierung des Rechts auf informationelle Selbstbestimmung", Neue Juristische Wochenschrift (NJW) 2001, 1463–1469.

Weitbrecht, Andreas, „Kartellrecht – Gestern, heute und morgen", Neue Zeitschrift für Kartellrecht (NZKart) 2020, 45–46.

Wiedemann, Gerhard, Handbuch des Kartellrechts, 3rd edition, Munich 2016 (cited: author, in: Wiedemann, Handbuch des Kartellrechts).

Zech, Herber, ""Industrie 4.0" – Rechtsrahmen für eine Datenwirtschaft im digitalen Binnenmarkt", Gewerblicher Rechtsschutz und Urheberrecht (GRUR) 2015, 1151–1160.

Ziemons, Hildegard/Jaeger, Carsten, Beck'scher Online-Kommentar GmbHG, 39th edition, Munich 2019 (cited: author, in: BeckOK GmbHG).

Internet Sources

Albers, Michael, "Der „more economic approach" bei Verdrängungsmissbräuchen: Zum Stand der Überlegungen der Europäischen Kommission", Lecture on the occasion of the Hamburg Antitrust Law Symposium 2006, available on the internet under http://ec.europa.eu/competition/antitrust/art82/albers.pdf (last accessed: 27/03/20).

Almunia, Joaquín, Speech "Competition – what's in it for consumers?" on the occasion of the European Competition and Consumer Day in Poznan, 24 November 2011, available on the internet under http://europa.eu/rapid/press-release_SPEECH-11-803_en.htm (last accessed: 11/03/20).

Almunia, Joaquín, Speech "Competition and personal data protection", speech at the Privacy Platform event: Competition and Privacy in Markets of Data, Brussels 26 November 2012, available under http://europa.eu/rapid/press-release_SPEECH-12-860_en.htm (last accessed: 09/02/20).

Art. 29 Data Protection Working Party, WP 259 – Guidelines on consent under Regulation 2016/679, available on the internet under https://iapp.org/resources/article/wp29-guidelines-on-consent/ (last accessed: 07/09/19).

Art. 29 Data Protection Working Party, Working Paper 203, Opinion 03/2013 on purpose limitation, available on the Internet under https://ec.europa.eu/justice/article-29/documentation/opinion-recommendation/files/2013/wp203_en.pdf (last accessed: 28/01/20).

Autorité de la concurrence and the Bundeskartellamt, "Competition Law and Data", May 10th, 2016, available on the internet under https://www.bundeskartellamt.de/SharedDocs/Publikation/DE/Berichte/Big%20Data%20Papier.pdf?__blob=publicationFile&v=2 (last accessed: 26/01/20).

Budzinski, Oliver, "Diskussionspapier Nr. 103 – Aktuelle Herausforderungen der Wettbewerbspolitik durch Marktplätze im Internet", available on the internet under https://www.tu-ilmenau.de/fileadmin/media/wth/Diskussionspapier_Nr_103.pdf (last accessed: 20/06/19).

Bundeskartellamt, "Big Data und Wettbewerb", October 2017, available on the internet under https://www.bundeskartellamt.de/SharedDocs/Publikation/DE/Schriftenreihe_Digitales/Schriftenreihe_Digitales_1.pdf?__blob=publicationFile&v=3 (last accessed: 23/01/20).

Bundeskartellamt, "Background information on the Facebook proceeding", available on the internet under https://www.bundeskartellamt.de/SharedDocs/Publikation/EN/Diskussions_Hintergrundpapiere/2017/Hintergrundpapier_Facebook.pdf?__blob=publicationFile&v=6 (last accessed: 27/03/20).

Bundeskartellamt, B6–113/15, "Arbeitspapier Marktmacht von Plattformen und Netzwerken", June 2016, available on the internet under https://www.bundeskartellamt.de/SharedDocs/Publikation/DE/Berichte/Think-Tank-Bericht.pdf?__blob=publicationFile&v=2 (last accessed: 23/08/19).

Bundeskartellamt, case summary of case no. B6–22/16 – *Facebook*, published February 15, 2019, available on the internet under https://www.bundeskartellamt.de/SharedDocs/Entscheidung/EN/Fallberichte/Missbrauchsaufsicht/2019/B6-22-16.pdf?__blob=publicationFile&v=3 (last accessed: 27/03/20).

Bundeskartellamt, press release "Bundeskartellamt prohibits Facebook from combining user data from different sources", February 7, 2019, available on the internet under https://www.bundeskartellamt.de/SharedDocs/Meld ung/EN/Pressemitteilungen/2019/07_02_2019_Facebook.html;jsession-id=832649993354525E65A66B820BEC5711.1_cid378?nn=3591568 (last accessed: 27/03/20).

Bundeskartellamt, press release "Bundeskartellamt initiates proceeding against Facebook on suspicion of having abused its market power by infringing data protection rules", March 2, 2016, available on the internet under https://www.b undeskartellamt.de/SharedDocs/Meldung/EN/Pressemitteilungen/2016/02_03_2 016_Facebook.html?nn=3591568 (last accessed: 27/03/20).

Bundeskartellamt, Working Paper, "Market Power of Platforms and Networks", June 2016, available on the internet under https://www.bundeskartellamt.de/Sh aredDocs/Publikation/EN/Berichte/Think-Tank-Bericht-Langfassung.pdf?__blob =publicationFile&v=2 (last accessed: 22/06/19).

Christensen, Clayton M./Raynor, Michael E./McDonald, Rory, "What is Disruptive Innovation", Harvard Business Review, December 2015, available on the internet under https://hbr.org/2015/12/what-is-disruptive-innovation (last accessed: 15/07/19).

Cooper, James C., "Privacy and Antitrust: Underpants Gnomes, the First Amendment, and Subjectivity", George Mason Law Review 2013, 1129–1146, available on the internet under http://www.georgemasonlawreview.org/wp-content/uploa ds/2014/03/Cooper_Website.pdf (last accessed: 24/01/20).

Crofts, Lewis/McLeod, Robert, MLex Interview: Margrethe Vestager, MLex Special Report, January 2015, pp. 2–8, available on the internet under https://mlexmar ketinsight.com/insights-center/reports/interview-with-margrethe-vestager (last accessed: 22/05/19).

Dietrich, Michael, "Will das Kartellamt zur Superbehörde werden?", March 11th, 2019, available on the internet under https://www.lto.de/recht/kanzleien-untern ehmen/k/facebook-entscheidung-bundeskartellamt-wettbewerbsrecht-datenschu tzverstoss-superbehoerde-zustaendigkeit-rechtsbereiche/ (last accessed: 01/09/19).

Dworschak, Manfred/Rosenbach, Marcel/Schmundt, Hilmar, "Planet der Freundschaft", May 7th, 2012, available on the internet under https://www.spiegel.de/s piegel/print/d-85586231.html (last accessed: 06/08/19).

Engels, Barbara/Grunewald, Mara, Institut der deutschen Wirtschaft, IW-Kurzbericht Nr. 57: "DAS PRIVACY PARADOX – Digitalisierung versus Privatsphäre", August 14th, 2017, available on the internet under https://www.iwko eln.de/studien/iw-kurzberichte/beitrag/barbara-engels-mara-grunewald-das-pr ivacy-paradox-digitalisierung-versus-privatsphaere-356747.html (last accessed: 09/09/19).

European Commission, Commission Staff Working Document, A Digital Single Market Strategy for Europe – Analysis and Evidence, SWD(2015) 100 final, available on the internet under https://eur-lex.europa.eu/legal-content/EN/TXT/ PDF/?uri=CELEX:52015SC0100&from=EN (last accessed: 23/08/19).

European Commission, Competition policy for the digital era – A report by Jacques Crémer, Yves-Alexandre de Montjoye and Heike Schweitzer, available on the internet under https://ec.europa.eu/competition/publications/reports/kd0 419345enn.pdf (last accessed: 01/04/20).

European Commission, Public Consultation on the regulatory environment for platforms, online intermediaries, data and cloud computing and the collaborative economy, September 2015, available on the internet under http://ec.europa. eu/newsroom/dae/document.cfm?doc_id=10932 (last accessed: 27/03/20).

European Commission, press release on the approval of case M.8124 Microsoft/LinkedIn, published 06/12/2016, available on the internet under http://e uropa.eu/rapid/press-release_IP-16-4284_en.htm (last accessed: 27/03/20).

European Commission, XXIIIrd Report on Competition Policy 1993, available on the internet under https://publications.europa.eu/en/publication-detail/-/publica tion/7db4a243-39f3-4ba4-a5b7-1cb48f8ca6d3 (last accessed: 05/09/19).

European Parliament, Challenges for Competition Policy in a Digitalised Economy", July 2015, available on the internet under http://www.europarl.europa.eu /RegData/etudes/STUD/2015/542235/IPOL_STU%282015%29542235_EN.pdf (last accessed: 15/07/19).

Evans, David S, "Multisided Platforms, Dynamic Competition, and the Assessment of Market Power for Internet-Based Firms", University of Chicago Coase-Sandor Institute for Law & Economics Research Paper No. 753, available on the internet under https://ssrn.com/abstract=2746095 (last accessed: 03/12/19).

Facebook Data Policy (Date of Last Revision: April 19, 2018), available on the internet under https://www.facebook.com/privacy/explanation (last accessed: 27/03/20).

Facebook, Facebook Reports Fourth Quarter and Full Year 2018 Results, available on the internet under https://s21.q4cdn.com/399680738/files/doc_financials/201 8/Q4/Q4-2018-Earnings-Release.pdf (last accessed: 03/09/19).

Facebook, Terms of Service, Date of Last Revision: July 31, 2019, available on the internet under https://www.facebook.com/legal/terms/update (last accessed: 22/09/19).

Federal Ministry for Economic Affairs and Energy, "Ein neuer Wettbewerbsrahmen für die Digitalwirtschaft – Bericht der Kommission Wettbewerbsrecht 4.0" (= A New Competition Framework for the Digital Economy – Report by the Commission Competition Law 4.0), available on the internet under https:// www.bmwi.de/Redaktion/DE/Publikationen/Wirtschaft/bericht-der-kommissio n-wettbewerbsrecht-4-0.html (last accessed 01/04/21).

Franke, Sten, "Das neue Social Media Prisma 2017/2018 – Wandel durch Disruptive Innovation", 16/10/2017, available on the internet under https://ethority.de/ 2017/10/16/das-neue-social-media-prisma-20172018-wandel-durch-disruptive-inn ovation/ (last accessed: 15/08/19).

Gabriel, Sigmar, "Unsere politischen Konsequenzen aus der Google-Debatte", May 16th, 2014, available on the internet under https://www.faz.net/aktuell/feuilleto n/debatten/die-digital-debatte/sigmar-gabriel-konsequenzen-der-google-debatte-1 2941865-p5.html (last accessed: 13/09/19).

Gersemann, Olaf, "Zerschlagt Facebook nicht!", April 4th, 2018, available on the internet under https://www.welt.de/print/die_welt/debatte/article175406752/Lei tartikel-Zerschlagt-Facebook-nicht.html (last accessed: 13/09/19).

Graef, Inge, "Stretching EU Competition Law Tools for Search Engines and Social Networks", Internet Policy Review 2015, available on the internet under https:// papers.ssrn.com/sol3/papers.cfm?abstract_id=2655555 (last accessed: 23/07/19).

Graw, Ansgar, "Facebook – Ein Monopol, das zerschlagen gehört", April 4th, 2018, available on the internet under https://www.welt.de/debatte/kommentare/article 175369044/Mark-Zuckerbergs-Werk-Facebook-ein-Monopol-das-zerschlagen-geh oert.html (last accessed: 13/09/19).

Hanfeld, Michael, "Was erlauben Facebook?", June 26th 2019, available on the internet under https://www.faz.net/aktuell/feuilleton/debatten/warum-facebook -wirklich-nach-regulierung-ruft-16253951.html (last accessed: 14/10/19).

Hartman, Philipp Max/Zaki, Mohamed/Feldmann, Niels/Neely, "Big Data for Big Business? A Taxonomy of Data-driven Business Models used by Start-up Firms", March 2014, available on the internet under https://cambridgeservicealliance.en g.cam.ac.uk/resources/Downloads/Monthly%20Papers/2014_March_DataDriven BusinessModels.pdf (last accessed: 12/09/19).

Hasse, Marc, "So entziehen Sie sich Googles Datensammlung", March 3rd, 2012, available on the internet under https://www.abendblatt.de/ratgeber/wissen/artic le107752170/So-entziehen-Sie-sich-Googles-Datensammlung.html (last accessed: 06/08/19).

Hein, Christoph/Hendricks, Frank, "Data-Driven-Company", Business Intelligence Magazine, available on the internet under https://www.bi-magazine.net/data-dri ven-company.html (last accessed: 12/09/19).

Herz, Martin/Vedder, Hans H.B., "A Commentary on Article 102 TFEU", available on the internet under https://papers.ssrn.com/sol3/papers.cfm?abstract_id=29771 95 (last accessed: 27/03/20).

Holzki, Larissa/Neuerer, Dietmar, "OLG Düsseldorf kassiert Vorwürfe des Kartel-lamts gegen Facebook", August 26th, 2019, available on the internet under https://www.handelsblatt.com/technik/it-internet/datenschutz-olg-duesseldorf-k assiert-vorwuerfe-des-kartellamts-gegen-facebook/24943100.html?ticket=ST-1078 0336-fQe2mQy0vL0ak5RT1F5e-ap4 (last accessed: 10/09/19).

House of Lords – Select Committee on European Union, Online Platforms and the Digital Single Market, HL Paper 129 2015–16, available on the internet under https://publications.parliament.uk/pa/ld201516/ldselect/ldeucom/129/129.pdf (last accessed: 22/06/19).

Huang, Elaine, "Facebook's US$1b data centre in Singapore to open in 2022", October 29th, 2018, available on the internet under https://www.edb.gov.sg/en/n ews-and-events/insights/innovation/facebook-s-us-1b-data-centre-in-singapore-to -open-in-2022.html (last accessed 01/10/19).

Hülsen, Isabell/Müller, Peter, "Haben sich die deutschen Autokonzerne abgesprochen, um Innovationen zu verhindern? Hier spricht EU-Wettbewerbskommissarin Vestager über ihre Ermittlungen und die Marktmacht von Facebook", April 12th, 2019, available on the internet under https://www.spiegel.de/plus/ma rgrethe-vestager-daimler-vw-und-bmw-haben-nun-zehn-wochen-zeit-a-00000000 -0002-0001-0000-000163403870 (last accessed: 12/11/19).

Hughes, Chris, "It`s time to break up Facebook", May 9th, 2019, available on the internet under https://www.nytimes.com/2019/05/09/opinion/sunday/chris-hug hes-facebook-zuckerberg.html (last accessed: 20/09/19).

IBM Institute for Business Value, Innovative analytics – *How the world's most successful organizations use analytics to innovate*, April 2015, available on the internet under ftp://public.dhe.ibm.com/software/pdf/de/Innovative_analytics_Ex ec_Report_v42.pdf (last accessed 20/09/19).

International Monetary Fund, "Measuring the Digital Economy", Policy Paper, April 5, 2018, available on the internet under https://www.imf.org/en/Publicatio ns/Policy-Papers/Issues/2018/04/03/022818-measuring-the-digital-economy (last accessed: 27/03/20).

Irish Data Protection Commissioner, Facebook Ireland Ltd. Report of Audit, December 21st, 2011, available on the internet under https://www.pdpjournals.com /docs/87980.pdf (last accessed: 06/08/19)

Kimmelman, Gene, "The Right Way to Regulate Digital Platforms", Harvard Kennedy School – Shorenstein Center on Media, Politics and Public Policy, September 18th, 2019, available on the internet under https://shorensteincenter. org/the-right-way-to-regulate-digital-platforms/ (last accessed: 11/11/19).

Knupfer, Gabriel, "Threema: Meistverkaufte App des Jahres", December 12, 2014, available on the internet under https://www.handelszeitung.ch/unternehme n/technologie/threema-meistverkaufte-app-des-jahres-709810 (last accessed: 30/03/20).

Kroes, Neelie, Speech "European Competition Policy – Delivering Better Markets and Better Choices", European Consumer and Competition Day, London, 15 September 2005, available on the internet under http://europa.eu/rapid/press-rel ease_SPEECH-05-512_en.htm?locale=en (last accessed: 12/03/20).

Kühl, Eike, "Zerschlagt, was euch kaputt macht", May 21st, 2019, available on the internet under https://www.zeit.de/digital/internet/2019-05/facebook-zerschlag ung-wahlkampf-monopol-soziale-medien-digitalkonzerne/komplettansicht (last accessed: 13/09/19).

Kuneva, Meglena, Keynote Speech at the Roundtable on Online Data Collection, Targeting and Profiling, Brussels, 31 March 2009, available on the internet under http://europa.eu/rapid/press-release_SPEECH-09-156_en.htm (last accessed: 01/05/19).

List of acquisitions made by Facebook, available on the internet under https://www .crunchbase.com/organization/facebook/acquisitions/acquisitions_list#section-ac quisitions (last accessed: 11/11/19).

Mansholt, Malte, "Zugriff auf Facebook-Daten: Hier sehen Sie, welche Apps bei Ihnen schnüffeln", March 21st, 2018, available on the internet under https://ww w.stern.de/digital/online/zugriff-auf-facebook-daten--hier-sehen-sie--welche-apps -bei-ihnen-schnueffeln-7908578.html (last accessed: 06/08/19).

Mielczarek, Detlef Conradi, "Digitale Diskriminierung – Ohne Facebook geht nichts mehr", November 19th, 2012, available on the internet under https://w ww.zeit.de/digital/internet/2012-11/leserartikel-ohne-facebook (last accessed: 09/09/19).

Miller, Rich, "Facebook's $1 Billion Data Center Network", February 2nd, 2012, available on the internet under https://www.datacenterknowledge.com/archives/ 2012/02/02/facebooks-1-billion-data-center-network (last accessed: 01/10/19).

Monti, Mario, Speech "The Future for Competition Policy in the European Union", Merchant Taylor`s Hall, London, 9 July 2001, extracts available on the internet under http://europa.eu/rapid/press-release_SPEECH-01-340_en.htm ?locale=de (last accessed: 12/03/20).

Monopolkommission, "Competition Policy: The challenge of digital markets", Special Report 68, available on the internet under https://www.monopolkommi ssion.de/images/PDF/SG/s68_fulltext_eng.pdf (last accessed: 28/01/20).

Monopolkommission, Policy Brief, Ausgabe 4 – Januar 2020, available on the internet under https://www.monopolkommission.de/images/Policy_Brief/MK_P olicy_Brief_4.pdf (last accessed: 27/03/20).

Monopolkommission, Wettbewerb 2018 – XXII. Hauptgutachten der Monopolkommission gemäß § 44 Abs. 1 Satz 1 GWB, July 3rd, 2018, available on the internet under https://www.monopolkommission.de/images/HG22/HGX XII_Gesamt.pdf (last accessed: 24/08/19).

Müller, Claudio, "Der große Google-Test", July 2nd, 2019, available on the internet under https://www.focus.de/digital/computer/chip-exklusiv/tid-18904/suche-d atenschutz-nutzbarkeit-der-grosse-google-test_aid_525753.html (last accessed: 06/08/19).

Nocun, Katharina, "Habe meine Daten runtergeladen: Was Facebook alles über mich weiß, hat mich schockiert", June 26th, 2018, available on the internet under https://www.focus.de/digital/experten/facebook-ich-wusste-dass-faceboo k-daten-speichert-doch-das-ausmass-hat-mich-erschreckt_id_9145326.html (last accessed: 06/08/19).

OECD, "Big Data: Bringing Competition Policy to the Digital Era", November 29–30, 2016, available on the internet under https://one.oecd.org/document/DA F/COMP(2016)14/en/pdf (last accessed: 22/05/19).

OECD, "Data-driven Innovation for Growth and Well-being – Interim Synthesis Report", October 2014, available on the internet under https://www.oecd.org/sti /inno/data-driven-innovation-interim-synthesis.pdf (last accessed: 22/05/19).

Paal, Boris P./Hennemann, Moritz, "Big Data as an Asset", available on the internet under http://www.abida.de/sites/default/files/Gutachten_ABIDA_Big_Data_as_a n_Asset.pdf (last accessed: 02/09/19).

Pantlin, Nick/Moir, Andrew/Young, Christine/Everett, Miriam/Wiseman, Claire, "Data use: Protecting a critical resource", available on the internet under https://www.herbertsmithfreehills.com/latest-thinking/data-use-protecting-a-critical-res ource (last accessed: 22/05/19).

Peterson, Rachel, "Data centers year in review", January 1st, 2019, available on the internet under https://engineering.fb.com/data-center-engineering/data-centers-2 018/ (last accessed: 16/09/19).

Podszun, Rupprecht, D'Kart Antitrust Blog, "Facebook @ BGH", June 23rd, 2020, available on the internet under https://www.d-kart.de/en/blog/2020/06/23/faceb ook-bgh/ (last accessed: 24/10/20).

Podszun, Rupprecht, D'Kart Antitrust Blog, "Facebook: Next Stop Europe", 25. March 2021, available on the internet under https://www.d-kart.de/en/blog/2021 /03/25/facebook-next-stop-europe/ (last accessed: 17/04/21).

Podszun, Rupprecht, D'Kart Antitrust Blog, "Facebook Case: The Reasoning", August 28th, 2020, available on the internet under https://www.d-kart.de/blog/20 20/08/28/facebook-case-the-reasoning/#comments (last accessed: 26/10/20).

PWC, "Big Data – Bedeutung Nutzen Mehrwert", available on the internet under https://www.pwc.de/de/prozessoptimierung/assets/pwc-big-data-bedeutung-nutz en-mehrwert.pdf (last accessed: 27/03/20).

Roßnagel, Alexander/Pfitzmann, Andreas/Garstka,Hansjürgen, "Modernisierung des Datenschutzrechts", report commissioned by the Federal Ministry of the Interior, Berlin 2002, available on the internet under https://pdfs.semanticsc holar.org/fa68/4e56317983fb6c379f29de8f61b4e22d3087.pdf (last accessed: 12/08/19).

Sasse, Robert, "A Micro-Economic Perspective on Social Media in Context of the New Economy", available on the internet under http://article.sapub.org/10.5923 .j.m2economics.20160402.03.html (last accessed: 01/10/19).

Statista, "Anteil der Internetnutzer nach Altersgruppen in der Generation 50plus in Deutschland in ausgewählten Jahren von 2011 bis 2017", available on the internet under https://statista.extdb.e-fellows.net/statistik/daten/studie/568561/ umfrage/anteil-der-internetnutzer-in-deutschland-in-der-generation-50plus/ (last accessed: 09/09/19).

Statista, "Bevölkerung – Zahl der Einwohner in Deutschland nach Altersgruppen am 31. Dezember 2017 (in Millionen)", available on the internet under https://st atista.extdb.e-fellows.net/statistik/daten/studie/1365/umfrage/bevoelkerung-deut schlands-nach-altersgruppen/ (last accessed: 09/09/19).

Stelzer, Dirk, "Digitale Güter und ihre Bedeutung in der Internet-Ökonomie", available on the internet under https://www.tu-ilmenau.de/fileadmin/public/iw m/diggut.pdf (last accessed: 01/10/19).

Temple Lang, John/O'Donoghue, Robert, "Defining Legitimate Competition: How to Clarify Pricing Abuses Under Article 82 EC", Fordham International Law Journal 2002, 83–162, available on the internet under https://ir.lawnet.ford ham.edu/cgi/viewcontent.cgi?article=1866&context=ilj (last accessed: 01/10/19).

Thierer, Adam, "The Perils of Classifying Social Media Platforms as Public Utilities", Journal of Communications Law and Technology Policy 2013, 249–297, available on the internet under https://scholarship.law.edu/commlaw/vol21/iss2/2/ (last accessed: 13/09/19).

Tim Wu, "In the Grip of the Internet Monopolists", November 13th, 2010, available on the internet under https://www.wsj.com/articles/SB10001424052748704635704575604993311538482 (last accessed 02/09/19).

Varian, Hal R., "Economic of Information Technology", available on the internet under http://people.ischool.berkeley.edu/~hal/Papers/mattioli/mattioli.pdf (last accessed 01/10/19).

Vestager, Margrethe, Speech at the EDPS-BEUC Conference on Big Data, Brussels 29 September 2016, available on the internet under https://wayback.archive-it.org/12090/20191129222113/https://ec.europa.eu/commission/commissioners/2014-2019/vestager/announcements/big-data-and-competition_en (last accessed: 27/03/20).

Vestager, Margrethe, Speech "Building a positive digital world", Digital Summit, Dortmund (Germany), October 29, 2019, available on the internet under https://wayback.archive-it.org/12090/20191130020041/https://ec.europa.eu/commission/commissioners/2014-2019/vestager/announcements/building-positive-digital-world_en (last accessed: 28/03/20).

Vestager, Margrethe, Speech "Competition is a consumer issue" in front of the BEUC General Assembly, 13 May 2016, available on the internet under https://wayback.archive-it.org/12090/20191129205633/https://ec.europa.eu/commission/commissioners/2014-2019/vestager/announcements/competition-consumer-issue_en (last accessed: 27/03/20).

Vestager, Margrethe, Speech "Competition in changing times" on the occasion of the FIW Symposium in Innsbruck (Germany), 16 February 2018, available on the internet under https://wayback.archive-it.org/12090/20191129215248/https://ec.europa.eu/commission/commissioners/2014-2019/vestager/announcements/competition-changing-times-0_en (last accessed: 27/03/20).

Vestager, Margrethe, Speech "Keeping the EU competitive in a green and gitial world", College of Europe, Bruges, March 2, 2020, available on the internet under https://ec.europa.eu/commission/commissioners/2019-2024/vestager/announcements/keeping-eu-competitive-green-and-digital-world_en (last accessed: 28/03/20).

Vestager, Margrethe, Speech "Shaping a digital future for Europe", Symposium on Digitalisation, The Hague, February 3, 2020, available on the internet under https://ec.europa.eu/commission/commissioners/2019-2024/vestager/announcements/shaping-digital-future-europe_en (last accessed: 27/03/20).

Waehrer, Keith, "Online services and the analysis of competitive merger effects in privacy protections and other quality dimensions", July 8, 2016, available on the internet under https://papers.ssrn.com/sol3/papers.cfm?abstract_id=2701927 (last accessed: 20/06/19).

Ward, Jonathan Stuart/Barker, Adam, "Undefined By Data: A Survey of Big Data Definitions", September 20, 2013, available on the internet under https://arxiv.o rg/pdf/1309.5821.pdf (last accessed: 22/05/19).

Wirtschaftswoche, "Welche Menschen die deutsche Internetwirtschaft bewegen", 07/05/2012, available on the internet under https://www.wiwo.de/technologie/d igitale-welt/plaetze-21-bis-100-plaetze-61-bis-100/6598926-2.html (last accessed: 15/08/19).

Yang, Qing/Ji, Yun, "The Platform Economy and Natural Monopoly: regulating or laissez-faire?", available on the internet under https://pdfs.semanticscholar.org/b 270/28b47b26656356b08115d52cb981b61e6358.pdf (last accessed: 01/10/19).

Zanfir-Fortuna, Gabriela/Ianc, Sînziana, "Data Protection and Competition Law: The Dawn of "Uberprotection", available on the internet under https://papers.ss rn.com/sol3/papers.cfm?abstract_id=3290824 (last accessed: 16/03/20).

Zech, Herbert, "Data as a Tradeable Commodity – Implications for Contract Law", available on the internet under https://papers.ssrn.com/sol3/papers.cfm?abstract _id=3063153 (last accessed: 24/09/19).

Table of Cases

Case law of the Court of Justice of the European Union:

Case law of the European Court of Justice (ECJ):

ECJ in case C-6/64, Costa v E.N.E.L., ECLI:EU:C:1964:66.

ECJ in case C-6/72, *Europemballage Corporation and Continental Can Company v Commission*, ECLI:EU:C:1973:22.

ECJ in case C-127/73, *Belgische Radio en Televisie v SV SABAM*, ECLI:EU:C:1974:25.

ECJ in case C-26/76, *Metro SB-Großmärkte GmbH & Co KG v Commission*, ECLI:EU:C:1977:167.

ECJ in case C-27/76, *United Brands v Commission*, ECLI:EU:C:1978:22.

ECJ in case C-85/76, *Hoffmann-La Roche v Commission*, ECLI:EU:C:1979:36.

ECJ in case C-28/77, *Tepea v Commission,* ECLI:EU:C:1978:133.

ECJ in case C-53/81, Levin v Staatssecretaris van Justitie, ECLI:EU:C:1982:105

ECJ in case C-322/81, *NV Nederlandsche Banden Industrie Michelin v Commission of the European Communities,* ECLI:EU:C:1983:313.

ECJ in case C-42/84, *Remia BV and others v Commission of the European Communities*, ECLI:EU:C:1985:327.

ECJ in case C-222/84, *Johnston v Chief Constable of the Royal Ulster Constabulary*, ECLI:EU:C:1986:206.

ECJ in case C-62/86, *AKZO Chemie BV v Commission of the European Communities,* ECLI:EU:C:1991:286.

ECJ in case C-41/90, *Höfner and Elser v Macrotron GmbH*, ECLI:EU:C:1991:161.

ECJ in case C-333/94 P, *Tetra Pak International SA v Commission of the European Communities*, ECLI:EU:C:1996:436.

ECJ in joined cases C-395 and 396/96 P, *Compagnie Maritime Belge Transport SA v Commission*, ECLI:EU:C:2000:132.

ECJ in case C-7/97, *Oscar Bronner GmbH & Co KG v Mediaprint*, ECLI:EU:C:1998:569.

ECJ in case C-453/99, *Courage Ltd. v Crehan*, ECLI:EU:C:2001:465.

ECJ in case C-418/01, *IMS Health GmbH & Co. OHG v NDC Health GmbH & Co. KG*, ECLI:EU:C:2004:257.

ECJ in case C-95/04 P, *British Airways v Commission*, ECLI:EU:C:2007:166.

ECJ in case C-238/05, *Asnef-Equifax v Ausbanc*, ECLI:EU:C:2006:734.

ECJ in joined Cases C-468/06 to C-478/06, *Sot. Lélos kai Sia EE and others v Glaxo-SmithKline AEVE Farmakeftikon Proïonton*, ECLI:EU:C:2008:504.

ECJ in case C-202/07 P, *France Télécom SA v Commission of the European Communities*, ECLI:EU:C:2009:214.

ECJ in case C-280/08, *Deutsche Telekom v Commission*, ECLI:EU:C:2010:603.

ECJ in case C-52/09, Konkurrensverket v *Telia Sonera Sverige AB*, ECLI:EU:C:2011:83.

ECJ in case C-209/10, *Post Danmark A/S v Konkurrencerådet*, ECLI:EU:C:2012:172.

ECJ in case C-457/10 P, *AstraZeneca AB and AstraZeneca plc v European Commission*, ECLI:EU:C:2012:770.

ECJ in case C-549/10 P, *Tomra Systems ASA and Others v European Commission*, ECLI:EU:C:2012:221.

ECJ in case C-131/12, *Google Spain SL and Google Inc. v Agencia Española de Protección de Datos (AEPD) and Mario Costeja González*, ECLI:EU:C:2014:317.

ECJ in case C-382/12 P, *Master Card Inc. and others v* Commission, ECLI:EU:C:2014:2201.

ECJ in case C-582/14, *Patrick Breyer v. Bundesrepublik Deutschland*, ECLI:EU:C:2016:779.

Case law of the General Court (GC):

GC in case T-30/89, *Hilti AG v Commission of the European Communities*, ECLI:EU:T:1991:70.

GC in joined cases T-374, 375, 384 and 388/94, *European Night Services and Others v Commission*, ECLI:EU:T:1998:198.

GC in case T-65/98, *Van den Bergh Foods Ltd v Commission of the European Communities*, ECLI:EU:T:2003:281.

GC in case T-52/00, *Coe Clerici Logistics SpA v Commission*, ECLI:EU:T:2003:168.

GC in case T-168/01, *GlaxoSmithKline Services Unlimited v Commission*, ECLI:EU:T:2006:265.

GC in joined cases T-213/01 and T-214/01, *Österreichische Postsparkasse and Bank für Arbeit und Wirtschaft v Commission*, ECLI:EU:T:2006:151.

GC in case T-201/04, *Microsoft Corp. v Commission of the European Communities*, *ECLI:EU:T:2007:289*.

GC in case T-321/05, *AstraZeneca v Commission*, ECLI:EU:T:2010:266.

GC in case T-79/12, *Cisco Systems and Messagenet v Commission*, ECLI:EU:T:2013:635.

Opinions of Advocate Generals (AG):

Advocate General *Jacobs in c*ase C-7/97, *Oscar Bronner GmbH & Co KG v Mediaprint*, ECLI:EU:C:1998:264.

Advocate General Jacobs in case C-53/03, *Synetairismos Farmakopoion Aitolias & Akarnanias (Syfait) and Others v GlaxoSmithKline plc and GlaxoSmithKline AEVE*, ECLI:EU:C:2004:673.

Cases of the European Commission (DG Competition):

European Commission, decision of June 2nd, 1971, case no. IV/26.760 – *GEMA*, OJ 1971 L 134/15.

European Commission, decision of December 21st, 1993, case no. IV/34.174 – *Sealink/B&I Holyhead*, OJ 1994 L 15/8.

European Commission, decision of July 20th, 1999, case no. IV/36.888 – *1998 Football World Cup*.

European Commission, decision of 21 April 2004, case no. COMP/C-3/37.792, C(2004)900 final – *Microsoft*.

European Commission, decision of 11 March 2008, case no. COMP/M.4731, C(2008) 927 final – *Google/DoubleClick*.

European Commission, decision of 14 May 2008, case no. COMP/M.4854, C(2008) 1859 – *TomTom/Tele Atlas*.

European Commission, decision of 13 May 2009, case no. COMP/C-3 /37.990, D(2009) 3726 final – *Intel*.

European Commission, decision of 3 October 2014, case no. COMP/M.7217, C(2014) 7239 final – *Facebook/Whatsapp*.

European Commission, decision of 27 June 2017, case no. AT.39740, C(2017) 4444 final – *Google Search (Shopping)*.

Case law of the German Federal Court of Justice:

German Federal Court of Justice, judgement of October 14th, 1986, VI ZR 10/86, NJW-RR 1987, 231

German Federal Court of Justice, judgement of December 1st, 1999, I ZR 49/97, NJW 2000, 2195.

German Federal Court of Justice, judgement of March 4th, 2010, III ZR 79/09, MMR 2010, 398.

German Federal Court of Justice, judgement of June 6th, 2016, KZR 6/15, *Pechstein*, NJW 2016, 2266.

German Federal Court of Justice, judgement of January 24th, 2017, KZR 47/14, *VBL-Gegenwert II*, NZKart 2017, 242.

German Federal Court of Justice, judgement of July 19th, 2018, VII ZR 19/18, ZfBR 2018, 775.

German Federal Court of Justice, judgement of August 30th, 2018, VII ZR 243/17, NJW 2018, 3380.

German Federal Court of Justice, decision of June 23rd, 2020, KVR 69/19, *Facebook*, GRUR-RS 2020, 20737.

Case law of the German Federal Constitutional Court:

German Federal Constitutional Court, judgement of February 2nd, 1990, 1 BvR 26/84, NJW 1990, 1469.

German Federal Constitutional Court, judgement of December 15th, 1983, 1 BvR 209/83, NJW 1984, 419.

Case law of German Higher Regional Courts:

Higher Regional Court Düsseldorf, decision of March 24th, 2021, Kart 2/19 (V) – Facebook.

Higher Regional Court Düsseldorf, decision of August 26th, 2019, VI-Kart 1/19 (V) – *Facebook*.

Cases of the Bundeskartellamt:

Bundeskartellamt, decision of February 6th, 2019, case no. B6–22/16 – *Facebook*.

Other official sources

European Commission, Commission Notice on Case Referral in respect of concentrations, OJ 2005 C 56/02.

European Commission, Communication from the Commission – Commission Guidance on the application of the referral mechanism set out in Article 22 of the Merger Regulation to certain categories of cases, Brussels, 26/03/2021, C(2021) 1959 final.

European Commission, Guidance on the Commission's enforcement priorities in applying Article 82 of the EC Treaty to abusive exclusionary conduct by dominant undertakings, OJ 2009 C 45/02.

European Commission, Guidelines on the application of Article 81(3) of the Treaty, OJ 2004 C 101/97.

Gesetzentwurf der Bundesregierung (Government Draft), Entwurf eines Neunten Gesetzes zur Änderung des Gesetzes gegen Wettbewerbsbeschränkungen, Parliamentary Publication (BT-Drucksache) 18/10207.

Bibliography

Federal Ministry of Economics and Energy, Ministerial Draft of the Federal Ministry of Economics and Energy for a Tenth Act to amend the Act against Restraints of Competition for a focused, proactive and digital competition law 4.0 (ARC Digitization Act), in German available on the internet under https://www.bmwi.de/Redaktion/DE/Downloads/G/gwb-digitalisierungsgesetz-referentenentwurf.pdf?__blob=publicationFile&v=10 (last accessed: 25/03/20).